M000251581

Tales and Tombstones
of Sunset Cemetery

Tales and Tombstones
of Sunset Cemetery

*Tracing Lives and Memorial Customs
in a Southern Graveyard*

JUNE HADDEN HOBBS *and*
JOE DEPRIEST

Photographs by Hal Bryant

McFarland & Company, Inc., Publishers
Jefferson, North Carolina

All photographs are by Hal Bryant unless otherwise indicated.

LIBRARY OF CONGRESS CATALOGUING-IN-PUBLICATION DATA

Names: Hobbs, June Hadden, 1948– author. | DePriest, Joe, 1944– author. |
Bryant, Hal, 1950– photographer.
Title: Tales and tombstones of Sunset Cemetery : tracing lives and memorial customs in a Southern
graveyard / June Hadden Hobbs and Joe DePriest ; with photographs by Hal Bryant.
Description: Jefferson, North Carolina : McFarland & Company, Inc., Publishers, 2022 |
Includes bibliographical references and index.
Identifiers: LCCN 2021044625 | ISBN 9781476686387 (paperback : acid free paper) ∞
ISBN 9781476644288 (ebook)
Subjects: LCSH: Sunset Cemetery (Shelby, N.C.)—History. | Cemeteries—North Carolina—Shelby. |
Sepulchral monuments—North Carolina—Shelby. | Shelby (N.C.)—Biography. | BISAC: SOCIAL
SCIENCE / Death & Dying | HISTORY / United States / State & Local / South (AL, AR, FL, GA,
KY, LA, MS, NC, SC, TN, VA, WV) | LCGFT: Biographies.
Classification: LCC F264.S54 H63 2021 | DDC 975.6/775—dc23
LC record available at https://lccn.loc.gov/2021044625

BRITISH LIBRARY CATALOGUING DATA ARE AVAILABLE

ISBN (print) 978-1-4766-8638-7
ISBN (ebook) 978-1-4766-4428-8

© 2022 June Hadden Hobbs and Joe DePriest. All rights reserved

*No part of this book may be reproduced or transmitted in any form
or by any means, electronic or mechanical, including photocopying
or recording, or by any information storage and retrieval system,
without permission in writing from the publisher.*

On the cover: the beautiful allée and central thoroughfare
of Sunset Cemetery's old section (photograph by Hal Bryant)

Printed in the United States of America

*McFarland & Company, Inc., Publishers
Box 611, Jefferson, North Carolina 28640
www.mcfarlandpub.com*

To the permanent residents
of Shelby

Acknowledgments

Much of the material for this book is drawn from years of field research in Sunset and other United States cemeteries and from informal sources such as church minutes, letters, family scrapbooks, pages torn out of notebooks, and commercial websites. We are inexpressibly grateful to all who have given us tips, encouraged our project, answered our questions, and provided professional expertise. These include Brownie Plaster; Tom Hanchett, history consultant; Rebecca Sitz, the *Shelby Star*; Zack Dressel, curator, The Earl Scruggs Center: Music & Stories from the American South; Dick Hamrick; William Lynch, Head Superintendent of Sunset Cemetery for 25 years and currently cemetery technician for the City of Shelby; Ann Wray; Brendan LeGran; the Cleveland County Memorial Library; the Dover Library at Gardner-Webb University; the Writing Across the Curriculum program at Gardner-Webb University; and Newspapers.com. Layla Milholen, our editor at McFarland, has been a model of clear guidance and good advice.

Hal Bryant, our wonderful photographer, has tramped Sunset Cemetery with us in heat, rain, and cold; kept us in stitches with his dry wit; taken and retaken "just one more photo" more times than we can count; and proven himself to be a man who will do nearly anything for friendship and banana pudding. He is an incomparable artist.

In addition, we have been privileged to interview many people, including Rebekah Adams, Mariel Camp, O. Max Gardner III, Laurel K. Gabel, Bobbi Gibson, Shellie Hamrick-White, William E. Harding, Mimi Elliott Hirsch, the Rev. Claude London, Scott Neal, Maida Scruggs, and Susan Scruggs.

Finally, we have many friends and family members to thank for personal support and encouragement. Joe thanks his wife, Jan DePriest, and June expresses her appreciation for friends from the Association for Gravestone Studies, who are her tribe. She is also grateful to her Collaborative Inquiry Team—Cody Sander, Mikeal Parsons, and Rochelle Martin—and to the Louisville Institute, which funded research into "a practical theology of corpse care" that required many hours of tramping cemeteries, holding focus groups, and brainstorming. She continues to rely on the unwavering support of her mother, Mary L. Hadden, and of her children: Kevin Hobbs, Nathan Hobbs, and Valerie Hobbs.

And to the permanent residents of Shelby, we say, as Joe often did when we finished a stroll: We've got your back.

Table of Contents

Preface by June Hadden Hobbs

Some time in the late summer of 2019, Joe DePriest sent a message asking if I knew about the witch buried in Sunset Cemetery in Shelby, North Carolina. I did not, so we made an appointment to take a look. Joe claimed her tombstone had a pentagram on it, and a cemetery worker had told Joe he found used candles and other paraphernalia suggestive of satanic rituals near her grave.

We had not known each other long after having become acquainted when the Association for Gravestone Studies met at nearby Gardner-Webb University, where I teach English, in June 2019. We quickly became friends because we share a special love for Sunset.

The gravestone for Kidder Cole Nichols, as it turns out, was indeed inscribed with a pentagram. But as I explained to Joe, the symbols in the pentagram told me that she was a member of a respectable Masonic organization for ladies known as the Order of the Eastern Star. The pentagram, in fact, is an allusion to the Star of Bethlehem in the story of Christ's nativity.

As far as I was concerned, that was the end of it, but not for an investigative journalist like Joe DePriest. He had to have the story of the woman herself, and he went digging. Eventually he uncovered the delightful story of a teen-aged Kidder Cole, the toast of Cashiers Valley in Jackson County, who was locked in a love triangle with two determined suitors. One rejected young man, who would go on to become Superior Court Judge Felix Alley, eased his heartbreak by writing a mountain ballad with a banjo accompaniment about Kidder Cole. Bascom Lamar Lunsford, the "Minstrel of the Appalachians," made it famous in a 1928 recording, and the rest, as they say, is history.

Joe grew up in Shelby and has written for most of the local newspapers as well as for the *Charlotte Observer*. He's always on the trail of the next great story, and he loves bringing the permanent residents of Shelby back to life with zesty details of the times in which they lived, including the music they would have heard and loved. I am an English professor who has spent her life studying tombstones and cemeteries just as I do literary texts, and I have sometimes joked to friends that I have no interest at all in the people buried in a graveyard. Like Huck Finn, "I don't take no stock in dead people."

But then Joe and I began to interpret the cemetery for each other through our different lenses. As we strolled, he told the stories of the fascinating people buried there, from a man who fancied himself one of the world's greatest bank robbers to two men who became governors of North Carolina. In turn, I explained to him why all the graves were in east/west orientation and why symbols of hands appear on so many nineteenth-century tombstones. He related the story of a notorious author and public figure as we looked at Thomas Dixon's tombstone. I was more interested in the fact that it was made of granite.

In truth, the tales and tombstones we focus on were not selected systematically. Instead, we approached Sunset Cemetery as one might a museum—a place to stroll and muse on what we found. And of course musing inevitably brings memories and new insights to the fore. Joe recalled the stories of people he knew, news stories he covered over the years, and legends of his hometown. I identified icons and epitaphs I had studied and written about and remembered the history of American cemeteries and deathways. We both asked questions about what was new and unfamiliar. I explain this process more fully in the section of Chapter IX titled "Cemeteries as Museums." We hope that this book will recreate some of our walks for our readers as we go back and forth between our two perspectives and that you will hear two distinctive voices conversing.

As we reached the final weeks of writing, however, the book took on a deeper significance. World events helped us see Sunset Cemetery afresh, as a remarkably vibrant microcosm of the Southeastern United States and of our world in general. A pandemic made the story of M.L. Heafner, a man who died of the 1918 flu pandemic and is buried in Sunset, particularly relevant. But more than that, a worldwide movement to address long-simmering issues of racial equality burst into Shelby just as it did across the nation. And here we were writing about the lives and memories of people who set the stage for all of it: Civil War soldiers, those who promoted the historical narrative of the Lost Cause, and those who lived in the Jim Crow South.

In addition to writing about the life and the gravestone of Thomas Dixon, author of the racist novel *The Clansman*, which became the movie *Birth of a Nation*, we had written about W.J. Cash, whose *The Mind of the South* argued for an alternative version of the War. Cash's version shocked those who romanticized the conflict. Both were part of a community of ordinary people who, we came to believe, were trying to find meaning in their lives, often expressed in songs, poetry, and art of all kinds. Few people realize, for example, that Cash's grandfather was a talented artist who honored the dead and made a living by carving some of the most beautiful tombstones in the cemetery.

It's easy to find historical records as well as the published words of public figures such as Cash and Dixon. But some who rest in the cemetery are left without a voice. They include ordinary folks who died before they had time to make a mark on society or whose lives, individual as fingerprints, are now largely forgotten though they were briefly the subject of front-page news. Some were fascinating women who couldn't even vote until 1920 and whose accomplishments may be forgotten altogether when their tombstones identify them only as "wife of." We felt a responsibility to show who they were and what their tombstones tell us about the culture in which they lived.

A bigger responsibility, though, was to give voice to the silenced, the enslaved people buried in the big "empty" field at the west end of the oldest part of the cemetery and the people of color buried there during the Reconstruction era and later. The old section of Sunset is clearly reserved for white people, not because no people of color are buried in it, but because people of color have been erased, both as individuals, and as a community. We hope to honor their memory and to emphasize our common humanity.

The most modern tombstones in Sunset are down the hill from the old section. Here we will introduce you to a beloved policeman, a baby who was "born sleeping," the white country musician Don Gibson, and the Black soul musician Bobby "Pepperhead" London. Modern technology allows us to "see" these Shelby residents in a way we could not before, but what we see is also shaped by the choices they or their families made about the shape, size, and decoration of their gravestones and the gifts left for the dead.

In this book you will hear two very different voices. They appear in the text in different type and different styles.

Joe DePriest, a long-time journalist, using this present font, tells the tales of those buried in Sunset Cemetery. Shelby, North Carolina, is his home town, and he knew some of the people he writes about personally. Others he "knows" through an imaginative rendering of the information he has learned through research. Joe brings the dead and their times to life for us, sometimes with the help of popular music or movies. His sections in the book are about the people.

June Hadden Hobbs, a long-time academic, uses this font to explain the tombstones, the design of the cemetery itself, and American memorial customs in general. Her voice is less narrative and more analytical. Although she has lived near Shelby for decades, her interests are more wide-ranging since she has studied tombstones and cemeteries all over the world. Her focus is on memory itself, how we create it, and what it reveals about us.

Cemeteries are sacred places where lives and memory meet. To understand, we need both the tales and the tombstones.

Introduction
to a Southern Cemetery

A graveyard is an old agreement made between the living and the living
who have died that says we keep their names and dates alive.
Thomas Lynch, "At the Opening of Oak Grove Cemetery Bridge"

Ballad of a Village Graveyard

Joe: In 1841, a wealthy planter donated most of the land for the seat of government in a new county created in the North Carolina foothills. As the village of Shelby

A panoramic view of Sunset Cemetery, founded 1841 in Shelby, North Carolina. The grid pattern of graves and defined family plots are clearly visible. The South Mountains are visible on the horizon. The beautiful sugar maples were planted at the direction of First Lady of North Carolina Bess Hoey, who is buried with her husband, Gov. Clyde R. Hoey, in Sunset Cemetery.

grew, so did its graveyard on part of the 40 acres another planter donated. The burying ground was tucked away northwest of the court square atop a hill overlooking the
South Mountains. One day this landscape of the dead was named Sunset Cemetery, a
park-like retreat for remembrance and reflection.

Like any graveyard, large or small, Sunset welcomed the rich and the poor, righteous and wicked, prominent and obscure. Sunset became a portal on the village's
past. Once spotless grave stones bore witness to the passage of time. Weathered,
lichen-smeared, cracked and broken, the aging relics survived. All the graves sing of
life's joys and woes to any passing pilgrim.

The music lingers in the imagination. In the soft early morning, harsh noontime
glare, or the ebbing afternoon light, the markers always declare themselves, forever
spinning ballads of life and death.

The Poetry of Graveyards

June: To think of a burial place as singing may seem crazy or just overly sentimental, maudlin even. But cemeteries act upon the human imagination in the same
way that poetry and music do.

Hollywood exploits this feature of cemeteries by setting scenes from horror mov-
ies in them. They terrify us and provide psychological satisfaction at the same time. As Stephen King said in a famous essay, "Why We Crave Horror Movies," it all happens on a subconscious level. We watch horror movies—and visit graveyards—to "keep the gators fed."

We all need to keep our darkest imaginings sated. But what of another unspoken need—the need for beauty and memory that binds us to others? The American landscape is filled with economically necessary but sterile places in terms of memory—think shopping malls and gas stations and fast-food joints. Marc Augé calls them

The Eugenia Poteat stone with an epitaph popular in colonial New England. The epitaph reminds viewers of their mortality.

"non-places." In contrast, cemeteries call upon a wealth of devices, from the orientation of the graves to the symbols and words on the gravemarkers, "to evoke memory and bind us together."

By the time Shelby was founded in 1841, the United States had undergone a cultural revolution that changed the way we understood cemeteries. In fact, no one was using the term "cemetery"—from the Greek for "sleeping place"—until this time in history. Before the early nineteenth century, places to dispose of the dead were simply "graveyards" or "burial grounds." And bodies were buried in coffins, not caskets, which were cases in which to keep something precious. The change in the way we viewed the dead was obvious by 1831, when Mount Auburn Cemetery, the first rural or garden cemetery in the United States, was consecrated in Cambridge, Massachusetts. The Rural/Garden Cemetery Movement, which swept the nation during the first half of the nineteenth century, advocated moving cemeteries from the centers of towns into the country, where they could provide an escape from the increasingly industrialized urban centers.

Rural/garden cemeteries also emphasized soul-consoling beauty in a "garden" of graves with beautiful trees and flowers and hopeful gravestones rather than the stark reminder of mortality in this popular colonial epitaph:

> Remember, friend, as you pass by,
> As you are now so once was I.
> As I am now, you soon shall be.
> So prepare for death and follow me

Though Cleveland County was hardly an industrialized metropolis in 1841, Sunset illustrates many of the features of rural cemeteries, including curving roads and family enclosures that emphasize a theme of reunion. Those features work upon our subconscious brains as poetry—or music—does.

I

A Glimpse of Life
a Century and More Ago

John Randolph Logan (1811–1884)

Joe: John Randolph Logan may have walked through Shelby on September 13, 1848. As Cleveland County's first surveyor, he had helped design the wider-than-usual dirt streets around the village square. That would have been an especially welcome asset on that September day because of a special attraction expected to arrive soon.

Not much happened in the village, still in its infancy, except the daily comings and goings of stage coaches. Officials hoped to get a railroad someday, but for now Shelby relied on the occasional fast-talking snake oil salesman, seedy vaudeville shows, or small circus for amusement. But today was different, and J.R. joined a crowd jammed onto the court square. People were likely restless, stepping out onto the streets, craning their necks, looking down a rutted road that led to Wilson Springs, a local landmark. Everybody knew the Post Road, the main route from Lincolnton, was nearby. And they knew the big show everybody waited on would come from that direction.

Newspapers had been spreading the word for weeks. A spectacle probably unlike anything local folks had ever witnessed: a traveling menagerie. It played the Gaston County town of Dallas on September 11; Lincolnton on September 12. Today, September 13, it was headed to Shelby. The crowd waited, and waited. Suddenly, someone may have heard the faint sound of music and hushed. Necks craned: there, in the distance, they spotted what might be carriages and carts. Tension mounted as the music grew louder. At last, the crowd could make out extra-large carriages creeping into the village. The first, pulled by eight large horses, hauled a band decked out in colorful uniforms and playing loudly.

At last, Raymond & Waring's Great Zoological Exhibition of New York City—America's oldest mobile menagerie—made a triumphant entrance into the village of Shelby. What a sight! A gigantic African lion pulled a carriage with a muscle-bound man gripping the reins. Onlookers already knew his name: John Shaffer, the Lion King.

The *Lincoln Courier* had been churning out descriptions of what villagers would experience on menagerie day—as long as they bought a ticket: 50 cents for adults, half-price for children and servants. An advertisement read: "Mr. John Shaffer, the daring lion tamer and his equally intrepid Lady will enter the cage with lions, tigers, leopards and panthers. He will drive a large African Lion harnessed to a car and will by various graceful and daring feats show his complete control over animals usually deemed of the most savage disposition."

The celebrated John Shaffer "has been styled by critics 'The Lion King,' as he has exposed his life heretofore in subduing the largest and most terrible lion ever caught. This animal is at present in his possession and has repeatedly saved his life when exercising the other beasts in the performing cage. His feats have been beheld by millions." This rolling zoological exhibit also transported "wild Tenants of the Forest":

> From the huge docile elephant, the majestic lions of African, the fierce Tiger of the Bengal jungles, the beautiful leopard, the playful but ferocious bear, gentle gazelle, the useful and patient camel, the curiously striped zebra, the grave robbing hyena, the stealthy panther, the savage wolf, the cunning fox, down through all the lesser grades, are here beheld with perfect safety, true to their nature at times, but perfectly subject to the control of man, the lord of creation.

The overripe ballyhoo always stressed who was in charge of all this wildness. Man, The Lord of Creation. Raymond & Waring's cast also included "fowls of the air and reptiles":

> The most beautiful, rare, varied and dangerous of their species are also comprised in this valuable collection; description is powerless and space too limited to admit it. Suffice it so say that the proprietors are of the oldest standing and highest celebrity, and have devoted years of toil and expense in the present collection, which is pronounced in Europe and American perfectly unparalleled.
>
> The moral and useful purposes which an exhibition like this can serve are perceived by all, and acknowledged by all moralists; the exhibition serves to entertain and instruct all in the wondrous works of the Supreme Being, and is particularly impressive on the minds of youth.

Like the other town folk, J.R. Logan wouldn't have missed a high-class show like this. Likely that night, after the menagerie was bedded down, he replayed the day's entertainment in his mind. Perhaps he heard the cries of jungle denizens in their cages at Raymond & Waring's encampment.

Logan may have worried if he had read about previous stops the menagerie made in American cities and towns. Just the previous July, in Poughkeepsie, New York, a Raymond & Waring rhinoceros ran amok when an elephant named Columbus tore off the iron bars of the rhinoceros cage. The animal bolted into nearby fields followed by a hunting party. Unable to catch the beast, they fired rifles but, according to a newspaper account, "They might as well have fired against the side of a stone wall, as his hide resisted the balls as effectively as if he had been encased in iron." The last Logan heard, the raging rhinoceros was still on the loose.

Then, in April of 1847, the menagerie had just closed a show in Philadelphia and animals were being taken across the Delaware River by ferry to Camden, New Jersey. Two elephants—one named Pizarro and the other Virginius—were skittish about boarding on a ferry slip, so their keeper decided to have them swim across the river. After being yoked together, they plunged into the water. A swift current in the river channel swept them downstream. Virginius began to sink, taking Pizarro down with him. The *Poughkeepsie Journal* commented: "We sympathize with Messrs. Raymond & Waring, in their loss, for the two elephants are said to have been worth nearly

$30,000. Virginius and Pizarro were well known to hundreds in this city, and many of their 'friends' (we think we may use this term) will read this announcement with regret—almost with sorrow."

Nothing apparently ran amok the night the menagerie slept in Shelby. Next morning, Logan may have waved goodbye as the Raymond & Waring outfit departed. By then, he was already looking ahead to an entirely different event that would take place on the court square in a few weeks.

On Saturday, October 28, 1848: Logan was among more than 2,000 people at a free public barbecue in honor of returning Mexican War veterans. At least two Cleveland County soldiers had died in the fighting, including James Ingram Love, son of James Love, who donated land for Shelby. Love was wounded on August 12 during the battle at National Bridge, in the state of Vera Cruz. He died on August 19 in Jalapa, the Vera Cruz capital. The *Lincoln Courier* printed a poem written by an officer in the 3rd Dragoons which served in Mexico. Company 12 distinguished itself during the battle at National Bridge where Love was fatally wounded. The final verse reads:

> If it is our fate to fall,
> Then we bid some soldier tell
> Our friends and dear ones, all
> "In the gallant charge we fell."
> O who would not wish thus to die,
> And sleep in the soldiers' grave!
> Until the world flies swiftly by
> And the trumpet wakes the brave!

In Shelby, the welcome mat at the free barbecue went out for Mexican War veterans from Cleveland, Gaston, Lincoln, Rutherford and Catawba counties. Just seven years after Cleveland County was formed, the court square in the center of the village had already become a popular spot for public gatherings. And they would continue down through the years—from barbecues and circuses to military exercises and band concerts.

At some point that day in October 1848, the *Lincoln Courier* reported that toasts were offered up to distinguished persons who were absent, beginning with the President of the United States, moving down through the U.S. Senate, House of Representatives, and the judiciary, moving on to the North Carolina governor, the army and navy. Toasts were extended to the memories of George Washington, Benjamin Franklin—a total of thirty, in all.

Someone even raised a glass to "the Fair Sex" and intoned: "May they ever be recognized as the noblest and most exquisite part of the human creation, while those who would degrade and under rate them as inferior and unfit for the society of man may go down to the dark shades of oblivion unwept and unsung." With a presidential election coming up on November 7, politics hovered in many minds. The Whig candidate was Mexican War hero Zachary Taylor. He faced Democrat Lewis Case, who was also a general officer in the Mexican War.

On that October day in 1848, standing on the village square, J.R. Logan raised a toast: "To Maj. General Zachary Taylor—the modest unpretending man; the hero that never surrenders; the idol of the soldiery, and the choice of the people for President of the United States. May his success be as certain as his career at Palo Alto, Resaca De La Palma, Monterey and Buena Vista was victorious, brilliant and glorious." Logan called the names of famous U.S. victories emblazoned in newspaper headlines throughout the nation.

The presidential race was close in November, but Old Zach came out on top. J.R. Logan's man went to the White House. Years raced by. A Civil War ravaged the nation, and then healing began. New presidents. New issues. The Old Guard falling away. Chester A. Arthur was president when J.R. Logan died in 1884. That's the same year Mark Twain was writing *Huckleberry Finn*, the Washington Monument was completed, and France presented the Statue of Liberty to America.

When Logan was buried in Sunset Cemetery, with a plain grave marker, Shelby had grown. The village had a population of about 900 and at long last

Tombstone for John Randolph Logan, the first Cleveland County surveyor, set in a family lot marked off by concrete coping.

business prospered. A railroad provided daily passenger service. Thirty-six years before J.R. came to Sunset Cemetery, he had stood on the court square watching the arrival of Raymond & Waring's mobile menagerie. A brass band from New York City filled the streets with music. An African lion in harness pulled a carriage around the court square for awestruck onlookers. Caged fowls flung tropical squawks all over town, drowning out Southern mockingbirds. Panthers hissed and hyenas laughed. Trumpeting elephants and groaning camels stirred dust. It all happened right there on the village streets. On the wide streets that J.R. designed. On the streets that remained his legacy.

Tombstones and Cemeteries 101

June: In sharp contrast to his life, J.R. Logan's tombstone is plain and unremarkable. It includes his name and dates, and not much else. Its most interesting feature is placement in a family lot marked off by concrete coping. Burial customs such as this were in flux in North Carolina and in most of the United States during Logan's lifetime, as the following overview shows.

A. Colonial Times to the Early Nineteenth Century

Characteristics: burials on family land or in churchyards, graves laid out in a grid pattern with east/west orientation, tombstones of indigenous materials, professionally carved/imported tombstones indicate wealth and status

Most burials during this period would have been on family-owned land or in churchyards. Cleveland County, North Carolina, alone has nearly 300 documented burial sites, many of them containing just a handful of burials and many without gravemarkers. Unless a family was very wealthy, graves might have been marked with field stones or with handmade markers of whatever was readily available. Sturdy gneiss is one possibility. This reliance on locally available material is typical of the colonies and the early Republic. Slate was the material of choice in the Northeast, for example.

People with enough money could import tombstones or hire a local stonecutter to produce a unique professional marker. Visitors can find locally produced professional stones in places such as Steele Creek Presbyterian Church Cemetery in Charlotte, which includes a remarkable set of stones carved by the Bigham Family workshop. These beautiful stones include secular

A row of field stones marks the graves of people buried in Sunset during the early years.

The Andrew Bigham stone in Steele Creek Presbyterian Church Cemetery in Charlotte, North Carolina. The design, based on the Great Seal of Pennsylvania, was carved in the Bigham workshop (photograph by June Hadden Hobbs).

images such as American eagles or coats of arms, even though North Carolina was a place where class distinctions were not what they were in, say, England. Daniel Patterson notes that stonecarvers sometimes created a coat of arms for a family in the American colonies or during the early days of the republic even though that family would not have been entitled to one in the old country. Many of these designs are carved on readily available soapstone.

Burial grounds themselves would have been called "graveyards" or perhaps "burying places." The day of cemeteries was yet to come. In churchyards, graves were laid out in a grid pattern, just as a farmer might sow a field. Earth burial is itself an important metaphor in an agricultural community. We expect what we "bury" in the ground to come back up.

Today we think of cemeteries as sacred places of memory. The graveyards of early settlers were much more utilitarian. They were obviously a necessity, but no one visited them just to stroll and refresh their souls. Still, graveyards could be an important teaching tool since they often were placed near a church, where people had to pass by the graves of their loved ones every time they attended.

In New England, in fact, *The New England Primer*, the most important elementary school textbook, emphasized the teaching value of graveyards. This textbook, first published around 1688 and used for decades after that, taught a combination of reading skills and Puritan values. Children learned their lessons by rote, which means that very young children would have been required to memorize verses such as this:

> I in the Burying Place may see
> Graves shorter there than I;
> From Death's Arrest no Age is free.
> Young Children too may die;
> My God, may such an awful Sight,
> Awakening be to me!
> Oh! that by early Grace I might
> For Death prepared be.

Although the *New England Primer* was the only textbook widely available in New England, we do not know if it was used in North Carolina. Still, its influence was enormous. It is the source of the first prayer many children learn, the one that begins "Now I lay me down to sleep."

B. The Nineteenth Century

Characteristics: More municipal graveyards, language changes ("cemeteries" instead of "graveyards," "caskets" instead of "coffins"), curving walkways, family plots, marble tombstones, emphasis on the community, beautiful plantings, hopeful icons and epitaphs such as fingers pointing to heaven and lines from Protestant hymns

The oldest sections of Sunset Cemetery reflect some features of an eighteenth-century graveyards with graves laid out on a grid pattern. A few of the gravemarkers also suggest an older way of marking graves. The crumbling brick vaults and box tombs on the westernmost edge are holdovers from an earlier day when such gravemarkers were clues to the status of those buried under them. Only wealthier inhabitants could afford these more elaborate ways to mark the graves of their loved ones. The bodies are still in the earth although vaults and box tombs give the appearance of an above-ground burial.

The Rural/Garden Cemetery Movement that formally began in 1831 with the consecration of Mount Auburn Cemetery in Cambridge, Massachusetts, was a response to cultural forces that changed American thinking and the American landscape. Fear of contagious diseases was one of them. In the early decades of the nineteenth century, people often assumed that fatal diseases such as typhoid and cholera were caused by fatal "miasmas," or bad odors that rose from places such as graveyards. Moving them into the country and away from the city was a way to ensure the health of the population.

But more than that, industrialization was changing the way people lived. Once railroads began to connect even small towns like Shelby, North Carolina, to the wider world, citizens' sense of time changed because railroads had to run on schedule. By the 1870s when the first railroad came to Cleveland County, cotton mills were beginning to employ many residents. Joining the industrial age meant that the South, like the Northeast, was living faster.

Crumbling box tombs and vaults on the west side of Sunset rise above the grave to signal the status of the deceased, who are buried in the ground.

A few years before the circus came to Shelby, Henry David Thoreau built a little cabin on the banks of Walden Pond just outside of Concord, Massachusetts, to "live deliberately" and escape the increasing demands of progress and civilization. The railroad was a particular target of his ire, representing as it did, both the gains and losses of industrialized America. It so took over life in progressive parts of the United States that Thoreau wearily proclaimed: "We do not ride on the railroad; it rides upon us."

The antidote was twofold, and both are represented in the cemeteries of the period. First, civic-minded citizens in Boston pushed to create cemeteries, literally "sleeping places" for the dead, in rural areas where people could escape the pressures of the modern world. Mount Auburn in nearby Cambridge became so popular for Sunday outings that it had to establish "rest stations" for the ladies outside the cemetery gates and limit the number of visitors who could come in at one time. It was the nineteenth-century equivalent of Disneyland for grownups.

The South soon followed suit, founding its own "pleasure gardens," as they were sometimes called. These burial places might more properly be called "garden cemeteries" than "rural cemeteries" in the South because the South was largely rural anyway at this point and gardening was already a treasured tradition. Riverside Cemetery in Asheville, Oakwood in Raleigh, and Oakdale in Wilmington are notable examples of garden cemeteries in North Carolina.

The older part of Sunset illustrates many of the features that made these new cemeteries attractive: curving walkways that take one "off the grid," beautiful trees

Curving walkways, typical of the rural/garden cemeteries, invite leisurely strolls that take visitors "off the grid" in the early Industrial Era.

and other plantings, attractive marble monuments, and hopeful messages about heaven and reunion in a heavenly home. They are very different from the utilitarian graveyards of a century earlier. Rural/garden cemeteries also generally have distinctive gates that separate the world of the living from the world of the dead. This world of the dead is not the domain of, say, zombies or horrifying glimpses of long bones dug up by animals. It is the world of heaven, where those gone on before live in peace and tranquility, protected from the passage of time. The gate at the entrance to Sunset Cemetery is not as elaborate as many, but it does a good job of distinguishing the two worlds.

The other antidote to industrialization was the Cult of Domesticity, which equated the middle-class home with respite from the world of work. The home was a place devoted to preservation of the family, not the unceasing quest for profit and progress. The Cult of Domesticity drove the emphasis on the family, especially the nuclear family, in a cemetery such as Sunset.

Family plots are often clearly marked off with coping or iron fencing—to the dismay of those charged today with upkeep of the grass. Blanche Linden-Ward notes that the nineteenth-century "fencing mania" had practical uses as well since it kept animals and strollers from damaging markers or plantings. And there are other ways to establish family connections. At least one tombstone in Sunset, for example, is marked with a family coat of arms for the Eskridge family. In the twentieth-century sections of the older part of Sunset, individual markers are often arranged around a large central grave marker with the family name on it. The idea

The authors and photographer pose at the entrance to Sunset Cemetery. The gates of a rural/ garden cemetery such as the older part of Sunset separate a sacred space from the stressful industrialized world. Left to right: June Hadden Hobbs, Joe DePriest, Hal Bryant.

is to create a place for reunion of living family members with those who have gone on before. In this way, the garden cemetery becomes a reminder of heaven—where time will be no more and loved ones will be reunited. Sadly, the Cult of Domesticity was an attainable ideal only for middle-class white people, not for those who were enslaved or impoverished.

The French philosopher Philippe Ariès has named the nineteenth century the "Age of the Beautiful Death." Calvinism was waning, especially after the Civil War, and without the fear that one might end up endlessly burning in a fiery

Wrought-iron fencing identifies a family plot in Sunset Cemetery. Emphasis on the middle-class family is characteristic of a rural/ garden cemetery.

The Eskridge family coat of arms emphasizes the importance of family connections in Sunset Cemetery.

pit, life after death started looking better and better. In fact, many people in places like Shelby began to imagine that it was very much like life on earth but without sorrow, physical imperfections, loneliness, or unfulfilled desires. Death became an experience to anticipate with pleasure, just like a stroll in Sunset Cemetery.

C. The Twentieth and Twenty-First Centuries

Characteristics: Less attention to cemetery aesthetics, abandonment of family plots, efficient use of space, mostly granite markers, highly individualized icons and epitaphs, emphasis on the secular, individualized grave goods

By the time land from T.D. Lattimore's dairy farm had been added to Sunset to form the new section, attitudes toward death and the afterlife had changed again. Ours is a time marked by an increasing reluctance to accept the inevitability of death at all. We find it unseemly, even morbid, to talk about it or to grieve too openly. Ariès calls modern times the era of "Forbidden Death." The landscape and tombstones in the new section of Sunset reflect these new attitudes by focusing attention on the lives of individuals rather than on the shared experience of anticipating the afterlife in a soul-restoring setting.

The newest section of Sunset is not meant to entice visitors to spend hours wandering the cemetery. The assumption is that people will come to bury and, perhaps, visit their loved ones, not to enjoy the cemetery itself. With few trees, it is too hot in warm weather and too bleak in cold weather to work as a "pleasure ground." Most modern cemeteries, especially the newest memorial parks, have a distinctly utilitarian feel to them although one more professionally polished than colonial graveyards.

The older sections of Sunset reflect attributes of a close-knit community and the influence of new-fangled ideas such as life insurance. According to James J. Farrell in *Inventing the American Way of Death, 1830–1920,* "life insurance refocused attention from the death of an individual to the lives of the survivors. The very name 'life' insurance reflected this purpose." Many of the fraternal organizations whose emblems adorn gravestones in the older section of Sunset also served as life insurance companies in that they paid burial costs or at least contributed to buying a tombstone for their members. The community was more important than the individual.

By the twentieth century, banding together to pay burial expenses, not to mention supporting widows and orphans, was no longer as crucial. Social Security, workplace benefits, and more women in the workplace made us more independent of each other and, sadly, more separated in the ordinary course of our lives. The counterculture of the 1960s also drove an emphasis on radical individualism as the Baby Boomers used their college campuses as sites of protest against the establishment.

The result is tombstones that focus on the interests and personalities of the individual, not on community values. These stones are almost always commercially produced granite markers. In addition to traditional gray, they come in a variety of colors, including rose and shiny black. The latter is especially suitable for laser-etched portraits of the deceased as they looked in life, perhaps engaged in their favorite activities or in their favorite settings.

Consider, for example, the tombstone for Timothy James Brackeen, a Shelby police office who died from wounds suffered in the line of duty in 2016. His tombstone is very different from those in the older section of Sunset. A photograph of Officer Brackeen in his uniform with his K-9 companion is etched into the top of the stone underneath his badge. Below his dates are characteristics that recall his life: "committed Christian, faithful husband, devoted father, honorable son and brother, respected police office, passionate K-9 Handler," and "HERO." At the foot of the grave is a rectangular footstone with the words "Good" and "Evil" separated by a blue line and Brackeen's badge number, 763. The symbolism of the police force— the thin blue line that stands between good and evil—could not be clearer.

Certainly these memorial stones evoke community values, but their overall focus is on Officer Brackeen as both public hero and honorable private man. The words "a just man made perfect" are an allusion to Hebrews 12:23, which describes the righteous perfected in heaven. This complex memorial is an attempt to capture the essence of the living man, not to dwell on his tragic death.

Brackeen's tombstone is surrounded by grave goods, gifts left by visitors that include a can of his favorite soda. Although adorning graves with flowers, a custom associated with the nineteenth century, is still important, the modern custom is to leave individualized gifts that complement the individualized markers. Near Brackeen's grave, recent visitors have found a bag of pinto beans, a bottle of Jim Beam, and

The tombstone for K9 Officer Timothy James Brackeen of the Shelby Police Department, who died from wounds suffered in the line of duty.

Matchbox cars on a child's grave. Perhaps grieving friends and family imagine that the spirit of the deceased is still earthbound, hovering somehow near the gravesite.

In contrast to the memorials for Shelby police officers Robert Shelton Jones and Edgar Hamrick, whose stories are told later, Officer Brackeen's family has taken care to ensure we imagine him properly. It's all right there on the tombstone.

Top: Footstone for K9 Officer Timothy James Brackeen emphasizing the "thin blue line" that stands between good and evil in the community. *Bottom:* Grave goods left as gifts for the deceased at the grave of Officer Timothy Brackeen.

Jesse Jenkins (1832–1889)
Hattie Jenkins Garloch (1835–1927)
Charles Coleman Blanton (1858–1944)
Ora Brewster Blanton (1858–1890)

Joe: When Jesse Jenkins died in 1889, he got a sleek obelisk in Sunset Cemetery, a monument befitting a distinguished soldier, banker and lawyer. A sturdy iron fence surrounded the spacious burial plot, but apparently nobody else was interred there. Jesse's wife, Hattie—an almost legendary figure in Shelby because of her indomitable personality—would most certainly have preferred to be buried beside the man she described in words carved on the obelisk: "My Darling Husband." How Hattie wound up buried alone under a plain marker out in San Diego, California, added extra fuel to her legend.

The vain and dramatic Hattie was the daughter of Joshua Beam, a rich planter and public leader. She grew up in a big house by Buffalo Creek, about two miles east of Shelby. Hattie was one tiny voice in a household of many other siblings. But she found her voice early on and let it be heard to advantage. How she met Jesse is a story buried in time. In 1855, they married and settled down in the village of Shelby, where he would become an up-and-coming figure after the Civil War. Jesse had barely survived the war. An officer in the Confederate Army, he was wounded on a Virginia battlefield severely enough to send him home for the duration.

After the war, Jesse rose rapidly as a businessman and founder of Shelby's first bank. People liked him so much they elected him to the North Carolina State Senate. In 1874, while in Raleigh with her husband, Hattie fell in love with a new house that featured the spectacular Second Empire design. She wanted one like it in Shelby and Jesse built her one on North Lafayette Street that became known as The Banker's House.

The stories of Jesse Jenkins and others are told in more detail in *Voices in Time: Stories of the Banker's House*. Hattie's new house came at a high cost. She had wanted so many expensive extras that upon completion, the overruns contributed to Jesse's already faltering financial situation. He and Hattie moved in, but only managed to stay there a couple of years before Jesse lost everything and their world fell apart.

As told in the Banker's House book, they still stuck together and moved to Meridian, Texas, where Jesse started a new career as a lawyer specializing in real estate. His winning personality made him popular there in the Lone Star State and voters elected him to the Texas State Senate. But the old solider who had dodged death back in the Civil War died at his Meridian home early on a December morning in 1889 at the age of 57. Hattie brought his remains back to Shelby on a train and had her "darling husband" buried in Sunset Cemetery.

Hattie stayed in Shelby—for a while. It took her until 1897 to find a new husband, this time a country doctor named W.A. Thompson. Like Jesse, the doctor had been an army officer in the Civil War. When his first wife died, his many children were grown and scattered. Thompson must have been lonely in his big house in the farming community of Belwood in northern Cleveland County. A question likely posed

The Jesse Jenkins stone. This granite obelisk honors the Confederate soldier, banker, and lawyer who built the Banker's House in Shelby. Tour guides sometimes tell visitors that the tallest monument in the older part of Sunset Cemetery is appropriate for the man who built the tallest house in town. The back of the monument includes a tribute from Jenkins' wife, Hattie: "MY DARLING HUSBAND."

by Shelby's gossip mill would have been: Why had the sociable, city-loving Hattie moved way off into the sticks with his old man? According to *Voices in Time*, local speculation was that Hattie married the doctor because she thought he had money and he thought the same thing of her; and it turned out both were wrong.

Voices in Time quotes from a fragmentary diary Hattie kept while living in the country, frequently describing how she despised her new husband. By 1903, they lived apart, Hattie in Shelby, the doctor in Belwood. However, they remained married up until his death in 1907. Six years later, Hattie boarded a train and headed to California. Five years later, she would send a letter to her hometown newspaper, the *Cleveland Star*, announc-

The Second-Empire-style Banker's House in Shelby, North Carolina. Built in 1874–75 by Jesse Jenkins and his wife Hattie, it is now an event site for weddings and other occasions managed by the Banker's House Foundation.

ing that the reason she had gone to California was to find a man just like her first husband, her beloved Jesse—and that she'd been successful.

The lucky man was a Mr. Thomas Garloch, about whom Hattie had little to say except that he was an officer in the U.S. Army and the "double" of Jesse. As told in *Voices in Time*, Hattie failed to say that Garloch was a private, not an officer, and 30 years younger than his new bride. Or that she had lied about her age to the magistrate who had performed the marriage ceremony. She had told him she was 61 which he put on the marriage license. In fact, she was 81, a fact documented on the marriage certificate.

They tied the knot in San Diego County and lived there happily ever after—so far as anybody in Shelby knew. Hattie never went back. What really happened in California is a mystery. When Hattie died in 1927, her husband erected a flat marker on her grave with this information: Hattie J. Garloch, 1835–1927. A month later, he remarried. Thomas Garloch and his third wife were buried in Fort Rosecrans National Cemetery, across San Diego Bay from Hattie. Her marker there had no hint of her colorful life and the passion she had felt for her first husband a continent away in Shelby's Sunset Cemetery. But Jesse's tall obelisk in Sunset stood as a monument to both of them, and their true love.

Charles and Ora

Like his friend Jesse Jenkins, Charles Blanton fell in love in Shelby and lived for a time in the same Texas town of Meridian. They rested near each other in Sunset Cemetery, but their wives were buried elsewhere—Hattie Jenkins in California, Ora Brewster in Tennessee. Charles and Ora met by chance in Shelby, had a whirlwind courtship, and started a new life together in Texas. Five years later, she died at the age of 31.

Charles must have replayed each step of their brief journey. He had been a bank president in Meridian and came home to Shelby for occasional visits. On one of these stops, relatives or friends may have introduced him to the petite Ora Brewster of Sweetwater, Tennessee, who taught music at the newly organized Shelby Female College. What happened during that encounter apparently approximated love at first sight.

Charles and Ora were married in 1885 in her hometown of Sweetwater, and Ora, the newcomer to Shelby, became Ora, the newcomer in the dusty cattle town of Meridian, Texas, down in Bosque County south of Dallas. Charles already had many friends there, including Jesse and Hattie Jenkins, former Shelby residents who had moved to Meridian in 1880 after Jesse's financial downfall and loss of their Second Empire home, The Banker's House. As told in *Voices in Time: Stories of the Banker's House*, Ora, as the wife of a bank president, would have likely been introduced to a wide network of local people and probably made friends quickly. Some connections, no doubt, came through her deep interest in music.

At some point, Ora developed serious, unspecified health problems. Charles took her to an Atlanta hospital where she underwent surgery and died on January 26, 1890. The *Atlanta Constitution* ran a short story headed "The Wife of a Texas Banker Dies After a Surgical Operation" and went on to say,

> Mrs. C.C. Blanton died in this city yesterday. Mr. Blanton, who is a wealthy banker from Texas, brought his wife here some time ago, accompanied by her brother, for the purpose of having a very delicate surgical operation performed.
>
> Mrs. Blanton had long been a sufferer and submitted to the ordeal as the last resort to preserve her life. The operation was successfully performed a few days since, but the shock was too much for her system and she continued sinking until her death occurred yesterday. The remains will be conveyed to Sweetwater, Tennessee, where the funeral will occur.
>
> Mrs. Blanton was a lady of many loveable traits of character and rare personal charms. Her death is a sad bereavement to her relatives here, and to those whom she loved and who loved her in her home in the west.

Ora's funeral may have been held in Sweetwater, but she was buried, probably at her request, in Knoxville's Old Gray Cemetery, where her mother and sister rested. Charles ordered a large Victorian angel for Ora's grave and was a frequent visitor, as described in *Voices in Time*. In 1895, Charles moved back to Shelby to work at the bank his father had acquired—the same one Jesse Jenkins had founded in 1874. Over

The tombstone for Charles Blanton, president of First National Bank of Shelby and one of the owners of The Banker's House.

the years, he served as bank president and became a respected business and civic leader in the community.

"Uncle Charlie," as nieces and nephews called him, never remarried and talked about Ora constantly. If he heard a musical piece like Edward Rimbalt's arrangement of Felix Mendelssohn's "Wedding March," Ora probably came to mind. It was one of her favorites. A Raleigh newspaper had once heaped praise on her rendition of "Wedding March" when she performed it, along with several of her students, at the Thomasville Female College commencement in 1884, the year before she came to Shelby.

Charles named two saddle horses after his late wife: Ora and Brewster. The *Cleveland Star* reported that he grieved when they died in a barn fire behind the Banker's House in October 1911. The years rolled on. In 1923 Charles named a new Shelby textile plant the Ora Mill in honor of his late wife. The preacher conducing Charles' funeral service in 1944 at Shelby's First Baptist Church mentioned Ora's name. She had always been a presence in Shelby. Charles was buried beside his friend Jesse Jenkins in Sunset Cemetery. Their beloved wives rested far away, but that distance shrank to nothing when cemetery visitors paused to remember the stories of these couples.

Charles Fromm (1828–1891)
Rosa Fromm (1830–1896)
Belle Fromm (1861–1927)

They were the only Fromms in the cemetery, Charles and Rosa, resting in a family plot with ample room for more relatives. But no more relatives were there. The two large markers behind a wrought-iron fence document Charles' birth in Germany and Rosa's in Ohio. Who were these people, and what brought them to Shelby? Another question also arises: Who did the Fromms hope might join them in the plot? A prime candidate would have been their daughter, Belle Fromm. Unlike her two sisters, Belle never married. For many years, she ran a women's clothing store on North Lafayette Street in Shelby and dabbled in local real estate.

A Shelby fixture, Belle most likely planned on being buried by her parents in Sunset Cemetery, and it might have happened if she had stayed in town. But Fate put her on a path that led all over the east coast and eventually to a pauper's grave in Atlanta. The Southern chapter of the Fromm family saga began in August 1880 when the Anderson (S.C.) *Intelligencer* reported on the recent death of a child:

> A few days ago Charlie Fromm, a little boy about ten years of age, son of Mr. Charles Fromm of this place, accidentally cut an artery in his thigh with a pocket-knife. The wound was dressed by physicians, but broke out two or three times, and on Wednesday at noon the physicians found it necessary to perform an operation to take up the artery, under which the patient died. The bereaved family have the sympathy of the community in their affliction.

Life moved on, and the following summer the *Intelligencer* had good news about the family:

> Professor C. Fromm, an experienced mineralogist who has resided in Anderson for the past two years, has made during that time numerous discoveries of valuable minerals, has consented to collect for Col. A.P. Butler, Commissioner of Agriculture for this state, specimens of the mineral of Anderson County to be exhibited at the Atlanta Exposition this fall.

Fromm also took charge of Anderson County's mineral specimens for the big exposition. He had already located copper, gold, asbestos, epidote, corundum, amethyst, beryl, garnet, rutile, mica, rock crystal, serpentine, manganese, kaolin, granite, tourmaline, chalcedony and chrysotile, among others.

It appeared that Charles had carved out a satisfactory niche for himself in South Carolina. But around 1884, the Fromm family packed up and moved to Shelby, North Carolina, where the local economy had, for whatever reasons, entered a boom time. Sizing up the town, 23-year-old Belle knew what she wanted: her own millinery shop uptown in the thick of things. While she got that up and running, her mineralogist father started manufacturing bricks, a potentially lucrative business given the local economic surge.

Whether by luck or instinct, Charles had managed to arrive at the birth of Cleveland County's textile industry. In August 1887, Shelby's *New Era* reported that "Mr. C. Fromm has already erected the 25-horse power machinery for making the brick for the new cotton factory." Six months earlier, he had made brick for the new Cleveland Mills. Then, in December of 1887, Charles' good fortune suffered a setback. Fire destroyed what the *New Era* called his "beautiful cottage." Around twelve o'clock, sparks from the kitchen chimney burned under the tin roofing and set the North Shelby residence ablaze. "As usual, the citizens of Shelby were on hand promptly and worked hard to save the house," the *New Era* reported. "Most of the furniture was saved. Mr. Fromm's loss is $1,200 on the house and $200 on furniture. He was insured for $1,000."

As Charles continued making brick for the growing town, Miss Belle Fromm made a name for herself in retail sales. She had plenty of local competition in the ladies' millinery line, and waged an aggressive advertising campaign. Her oft-repeated message: quality goods, the cheapest prices. Belle loved the word "cheap." Her newspaper ads read: "Cheaper than the cheapest," "The Cheapest Store in Cleveland County," "Cheaper Than Ever."

Cheap drew the customers. And some, like Hattie Jenkins Thompson, became Belle's friends. Belle especially hit it off with Hattie, who had returned to Shelby from Texas in 1889 after the death of her first husband, Jesse Jenkins. Before the Fromms moved to Shelby, Hattie topped the A-list of Shelby elite. Her husband had founded the town's first bank, served in the state legislature, and built his wife a fine new Second Empire house on North Lafayette Street. But everything went down the drain when Jesse went bust and the couple moved to Texas. Back in town after Jesse's death, Hattie shopped at Miss Belle's store, and they took a liking to each other despite an age difference of nearly 30 years. The two women visited in each other's homes. Belle, the younger of the two, may have talked about her various business deals; Hattie could have let off steam about her second husband, a man she would describe in a secret diary now in the archives of the Earl Scruggs Center in Shelby as "that old hypocrite."

In March 1899 they had plenty to talk about: Shelby news circulating statewide. The *Asheville Citizen* reported:

> While the storm of Saturday night was raging in all fierceness and the wind was roaring and howling, and the lightning flashing and crashing, burglars entered the stores of J.C. Morrison, T.K. Barnett and Miss Belle Fromm. They effected entrance in each case by raising a window, using a screw driver as a prize. In Mr. Morrison's store they helped themselves to watches and jewelry to the amount of $50. In Mr. Barnett's they stole his cash drawer, but fortunately he had not left any funds in the drawer.

The story didn't mention what the burglars took from Miss Belle's store. Belle would surely have told Hattie about it. The women would have discussed the fire in uptown Shelby early on the morning of July 18, 1904. According to the *Charlotte Observer*, the alarm sounded at 1:30 a.m., alerting the populace that several stores, including T.W. Hamrick & Co. china and glassware and T.K. Barnett hardware, had gone up in flames. A brick building survived, but the wooden buildings didn't stand a chance. "It was impossible to save anything, as everything was burning by the time the citizens arrived," the *Observer* reported. "The buildings belonged to the estate of D.C. Webb and Miss Belle Fromm, and there was no insurance on them."

Belle and Hattie knew all too well about life's ups and downs. And they knew how to keep on keeping on. The new century had handed Belle some hard knocks, but her clothing business kept packing in the customers who couldn't get enough of cheap, cheap, cheap. "Miss Belle Fromm has, for a number of years, been thoroughly identified with the business interests of Shelby," the *Shelby Aurora* observed in December 1906. "She handles a full line of millinery goods and notions. She has been quite successful in business. Don't fail to see her when in need of anything in her line."

So why did Miss Belle, nearing the age of 50, walk away from it all and leave Shelby? Hattie would have known. And she likely shared with Belle a dream of leaving town. Part of the answer may be in a brief that ran in the *Cleveland Star* in May 1909 under the headline "Fourteen Years-old Girl Runs Off and Is Married":

> Last Monday, Shelby people were surprised to hear of the unexpected marriage of little Miss May Lowry, the adopted orphan child of Miss Belle Fromm, to Kid Golden of Lynchburg, Va. The affair is an excellent illustration of cupid's capers and the young couple was so deeply pierced with love arrows they could not live without each other and went across the line to Grover and committed matrimony before Squire Mullinax. The bride was only 14 years old.

How Miss Belle Fromm's adopted orphan girl came under the spell of an older man and ran off with him must have kept the Shelby gossip grinding away for years. Meanwhile, Miss Belle left Shelby. By September 1911, she lived on West Depot Street in Concord, North Carolina, and took out an ad in the *Charlotte Evening Chronicle* offering her "valuable residence in Shelby to sell or exchange for store room." In October, she took out a notice in the *Concord Daily Tribune* offering to sell her house and millinery store on West Depot Street.

She lived in Baltimore in March 1915, when she sold a Shelby storeroom occupied by W.B. Nix to shoe salesman W. Hugh Wray. Maybe by then Belle had heard from 80-year-old Hattie announcing that she had settled in San Diego to look for a new husband. From 1915, Miss Belle disappeared from the record. She died on the morning of August 24, 1927, in the Old Woman's Home at 891 West End Avenue, Atlanta. Her plain grave marker tucked away by a stone wall in a far corner of historic Oakland Cemetery gave only her name and the dates of her birth and death. The birth year was listed as 1871 when it should have read 1861. Miss Belle was only 63 when she died from a cerebral hemorrhage, according to her death certificate.

Did she know that her old friend Hattie, living out in San Diego, had died at age 92 in April 1927? Did Belle ever find out if adopted daughter Mary Lowry had a long and happy marriage? Sitting there in the Old Woman's Home, did Belle think of the song Canadian tenor Henry Barr made popular that long ago year when the 14-year-old Mary ran off?

> When other lips
> And other hearts their tales of love
> Shall tell in language whose excess imparts
> The power they feel so well.
> There may perhaps in such a scene some recollection
> Be of days that have as happy been
> And you'll remember me
> And you'll remember me
> You'll remember me.
>
> When coldness or deceit
> Shall slight the beauty now they prize

And deem it but a faded light
Which burns within your eyes.
When hollow hearts shall wear a mask
'Twill break your own to see
In such a moment I but ask
Then you'll remember me
Then you'll remember me.
You'll remember me.

Dr. Jonathan Chauncey Gidney (1835–1889)

They laid Dr. J.C. Gidney to rest in the oldest part of Sunset Cemetery under a Woodmen of the World tombstone shaped like a tree trunk. Marble ivy and toadstool adorn the monument, possibly ordered from a catalog. The open pages of a large stone book atop the marker may have listed the doctor's accomplishments. But lichen and acid rain have made all that unreadable most of the time.

As years passed, the doctor's name remained intact on the front of the stone, yet his reputation faded from local memories. Once, Dr. Gidney had been Cleveland County's Superintendent of Health and served as treasurer for the City of Shelby. He was also a physician who ran a drug store. In September 1887, he placed an advertisement in a local newspaper, the *New Era,* announcing he had resumed his drug store business at the corner of Warren and LaFayette streets in Shelby. The newspaper reported the particulars. It seemed that

Tree stump monument for Dr. J.C. Gidney. The monument is covered with simulated bark and displays carved ivy and a toadstool. At one time it had a readable Woodmen of the World logo. Tree-stump monuments were very popular in the late-nineteenth and early twentieth centuries.

Dr. John H. McBrayer had sold to Dr. Gidney the drug business that Gidney had sold to McBrayer a few months earlier.

"Dr. Gidney will continue to conduct business at the old stand," the paper continued. "Dr. McBrayer will soon engage in the manufacture of patent medicines in one of the largest cities of the south. Dr. Gidney stated he would be 'glad to see his old friends and customers.' 'My stock of medicines is pure and fresh. PRESCRIPTIONS carefully compounded,' he said." In addition to drugs, the doctor offered paints, oils, tobacco, varnishes, snuff, cigars, toilet, and fancy articles. He also had soap, perfumes, window glass, putty, lamps and window goods. Almost daily, the *New Era* ran notices about the doctor's products, which came from the Acker Company. The brief, over-the-top descriptions of these cure-all concoctions created a curious kind of poetry. However far-fetched the claims, Dr. Gidney apparently gave his blessing.

Almost daily, the *New Era* carried notices like this one from March 1889: "People everywhere confirm our statement when we say that Acker's English Remedy is in every way superior to any and all preparations for the throat and lungs. In whooping cough and croup it is magic and relieves at once. We offer you a simple bottle free. Remember, this remedy is sold on a positive guarantee by Dr. J.C. Gidney."

From the *New Era* in May 1889: "Another child killed by the use of opiates given in the form of soothing syrup. Why mothers give their children such deadly poison is surprising when they can relieve the child of its peculiar troubles by using Acker's Baby Soother. It contains no opium or morphine. Sold by Dr. J.C. Gidney."

Then from the following month: "Acker's blood elixir has gained a firm hold on the American people and is acknowledged to be superior to all other preparations. It is a positive cure for all blood and skin diseases. The medical fraternity endorse and prescribe it. Guaranteed and sold by Dr. J.C. Gidney."

In July 1889, the doctor targeted pimples on the face, which "denote an impure state of the blood and are looked upon by many with suspicion. Acker's Blood Elixir will remove all impurities and leave the complexion smooth and clear. There is nothing that will so thoroughly build up the constitution, purify and strengthen the whole system. Sold and Guaranteed by Dr. J.C. Gidney." The *New Era* was owned by brothers George and Charles Fromm, who had moved to Shelby from Baltimore around 1885. In addition to reporting the news, they injected a little humor into their pages from time to time, like this item from June 1888:

> Noticing an extended throng around Dr. J.C. Gidney's drug store last week, the editor hastened to ascertain what was wrong. He found the doctor and his energetic assistant Mr. Kemp Kendall hard at work resuscitating a young men who has just finished two glasses of soda water from the magnificent new soda fountain lately purchased by Dr. Gidney. After hard work, the life of the youth was saved. Mr. Kendall says that hereafter he will guarantee not to freeze anybody to death.

Kendall resigned from his drug store job in December of that year and moved to Rock Hill, South Carolina, where he went to work with druggists Fewell & Co. A.M. Whisnant took Kendall's place in Dr. Gidney's store. On October 3, 1889, the *Charlotte Observer* ran a short notice about the 54-year-old Dr. Gidney's death from heart trouble. The story noted that he was secretary of the Masonic lodge and was buried with Masonic honors. "He leaves a widow," the *Observer* reported, without naming her. No other survivors were listed. Dr. Gidney and his wife, Mattie, had grieved over the loss at early ages of two children, Myrtle and Chauncey, both of whom are buried beside them. The passing of a man of Dr. Gidney's prominence would have likely grieved the town of Shelby and brought many of his friends and customers to his gravesite in early October 1889, when he was buried in Sunset Cemetery. (Mattie remarried to Burton C. Houser, but was buried with the doctor after her death in 1930.)

The day after the doctor's passing the *Lincoln Courier* ran a patent medicine advertisement that, even though a bit verbose, surpassed those notices he had put into the *New Era*. It could well serve as an epitaph for the druggist part of his career, at least.

> If we know all the methods of approach adopted by an enemy we are the better enabled to ward off the danger and postpone the moment when surrender becomes inevitable. In many instances the inherent strength of the body suffices to enable it to oppose the tendency toward death. Many however have lost these forces to such an extent that there is little or no help. In other cases a little aid to the weakened lungs will make all the difference between sudden death and many years of useful life. Upon the first symptoms of a cold, croup or any trouble of the throat or lungs, give that old and well-known remedy—Boschee's German Syrup—a careful trial. It will prove what thousands say of it to "be the benefactor of any home."

Dr. Gidney would probably have liked that.

Woodmen of the World and Trees in the Cemetery

June: Before it became too worn to read, Dr. J.C. Gidney's tree-stump monument bore the carved logo of the Woodmen of the World. For over three decades at the turn of the twentieth century, this fraternal organization provided subsidized tombstones for all of its members. The first iteration of the society was the Modern Woodmen of America, founded in 1893 by Joseph Cullen Root. Professor Annette Stott explains that a "sermon about the pioneers chopping down trees to build cabins for the protection of their families" inspired the name and what came to be known as "woodcraft," although the organization had nothing to do with the lumber business. Instead, Root's purpose was to promote civic virtues such as "self improvement and neighborliness" and to provide a way to mark the graves of ordinary hard-working citizens. After a falling out with other members of the organization, Root eventually left and, in 1900, reformatted his organization in Omaha, Nebraska, as the Woodmen of the World.

Omaha was also the home of one of the most memorable characters in children's fiction, the Wonderful Wizard of Oz, who came to life in a novel of the same name published in 1900 by newspaperman, author, actor, and women's-suffrage advocate L. Frank Baum. Most people remember the story, of course, from the 1939 movie starring Judy Garland. In an intriguing 1964 article called "*The Wizard of Oz*: Parable on Populism," a high school teacher named Henry Littlefield describes how the novel encodes the progressive ideals of turn-of-the-century Populism, the ideology of a political party that promoted the worth and value of the common citizen, the very man Root wanted to honor in death. This ideal American exemplifies the values of the country or small town rather than those of the big city. Joseph Cullen Root, in fact, specifically excluded "ANYONE living in a city" from the original Woodmen of the World, according to Laurel Gable. He offered its benefits only to healthy residents of small towns and rural areas in the Midwest at first.

In Baum's novel, Littlefield argues, the scarecrow symbolizes the American farmer, the sort of person who would chop down a tree and build a house with his own hands to protect his family. He fears only the forces of nature he cannot control such as wildfires. Like the iconic farmer, the scarecrow is loyal and kind, a good friend to the other travelers. He travels to Oz on the yellow brick road to ask the Wizard, who is himself only an ordinary man, for brains. The Wizard, of course, can only simulate such a gift by stuffing the scarecrow's cloth head with pins and needles to make him "sharp." As the Wizard explains to Dorothy, who accuses him of being "a very bad man," he's really a "very good man" though a "very bad Wizard."

And the truth is, of course, that the scarecrow already has brains. In the novel he is the one who solves problems—often using classical syllogisms—for his companions. As members of the Populist Party, organized in 1892, saw it, what ordinary people like the scarecrow lacked was not brains but confidence in themselves and their own worth. That is why the Populist platform included planks such as initiative—the right for ordinary citizens to place new legislation on a ballot—and referendum—the right to repeal legislation and recall elected officials. Oklahoma, which became a state in 1907, was one of several that incorporated these ideals into their constitutions.

Root's ideal of the hardy pioneer who should be honored in death as in life was very much in line with this thinking. After the Populist candidate William Jennings Bryan lost the 1896 president election to William McKinley, the Populist Party fell apart, but its ideals lingered in American culture and in cemeteries where Woodmen of the World monuments were erected. Why should impressive monuments be reserved only for the rich and famous? People like Dr. Gidney, who worked hard to cure the ills of his fellow Shelbyans, was worthy of memory as well. Although he had status in a small town like Shelby, he was one of the little people in the social scheme of the Gilded Age. But as Annette Stott affirms, "membership in Woodmen of the World made ordinary people special."

Stott explains that Woodmen of the World memorials were produced in various ways—by contracting with a local company, by supplying patterns for use by local craftsmen, and by ordering stones from catalogs such as the *Sears Tombstones and Monuments Catalog* or the similar options offered by the Montgomery Ward catalog. They might be made of marble, limestone, or, eventually, granite. After the cost of production rose too much to make buying tombstones outright feasible, the Woodmen of the World subsidized the monuments instead of donating them outright. Mail-order catalogs and the ability to ship almost anything via rail democratized the monument business, making the same monuments available in Chicago accessible to people living in small-town Shelby. Today, the modern version of Woodmen of the World still exists as WoodmenLife, a fraternal benefits organization that offers insurance to its members.

Although tree-stump monuments were only one of the options offered to the earlier Woodmen of the World, they were very popular during this time period, and not all of them were erected to honor Woodsmen of the World. The folklorist Susanne Ridlen defines a tree-stump tombstone as "a rustic funerary memorial which places emphasis upon the representation of a tree or portion thereof in its natural exterior state." What makes it unique in a cemetery is the simulation of bark. According to Douglas Keister, the turn-of-the-century fad for rustic lawn furniture made of cast-iron "twigs" is part of the same decorative art movement. It was ideal for funerary monuments in rural/garden cemeteries that emphasized the consoling benefits of nature and the idea that death is simply a return to nature. Tree-stump monuments are particularly common in the Chicago area, the home of the Sears catalog, and in the Midwest in general.

When the monument for a Woodman of the World is not a tree stump, the logo carved on it or attached on a bronze plaque includes a tree stump and the words "*Dum Tacet Clamat*," usually translated "Though silent, he speaks." The motto emphasizes the idea of giving voice to a worthy member of society, whose monument speaks on his behalf of the value of "woodcraft." Dr. Gidney's tree-stump monument enhances this idea by making the monument look like a rustic pulpit with a book on top. The names and dates of Gidney and his wife are still visible on the book when it is wet with rain or the sunlight hits it just right. Stott explains that F.A. Falkenburg, who collaborated with Root in forming the Woodmen of the World, once gave a speech called "The Altar of Woodcraft Is a Stump," in which he proclaimed that the founding fathers used tree stumps as pulpits to proclaim "the inalienable rights of man and his absolute equality with his fellow man."

The idea of a sturdy tree cut down is itself provocative. Stott suggests that it symbolizes masculinity since a tree can be the sturdy base around which clinging ivy (presumably the wife and children) twines itself. Certainly the turn-of-the-twentieth-century was a time when some Christian men began to separate themselves from what they considered to be an overly feminized religion of emotional attachments to Jesus and an inordinate concern with the after life. The Social Gospel Movement, in contrast, focused on a more practical, manly version of religion that advocated social justice and societal changes that improved life here on earth. The YMCA, founded in the middle of the nineteenth century, became a bastion of this practical Christianity by offering services for young men from all walks of life.

Trees and shrubs in general have been associated with burial places for centuries. Oak and yew trees are traditional cemetery plantings, and the smell of boxwood pervades many Southern cemeteries. Sunset Cemetery is known for its beautiful trees, especially in autumn when the sugar maples planted at the direction of former North Carolina First Lady Bess Hoey, are ablaze with color. Many cemeteries are also world-class arboretums. A notable Southern example would be Cave Hill Cemetery in Louisville, Kentucky. The website for Oakdale Cemetery in Wilmington, founded in 1852, advertises it as "Oakdale Cemetery—Cemetery, Arboretum and Outdoor Museum."

An older symbol involving a tree is the urn-and-willow motif on the tombstone for Anne Irby, who died in 1847. James Deetz and Edwin S. Dethlefsen date this

Tree stump monument in Crown Hill Cemetery of Indianapolis, Indiana. This memorial for the Smith family also features the hands icon popular in the nineteenth and early twentieth centuries. In this case, male and female hands grasp the chain that binds them even in death (photograph by June Hadden Hobbs).

Opposite, bottom: The carved logo on the tombstone of Kemper Kendall (1867–1931) identifies it as a "Woodmen of the World memorial" rather than as having been erected by the Woodmen of the World. By the 1930s, the Woodmen organization subsidized memorials instead of paying for them to be erected.

neoclassical design to the Greek Revival movement of the 1760s. Urns were associated with classical burials and also with European aristocrats and royalty, who sometimes used them to bury the heart of the deceased in a place apart from the rest of the body, according to Blanche Linden. Willow trees also have a rich history and can be associated with the Christian gospel since they "flourish and remain whole no matter how many branches are cut off," as Douglas Keister points out. It probably does not hurt that, true to their name, their long branches make it appear that the tree is weeping and mourning.

Woodmen of the World logo on the tombstone for Walter J. Fulenwider (1860–1907). The brass plaque indicates that the monument was "erected by the Woodmen of the World." The Woodmen motto, *Dum Tacet Clamat*, is usually translated "Though silent, he speaks."

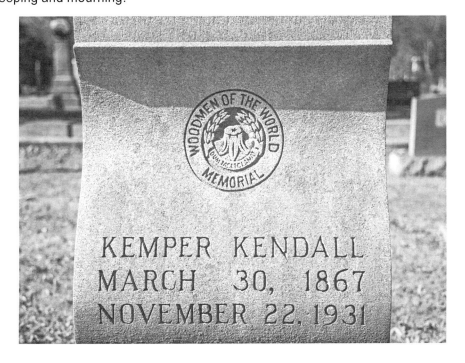

The urn-and-willow icon was especially popular in the late-eighteenth and early nineteenth centuries during the time when it was fashionable to borrow classical designs for the new American democracy from ancient Greece. Unlike other common tombstone icons, they emphasize secular rather than religious values, perfect for a new republic that valued the separation of church and state.

In a rural/garden cemetery like the older part of Sunset, living trees and tree-related icons such as carvings of palm branches and acorns on gravestones remind the visitor that death and renewal are the expected

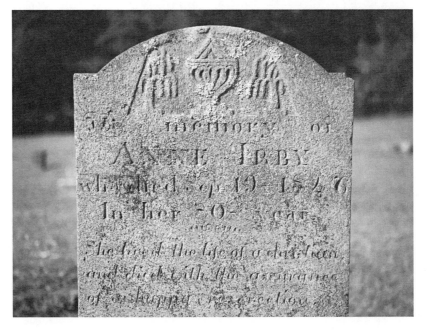

Top: A classical egg-and-dart motif on a bench in Sunset Cemetery. This architectural pattern alternates eggs, signifying birth, and darts, representing death. It symbolizes the cycle of life. *Bottom:* The Hamilton stone includes a modernized version of the architectural design known as "egg-and-dart." Subway restaurants use a version of this design on the molding in their buildings. They are a common feature of many monuments, buildings, and objects such as picture frames.

Opposite, top: Dr. J.C. Gidney's footstone is a small tree stump. His headstone resembles a rustic pulpit topped by an open book inscribed with his names and dates and those of his wife. *Opposite, bottom:* The urn-and-willow motif on Anne Irby's tombstone is a neoclassical design popular in the late-eighteenth and early-nineteenth centuries. Neoclassical designs linked the new American democracy to the ancient Grecian democracy.

patterns of all life. Perhaps no tombstone detail represents this idea more clearly than a small architectural design known as "egg-and-dart." It is so common as part of ornamental molding in everything from Subway restaurants to park benches that most people never see it. Egg-and-dart is a repetitive series of round or oval "eggs," signifying birth, separated by pointed darts, which have represented death since classical times. Like tree stumps, they are both sobering mortality symbols and hopeful reminders that nature is cyclic. Life and death follow each other with predictable regularity.

Dr. William Perry Andrews (1823–1903)
Susan Ann Love Andrews (1832–1874)

Joe: Wedding bells tolled on May 28, 1851, at the Shelby First Baptist Church. It was probably the talk of the village, population 400: Dr. William Perry Andrews and Susan Ann Love getting married in the first big wedding with bridesmaids and groomsmen and who knows what else. First Baptist had the largest congregation in Shelby, but that wasn't saying much. The new village hadn't amounted to much yet as evidenced by the abundance of unsold lots around the court square, according to J.R. Logan's 1850 map.

Down on North Lafayette Street, the Baptists had put up a small frame building that served as a house of worship. On this fine day in May, the church probably seemed to take on new life as two well-known young people became man and wife. Performing the marriage ceremony was the Rev. Wade Hill, the area's leading preacher and early champion of temperance. Not everybody shared his view on that subject, and some in attendance at Shelby First Baptist Church on May 28 may have even entertained the notion of taking a drink afterwards. If they did, they didn't let on to the outspoken Rev. Wade Hill. A church history noted that as vows were exchanged before the preacher, other married couples who knew Dr. Andrews and his bride "stood up" to show their support of two outstanding citizens. W.P. Andrews was Cleveland County's first surgeon and Susan came from a prominent family. He was 28, and she was 18.

Six children were born of the union, most given unordinary names: Sons like Salola McClintock "Clint" Andrews and Flabanica Anifesto Andrews; daughters Quintina Quillana Andrews, Kansas Andrews, and Eulalia Velsasa Andrews. Kansas would marry Judge James L. Webb. Their daughter, Fay Webb, would become the wife of North Carolina's future governor, O. Max Gardner.

The Civil War came and went and Reconstruction settled in. Around 1870, Salola McClintock Andrews got caught up in the Ku Klux Klan's reckless doings. According to *History of First Baptist Church*, edited by Grace Hamrick and published in 1969, Salola was accused of a crime that he denied doing. Still, he deemed it right to leave Shelby. He ended up in Arkansas, where he became a deputy sheriff in the small town of Cut Off, 200 miles south of Memphis. On November 2, 1873, Deputy Clint Andrews tried to arrest a man for a relatively minor offense. The suspect resisted, pulled a gun, shot Andrews and killed him. According to Grace Hamrick's church history, Dr. W.P. Andrews made the long journey to Arkansas to bring back his son's body for burial in Sunset Cemetery.

"While there, he ate some pecans, the first he'd ever seen," Hamrick wrote. "He brought several of the nuts back with him and planted them in the yard of his home on South Washington Street (D.W. Royster residence) where they became huge trees and still bore nuts in 1969." One year after 21-year-old Salola was laid to rest, his mother, Susan Ann Andrews, 42, joined him in Sunset Cemetery.

Before Dr. Andrews' death in 1903, he would have visited their graves in a fenced-in family plot. Perhaps, in those moments of silence, a sentimental tune visited him from out of the past: "Ah, May the Red Rose Live Alway," a parlor ballad written the year the doctor and Susan were married in Shelby First Baptist Church. It was penned by the "Father of American Music,"—Stephen Foster.

> Lulled be the dirge of the cypress bough,
> That tells of departed flowers!
> Ah! That the butterfly's gilded wing
> Fluttered in evergreen bowers!
> Sad is my heart for the blighted plants
> Its pleasures are aye as brief
> They bloom at the young year's joyful call,
> And fade with the autumn leaf:
> Ah! May the red rose live always,
> To smile upon earth and sky!
> Why should the beautiful ever weep?
> Why should the beautiful die?

M.L. Heafner (1873–1918)

In late October 1918, M.L. Heafner felt well enough to go back to his job at a Shelby textile mill. The *Cleveland Star* reported he had been down and out for a short while with influenza, a viral infection that struck fear in the hearts of millions that autumn just before World War I ended. A vicious pandemic swept the United States leaving thousands dead in its wake.

Cleveland County went under quarantine. The *Cleveland Star* reminded readers that a decree wasn't sufficient and that "careless sneezing, coughing and spitting should be avoided. If you must do these things, use your handkerchief." Trucks sprayed disinfectant on Shelby's streets twice daily while obituaries continued to fill columns in the *Cleveland Star*. There were many horror stories. For example, the McSwain family of Shelby lost six members within days. Mrs. Floyd McSwain and four of her children died one week and were buried in the same grave. A few days later, her fifth child, an 8-year-old son, fell victim to the flu.

On it went—the grim reaping, the cemetery filling. Yet M.L. Heafner returned to work. How long he stayed at it wasn't clear in the newspaper obituary that appeared on October 29. Heafner, 45, had suffered a relapse, developed pneumonia and died. He was laid to rest in Sunset Cemetery, leaving behind a wife and child.

The same day of Heafner's death, the *Cleveland Star* reported that the Spanish influenza situation in Cleveland County had improved and the worst over. "Barber shops opened Monday for business as usual and everything in Shelby is beginning to assume normal proportions," the *Star* said. However, it was still wise to watch out for germs. "The essential thing is to take care of yourself as soon as you discover that you have a cold," reported the *Star*. "The 'flu' doesn't amount to much unless you fail to take care of yourself and pneumonia develops."

One hundred and two years later when coronavirus savaged the globe, was that the voice of M.L. Heafner down in Sunset Cemetery that we heard, whispering, "take care of yourselves"?

Dr. Thomas Williams (1806–1879)
Permelia Williams (1821–1897)
Mary C. Elliott (Unknown–1858)

Dr. Williams and his wife Permelia, didn't really need the two-story house opposite Shelby's court square. A more modest place might have better suited a young couple starting out in a new village. They had no children yet, but obviously expected a houseful someday. But the children never came. There was only Mary, the little orphan, and the couple didn't get to keep her for very long.

Dr. Williams was one of Shelby's first doctors, a much-respected civic and leader at the Shelby First Baptist Church. Yet he and his family were lost in time. Time was unkind to their gravestones: the doctor's on the ground and Permelia's propped against what's left of a vandalized decorative wrought-iron fence around the family plot. Mary's stone also has also fallen to the ground. Her shattered marker bore an inscription, but crabgrass, Carolina red clay, and fire ant nests have obscured it most of the time. Only when the light angles perfectly can words be deciphered.

At that moment, all of what will probably ever be known about Mary C. Elliott flashes before our eyes: How she was found in the state of Mississippi, orphaned and in a state of destitution, by Dr. Thomas Williams in the year 1853; how he carried her home with him and raised her in the fellowship of Shelby First Baptist Church. That Mary died on December 16, 1857. Light shifts and the story of her life vanishes.

For the five years Mary lived with the doctor and Permelia in their rambling house, there is no record of her life. Villagers probably knew about Mary: what she was doing in Mississippi; what killed her parents. And they would likely know the cause of Dr. Williams' westward journey to fetch Mary back to Shelby. Mary probably made friends in the village, especially at Shelby First Baptist Church, where the doctor was a founding member and deacon. Mary came to the Williams household an unexpected joy in the lives of the childless couple. But a day came when the joy abruptly ended, and they buried her in Sunset Cemetery. The doctor joined Mary there in 1879; Permelia came in 1897.

In February of the following year, the *Cleveland Star* ran this item: "The old homestead of Dr. Thomas Williams, one of the oldest houses in Shelby, and the only piece of property that has never changed hands since Shelby has been a town, was sold Monday at public auction and bought by J.L. Webb, Esq., for $1,125. The old house standing on the corner of this lot is the one occupied by Dr. Williams when he

The Permelia Williams stone illustrating the common nineteenth-century motif of a hand with the finger pointing up toward heaven.

was first married, and the one in which he and his wife both died. The lot is a beautiful one and is a valuable piece of property."

Dr. Williams, Permelia and their little Mary sleep on in their family plot gradually ravaged by time and uncaring hands. Sympathetic strangers—saddened by the neglect and abuse—may have occasionally paused to pay respects. Was that music they heard when wind stirred nearby trees? Perhaps Permelia was singing blind hymn writer Fanny Crosby's most famous composition to little Mary.

> Safe in the arms of Jesus
> Safe on his gentle breast
> There by His love o'er shaded,
> Sweetly my soul shall rest.
>
> Hark 'tis the voice of angels
> Borne in a song to me
> Over the fields of glory
> Over the jasper sea.

The sounds, faint and wavering, fade. Only mystery remains.

Hands

June: Nineteenth-century Americans were obsessed with hands. Tombstones in Sunset Cemetery illustrate some of the most common uses of this icon: hands with fingers pointing to heaven such as the icon on Permelia Williams' stone; hands descending from clouds to break a chain; hands holding ribbons with comforting mottoes such as "Gone Home." Tombstones in other cemeteries across the United States include a dizzying array of clasped hands, hands holding or plucking up flowers, hands clutching anchors or a cross, hands emerging from books. Jewish cemeteries have their own versions with Kohanim hands offering blessings and Levite hands holding water pitchers.

Hands and parts of hands were such a potent part of American culture, especially in the latter half of the 1800s, that they show up in many popular novels, poems, and hymnals. The plot in Nathaniel Hawthorne's *The House of the Seven Gables* (1851) begins with the hanging of Matthew Maule, a man accused of witchcraft in colonial Massachusetts. On the gallows, he curses his accuser, Colonel Pyncheon: "'God' said the dying man, pointing his finger, with a ghastly look, at the undismayed countenance of his enemy,—'God will give him blood to drink!'" Maule's words and hand activate a curse that dooms Colonel Pyncheon and his descendants. Col. Pyncheon dies from a throat hemorrhage, and an ominous bloody hand print appears on his ruff. Mysteriously, when old Maule's body is disinterred, his right hand is missing.

A Southern novelist, Mrs. E.D.E.N. Southworth, made an even bigger splash in 1859 with her serialized novel T*he Hidden Hand or Capitola, the Madcap*. This now-forgotten story was so popular that many little girls and a town in California on the coast of Monterey Bay were named "Capitola" for Southworth's heroine, who has a birthmark that looks like a small red hand on her palm. She delightfully "takes matters into her own hands," rescuing a damsel in distress, catching a notorious criminal, and even fighting a duel on her own behalf.

And then there were the hymns. Almost all of the popular Protestant hymnals of the day included hymns with titles such as "Parting Hand," "His Guiding Hand,"

and "Beautiful Beckoning Hands." Singing "Parting Hand" is and was a popular way to end shape-note singings in the South. After hours of creating four-part harmony with beloved friends, singers shake hands and sing "Parting Hand." "His Guiding Hand" refers to God's benevolent guidance. "Beautiful Beckoning Hands," however, is a creepy invocation of dead hands calling the singer to heaven from beyond the grave.

Hands in literature and on gravestones refer in one way or another to what is called "agency," the ability to act on one's own behalf. The hand reaching down from a cloud to break a chain on Sophia M. Wray's stone is the time-honored *Manus Dei*, the hand of God reaching from beyond to break the chain binding

a person to earth so her spirit can return to heaven. Fanny J. Crosby described the soul's liberation in her popular hymn "Some Day the Silver Cord Will Break," published in 1891.

By the mid-nineteenth century, the emerging evangelical movement shifted the burden for securing salvation to the individual believer, who had to choose whether to believe. In earlier times, Calvinists such as the Puritans and other Europeans who colonized North American, believed that God had all the agency and could elect or predestine some people for heavenly salvation and others for eternal damnation. Personal choice played no part in the matter. In contrast, the hand reaching down from heaven on Sophia Wray's stone suggests that her family has hope because she chose to be a believer. Permelia

The Sophia Wray stone shows the hand of God, the *Manus Dei*, reaching down from heaven to break the chain the binds the living to earth. This photograph by June Hadden Hobbs was taken around the year 2000. The stone today, fallen and shattered, is barely recognizable.

Williams' stone shows the ever-popular hand with a finger pointing up. No doubt people who visited this grave a century ago immediately thought of her eternal place in heaven. The beautiful marble stone for Little Georgie Clower makes the point explicitly. The hand on her stone points to heaven and holds a ribbon with the words "Gone Home."

But hands on the gravestones for middle-class white women and children often suggest another meaning as well. Not only do women and innocent children have spiritual agency to make heaven their eternal home, but they also have spiritual authority to point others in the right direction. Often hands on tombstones have frilly cuffs, suggesting that they

Little Georgie Rebecca Clower's marble stone illustrates a common epitaph for the young, "budded on earth to bloom in heaven," and the icon of a finger pointing to heaven.

are gendered female. One result of the industrial revolution was a separation of "spheres" of influence. While men increasingly went out to work in the corrupt and corrupting marketplace, women and children stayed in the home, where they could maintain "spiritual purity."

Though the social power of women and children was limited, they had enormous spiritual influence in the nineteenth century, power enhanced by the popularity of Spiritualism. The Spiritualist movement in the United States began in 1848, and after the Civil War, its most potent ideas began to be incorporated into mainline Protestantism. Spiritualism denies the full reality of death with a belief that the dead are "translated" into another realm beyond earth, from which they can comfort and guide the living. Dead children and mothers were considered especially powerful in watching over the living from beyond the grave.

The attention to women and children as an antidote to the ills of the marketplace influenced other uses of hands as well. Women often defined themselves in the nineteenth century in terms of successful relationships with friends and family. Their place in the social fabric emphasized cooperation over the competition encouraged by capitalism. Ironically, while many people valued the competitive marketplace, others saw it as soul destroying and embraced membership in fraternal organizations as an antidote. As the 1871 handbook, *Morals and Dogma of the Ancient and Accepted Scottish Rite of Freemasonry*, put it, "Ties of friendship and love" bind us together and keep us from being "a raging multitude of wild and savage beasts of prey."

Hands clasped in fellowship or brotherly love are one symbol of both Masons and Oddfellows. Masonic literature emphasizes the numerology of joining two hands with ten fingers together since ten is a sacred number in Pythagorean mathematics. Oddfellows often used clasped hands over their signature symbol of three interconnected circles. They also use a raised hand with a heart in its palm as a symbol of benevolence and charity toward the needy. Male and female hands clasped are a more generic version of the icon and could mean anything to the viewer from "farewell" to "reunion."

Hands appear only occasionally on twentieth- and twenty-first-century tombstones in Sunset and other cemeteries. One exception is the graphic representation of a line from an early twentieth-century hymn, Thomas Dorsey's "Precious Lord, Take My Hand." These stones usually show a hand or hands reaching up to grasp

A modern version of the hands icon so popular in the nineteenth century. Many of these designs, which are well represented in Sunset Cemetery, refer specifically to the hymn "Precious Lord, Take My Hand." The hymn was written by Thomas Andrew Dorsey, the "Father of Black Gospel Music," in 1932 after the death of his wife and baby son.

a hand coming down from a cloud. This gospel song emphasizes a relationship between the believer and God rather than personal relationships with other people or a need to establish a sense of personal agency in a chaotic world during the Industrial Revolution or after the Civil War.

Nineteenth-century people did not choose the icons for their tombstones with these Big Picture ideas in mind, of course. No one visited a stone carver requesting a symbol of personal agency. Most likely, they had seen other stones they found meaningful and asked for something similar or looked through pattern books for something that seemed appropriate. It is left to their descendants to see the patterns and draw conclusions about what their deathways tell us about them and about ourselves.

John Fay (c. 1891–1931)

Joe: The wandering showman came to town in a year of Depression. His name was John Fay, and he rode horses in a Wild West Show traveling with Model Shows of America playing the Cleveland County Fair. It was October 1931. The Depression might have been on, but people still craved their fun even though money was tight. Fay worked for a class act. Model Shows billed itself in newspaper advertisements as the world's largest outdoor midway attraction—the "aristocrat of the tented world."

In those days, many carnivals traveled by rail and Model Shows was among them. The show train rolled into Shelby and parked for the duration of the fair. Equipment and animals were transported from the train to the fairgrounds, located two miles eastward. Some fair workers lived aboard the train, and there was constant coming and going from the fairground. The *Charlotte News* reported that Fay left the fair around 2:30 a.m. one morning, riding in a wagon pulled by a trick mule from the wild west show. They crept along two-lane Highway 20, a usually busy east-to-west route lightly traveled in the early morning hours. But in case anybody else was out that late, Fay had attached a light to the wagon.

Approaching headlights on the lonely highway would have grabbed Fay's attention. As they drew closer, did he begin to understand what was about to happen? The lights rushed on top of him and that's when the oncoming car crashed into the wagon. Fay suffered a fractured skull and broken collar bone, along with other injuries. The badly injured mule had to be put to sleep.

According to the *Cleveland Star*, Fay lingered in a semi-conscious state in Shelby Hospital for weeks before he died. Palmer Mortuary of Shelby got the body, but no relatives could be reached. Members of the show troupe recalled Fay's parents once lived in Cincinnati, Ohio. No trace of them could be found. Nobody ever claimed the body. Fay's funeral service was held at Palmer Mortuary, and the Wild West Show agreed to pay a portion of burial expenses. Fay was buried in Sunset Cemetery. A group of Shelby mothers sent wreaths to cover his grave and the *Star* wrote, "Kind-hearted Shelby people formed a funeral cortege for a young show trooper who had no relatives or friends of his own here to see him in his last resting place." The wanderer had found a home.

II

Women You'd Want
to Have Coffee With

Kidder Cole Nichols "Mama Nick" (1878–1947)

Joe: Kidder Cole: Belle of the North Carolina Mountains. Her name once sent melodies echoing up and down lonely valleys and coves. Even her gravestone in Sunset Cemetery might have made music for those who knew the story. That story reached back to the Cashiers Valley of Jackson County where three teenagers were locked in a love triangle.

Song lyrics would spin the tale. How two friends—Felix Alley and Charlie Wright—had a falling out over the affections of Kidder Cole. To Felix's mind, she was already his girl. He hurried to a dance one autumn night certain he would dance with Kidder all evening. But Charlie Wright got to Kidder first—and wouldn't let go. Shocked and shattered, 16-year-old Felix moped back home and penned a banjo tune about the disaster at the dance. The result, called "The Ballad of Kidder Cole," blossomed into one of the most popular mountain songs ever written. In 1928, it gained national attention from a recording by Bascom Lamar Lunsford, the "Minstrel of the Appalachians." Lunsford personally knew all the folks involved—Kidder, Felix and Charlie—and spoke with authority.

Bascom's banjo strummed a lilting tune as he sang:

> My name is Felix Eugene Alley,
> My best girl lives in Cashiers Valley.
> She's the joy of my soul.
> And her name is Kidder Cole.
>
> I don't know—it must have been by chance.
> Way last fall when I went to a dance.
> I was to dance with Kidder the livelong night
> But I got my time beat by Charlie Wright.

The story continued, with the ballad's author repeating that for all his grief at being outdone by his former friend, his heart was still captive to the mountain girl:

> Kidder Cole is the prettiest girl
> I know there is in the whole wide world
> She's the joy of my soul
> Oh, how I love that Kidder Cole.

The twists and turns of fate wrapped things up like this: Neither Felix Alley or Charlie Wright married Kidder. The daughter of a Jackson County merchant who also served as sheriff, she went off to school in Anderson, South Carolina, and eventually became the wife of A.S. Nichols, living in Asheville. Kidder worked at the Bon Marche and Denton's department stores and the George Vanderbilt hotel. When Kidder died in 1947 at the home of her sister in Sylva, she rated coverage in the *Asheville Citizen*, which also ran a photo with the story.

"Member of a pioneer Jackson County family, her name became familiar in every cove and 'holler' of this highland region as the 'purtiest' girl in Cashiers valley," the newspaper reported. "Judge Alley put to song the story of her beauty and her versatility as a dancer of the old reels and square dances in her girlhood days."

Kidder was buried in Shelby where her daughter, Mrs. Robert Cooke, lived. Meanwhile, Felix Alley had a long career as a lawyer and Superior Court Judge in Waynesville. He died in 1957 at 83. A story in the *Asheville Citizen* called him "a mountain man with a thousand stories and a thousand legends." By the time of the judge's death, "The Ballad of Kidder Cole" was a classic of North Carolina folklore.

Kidder's gravestone faces the South Mountains and, far beyond, Cashiers Valley in the Blue Ridge. Here stands a symbol for all of Sunset Cemetery's thousands of stories and legends—each as lilting and haunting as an old banjo tune from Cashier's Valley:

> Kidder Cole is the prettiest girl
> I know there is in the whole wide world.
> She's the joy of my soul
> Oh, how I love that Kidder Cole

Fraternal Symbols on Gravestones

June: Kidder Cole may have enchanted Felix Alley, but the symbol on her tombstone does not support local legends that she was a witch. The five-pointed star is, instead, the emblem for a fraternal organization, the Order of the Eastern Star. Although Freemasons are male, membership in Eastern Star is a way for women related to Masons to engage in Masonry. It does involve secret rituals and may look to outsiders as if it has occult origins.

However, the very name "Eastern Star" is a biblical reference to the star of Bethlehem described in Matthew 2:2. Past Worthy Grand Matron Effie H. Lahr, one of Kidder Cole Nichols' contemporaries in North Dakota, said that "The Order of the Eastern Star is essentially a Religious Order. It is founded upon the Holy Scriptures, and its Symbols, Teachings and Precepts, are all found within the pages of the Bible." The five symbols in the star points arranged around an icon of an altar with a book refer to five Biblical women:

- Adah, daughter of Jephthah in the book of Judges (a sword and veil).
- Ruth, the heroine of the book of Ruth, (a sheaf of barley).
- Esther, the queen from the book of Esther (a crown and scepter).
- Martha of Bethany, whose story is in the book of Luke (a broken column).
- Electa, the martyred "elect" lady from II John (a chalice).

The Kidder Cole "Mama Nick" Nichols stone with the symbol for Eastern Star, a Masonic organization for women. A teen-aged Kidder Cole was the subject of a mountain ballad by Felix Alley.

These symbols are rendered rather crudely on Kidder Cole Nichols' granite stone.

Other Eastern Star symbols on gravestones in Sunset Cemetery also include the letters "F.A.T.A.L.," one letter for each of the star points. The acronym stands for "Fairest Among Thousands, Altogether Lovely," a reference to Song of Solomon. Douglas Keister's *Stories in Stone: A Field Guide to Symbolism and Iconography* speculates, perhaps tongue-in-cheek, that the word "fatal" may also be a warning to any Eastern Star member who betrays the secrets of the organization.

Eastern Star was obviously popular in the Shelby community—and across the state and nation. Tombstone scholar Laurel K. Gable estimates that by the 1920s, when "Mama Nick" would have been in her forties, "nearly half of the entire population of the United States belonged to at least one secret order or fraternal society." Other popular fraternal symbols in Sunset are emblems for Masons, the Woodmen of the World, and the Shriners. The most common fraternal symbol is the square and compass for Freemasons, more commonly known as "Masons." In the center of the design, a "G" stands for God and geometry, both of which are sacred to the fraternity.

Although many of these organizations are still alive, their symbols are now obscure enough to make people think they have sinister meanings. Instead, they speak to a time when people in a newly formed village needed to band together for education, mutual encouragement, and public service. Many fraternal

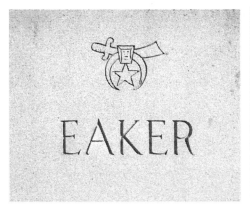

Left: A Shriners symbol on a gravestone. The Shriners logo parodies Islamic symbols. Members of this nineteenth-century spin-off of the Freemasons are known for amusing antics such as riding small motorcycles while wearing fezzes in local parades. They are also known for benevolence, especially in aid of children's hospitals. *Right:* The square and compass symbol of the Freemasons. The Masons, as they are commonly known, employ a number of symbols on gravestones and elsewhere, including the all-seeing eye. The square-and-compass with a "G" in the center for God and geometry is their most common symbol.

organizations and secret societies provided burial insurance in a time before insurance benefits were part of most people's jobs. Tombstones like Kidder Cole Nichols' also testify to the important role these organizations played in creating identity as part of a community.

Attie Bostick League (1875–1965)

Joe: When the Swedish ocean liner M.S. *Gripsholm* passed by the Statue of Liberty in early December 1943, Attie Bostick did a little dance on deck. The 68-year-old Baptist missionary to China couldn't contain her joy: Soon she would set foot on American soil again, this time for good. Attie was among the more than 1,900 former prisoners of Japan who had arrived safely in New York after being held for years in internment camps. She and the others on the refugee ship *Gripsholm* were part of an exchange program with the Japanese.

"Danced as Refugee Ships Reached Port," read the headline on the *Charlotte Observer's* story about Attie's return. After a brief stay in New York, Attie would take a train to Gastonia, North Carolina, where friends and relatives waited to welcome her back for only the fourth time in 43 years. The final destination would be her home in Shelby.

The *Observer* reported that in New York, someone had given her a book for the long train ride, but Attie probably couldn't concentrate on reading. Instead, she watched the beautiful scenery rushing by her window. Hour after hour, the images blended together as humming rails lulled Attie into a reverie that likely took her back over an epic career as a missionary to China. She had left Shelby in 1900, a 24-year-old single woman headed to a foreign land on a great adventure. Unescorted single women didn't do that sort of thing. But Attie didn't hesitate because she had

had The Call. It had come to her at the age of 14: Go out to China and do the Lord's work. In preparation, she graduated from college and taught school in a Gastonia textile mill neighborhood. Finally, under the sponsorship of her home church, Gastonia First Baptist, Attie got her wish: she boarded the ocean liner *Empress of China* and answered The Call.

During the voyage out, she met two missionaries who were returning to China following their furlough in the States: T.J. League and his wife Florence Nightingale League. Attie also had time to reflect on the possible dangers that awaited her. The Boxer Rebellion, a bloody uprising against foreigners, still raged in China and foreigners were dying. Attie's mother had begged her not to go but couldn't crack her daughter's determination.

The *Empress of China* finally docked in Shanghai, and Attie stepped off the liner into a new world and new life. The Boxer Rebellion would pass, but new trouble of some sort always flared in China. Attie performed her mission work facing famines, uprisings, rebellions, civil wars, and invasions. She labored alongside her missionary brothers, George and Wade. On infrequent furloughs to the States, Attie spoke to church groups about her challenges as a missionary. Audiences listened in admiration. Yet how could they really understand the hardships she endured? Attie did her best to explain, to open their eyes, to make them see. And then she went back across the ocean.

And then came December 7, 1941: Japan's surprise attack on Pearl Harbor. The Japanese had invaded China in 1937, but the status of missionaries really changed after Pearl Harbor. Attie and others were arrested and interned in various locations. By March 1943, The Civilian Internment Center in Weihsien, Shantung Province, 200 miles from Peking, was her home. Attie, 63, may have known a 24-year-old American teacher named Langdon Gilkey who was also interned at Weihsien. The year after her death in 1965, his book about the internment camp was published: *Shantung Compound: The Story of Men and Women Under Pressure*. Attie wasn't mentioned in the text, but Gilkey described what life would have been like for her and the 2,000 other civilian internees at Weihsien. They weren't beaten or tortured, but they endured overcrowded and unsanitary conditions along with the scarcity of food.

Someone wrote a song satirizing living conditions there called "Wiehsien Blues." Attie thought enough of it to keep a copy, which is quoted in her biography.

> We used to be executives and labored with our brains,
> With secretaries neat and quick to spare us any pain.
> But if the ticker tape ran out we didn't touch the thing,
> The office staff could see to that, we did the ordering.
> Chorus
> Now we're in Weihsien, nothing's too dirty to do.
> Shops, spots or garbage, or stirring a vegetable stew.
> To shine in this delightful camp, you join the labor camps.
> Where if you do your work too well, they work you more and more.
> For since we've come to Weihsien camp, they've worked us till we're dead.
> Though now we're called the labor corps, we'll be a corpse instead.
> You'd think to hear those fellows sing the men did all the work
> But I am here to tell you now the ladies do not shirk.
> We clean the leeks, we cut the bread, But then what really hurts.
> When they have done the dirty work, we have to wash their shirts.

Attie kept an internment diary with brief entries that focus not on hardships but daily routine:

> December 13: We cleaned up, beating the rugs. Devotions. Men cut wood, exercise, study.
> December 17: Beautiful day. Hair washing.
> December 22: Monday. Wash day, Preparations made for Christmas.
> December 23: Monday. Guards changed. [The guards] got drunk and went upstairs in the night.
> December 25—Christmas morning. Oranges for breakfast and a present at everybody's plate. Decorations of red paper and sweets given to guards. Bro. Thiessen gave Christmas message. Had a big chicken dinner, with fruit, cake, apples, oranges and candy. Hymn singing carols.
> December 26—North wind snow and cold—put up the little stove in the dining room. Reading and games.

At times, Attie made internment sound like a church camp. The world might be coming apart, but she never wavered.

In the 2006 biography *Called to China: Attie Bostic's Life & Missionary Letters from China 1900–1943*, author Becky E. Adams wrote of her great-aunt:

> I discovered the fascinating story of a woman of incredible determination who became a missionary to China despite the prevailing societal pressures for her to marry for protection and security. The way she dealt with uncertainty of the financial support of her ministry and her accounts of the famines and bandit attacks in China were inspiring. When she was interned by the Japanese and was erroneously told numerous times that she would be allowed to return to the United States, she relied on her faith in God to give her the strength to endure.

Attie endured, and she made it back to Shelby. Home again and retired after an absence of 43 years. Attie continued speaking at churches about her experiences in China. At some point, as years rolled by, she renewed her acquaintance with another former missionary, a man she had first met aboard the Empress of China way back in 1900: Mr. T.J. League. League's first wife, Florence Nightingale League, had died in China. On January 7, 1947, 72-year-old Attie married T.J. League, 84. They had plenty in common to talk about in the seven years they had together. League died in 1953. Attie suffered a stroke in 1965 and moved to a rest home. Becky Adams wrote in *Called to China*: "Even at the rest home the cause of missions remained foremost in her mind." Attie asked a niece to "write a check for $100 to the Lottie Moon offering, to which she had been giving a month's salary each year while in China."

On May 7, 1965, Attie died at the age of 89. The old missionary had crossed vast oceans on the Empress of China and the M.S. Gripsholm, hiked barren mountain slopes and stared unblinking into the faces of warlords, but on a certain day in May she had docked forever on the shores of Sunset Cemetery. Beside her missionary brother Wade, they buried her in a robe she had worn when speaking to groups about China. And in her hands they placed a well-worn Bible. The marker reads: "Missionary in China for 43 years."

Few who stop by the grave will know much more. If the wind played a satiric verse from "Weihsien Blues" they would be mystified.

You'd think to hear those fellows sing the men did all the work
But I am here to tell you now the ladies do not shirk.
We clean the leeks, we cut the bread, But then what really hurts.
When they have done the dirty work, we have to wash their shirts.

Christianity in the Cemetery

June: The tombstone for Attie Bostick League is notable for identifying her by her profession as a missionary to China as well as by her relationship to her husband. She was a missionary for forty-three years and married for only seven, but her position as a wife gets top billing. The fact that her service as a missionary is included at all at a time when women were usually identified only by relationships shows what a big deal it was in her community.

The business of missions was one of the few ways in the late-nineteenth and early twentieth centuries that a woman could gain power and respect in a profoundly patriarchal Southern Baptist church in North Carolina. Baptist women had been supporting missionaries since 1800, when a paralyzed woman in Boston named Mary "Polly" Webb organized the first American missionary society. Baptist women in the South followed suit in 1811 with the formation of the Wadmalaw and Edisto Female Mite Society in South Carolina.

These societies were marvels of female ingenuity. "Mite" societies recalled the biblical story of the widow's mite. They emphasized the idea that even the small amounts women could control from the household budget could make a difference. Most thrifty women could manage to put a few pennies aside here and there—in some cases by devoting the money earned from selling eggs from the "missions hen" or those laid on Sunday to aid the cause of sending missionaries to foreign lands.

The women met to pray and gather supplies for missionaries, and they published popular newsletters such as *The Heathen Helper* and *The Baptist Basket* to tell stories of missionaries and play on the

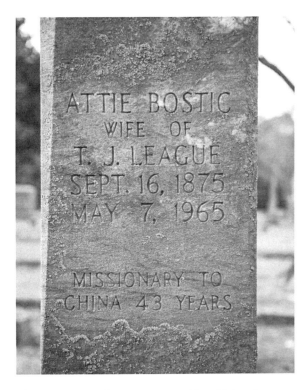

The Attie Bostick League stone identifying her as a Baptist missionary to China. Her stone is unusual in identifying a woman by occupation as well as by relationship. "Bostick" was also spelled "Bostic."

heartstrings of men and women who could give money or answer a call to leave their families behind and face unknown privations to spread the gospel. An American woman who felt called to minister in the United States was restricted to a supporting role, perhaps as a minister's wife. But as a missionary, she could do anything a man could do, including, if she were a single woman, preach. Few single Baptist women responded to such a call, but those who did were both criticized and adored.

The closest thing Baptists have ever had to a saint, in fact, is Charlotte Digges "Lottie" Moon, who was appointed a missionary to China in 1873, just before Attie was born. Lottie Moon was determined to evangelize in the same way that male missionaries did, and because she had no husband, she was able to gain a measure of autonomy that was rare for a late-nineteenth-century woman. Her letters home galvanized Baptist congregations in the South, inspiring many little girls to dream of being like Lottie Moon. Her ashes are buried today in Crewe, Virginia, and Crewe Baptist Church boasts stained glass windows depicting the life of Lottie Moon in much the same way that a Catholic church might show images of a St. Agatha or a St. Theresa.

Even in the South during Reconstruction, missions were a way for women to escape being dominated entirely by men in their churches. Catherine Allen, official historian of the Baptist Woman's Missionary Union, observes that "defeat in the Civil War, humiliation during Reconstruction, and devastation of culture left many male southerners ill-humored, and they took their anger out on the women." When the various Baptist women's missionary societies in the South decided to unite and form Woman's Missionary Union in 1888, they reached their decision at a Methodist Church in Richmond, Virginia, while the all-male Southern Baptist Convention met at the First Baptist Church a block away to debate whether to allow the women to organize.

Men who were terrified of the women's power had to express their misgivings for hours while the women calmly went about creating their organization. According to Allen, a Baptist man from Kentucky argued that "you can't overthrow Paul and Paul said, 'If you vote for this organization, God only knows what the women will do. Nobody on the face of this earth will be able to manage them, and they will be in danger of wrecking the whole business.'" Attie was thirteen years old during the debate.

Within two years, Southern Baptist men in North Carolina "allowed" their sisters to join Woman's Missionary Union officially, urged on by the redoubtable Miss Fannie Exile Scudder Heck of Raleigh, whose writing and advocacy for missions influenced women across the South. Perhaps Attie heard her speak at some point. One young woman described her skill at oratory like this: "As one listened, one felt as if one could lay down her life the for the cause she presented." Attie left for China with just that kind of determination.

Attie's tombstone noting her forty-three years as a missionary to China is much more than a occupational tombstone. It is a condensed story of what she exemplifies: a woman who broke the norms of an extremely conservative religious organization to follow her call. Other tombstones in the cemetery show what she was up against, a culture devoted to a version of Christianity that, in the South, included traditions of both repression of women and support of slavery. The Southern Baptist Convention was itself formed in 1845 when American Baptists split over whether slave owners could be commissioned as missionaries.

That the older part of Sunset is the final resting place for Christians is obvious. Quotations from scripture and from Protestant hymns such as "Safe in the Arms of Jesus" and "Come, Ye Disconsolate" are common. Some graves of Confederate soldiers are decorated with the Southern Cross of Honor, a variation of the Maltese Cross used by the Knights of St. John of Jerusalem, also known as the Knights of Malta, during the Crusades. The crosses are adorned with the Confederate battle flag and "CSA" on one side and the dates of the Civil War (1861–1865) plus the motto of the Confederacy, "*Deo Vindice*" and a laurel wreath on the other. "*Deo Vindici*" combines Christian assumptions about the regional allegiance of the Almighty with Lost Cause ideology. The Latin words mean something like "With God as our Defender."

More subtly, the graves in Sunset are oriented east to west, with the heads of the deceased at the west end of the grave and the feet at the east. The idea is that, on the Day of Judgment, as described in Matthew 24:27, the risen Christ will appear in the east. The dead will thus be perfectly positioned to rise from their

The Southern Cross of Honor on the grave of a Confederate soldier. "CSA" for Confederate States of America and the Confederate battle flag adorn the front of the marker. The dates of the Civil War, a laurel wreath, and the motto *Deo Vindice* ("with God as our Defender") are on the back.

graves to face him. Or so Christians have interpreted the scripture, making that interpretation a material reality in their cemeteries. Some scholars claim that east/west orientation predates Christianity and is a way to ensure that bodies called forth from their graves will face the rising sun.

Beyond the generically Christian bent of burials in Sunset Cemetery, the tombstones tell visitors that the culture is overwhelmingly Protestant. One indication is that Sunset has very few grave markers shaped as crosses, which are generally favored by Catholics and those of the Anglo-Catholic tradition (i.e., Episcopalians). When Protestants put a cross on a tombstone, it is almost always combined with another symbol such as a crown, ivy, or the opening gates of heaven.

The opening gates of heaven by itself is a popular tombstone icon beginning in the late-nineteenth century, and there are several in Sunset Cemetery. It is one of the few nineteenth-century icons that has remained popular even in our own time. The source of the design is a trilogy of novels by Elizabeth Stuart Phelps, a nineteenth-century Spiritualist. The first of her novels, *The Gates Ajar*, was published in 1868 and became an instant success. Phelps explains in her autobiography that she composed it to comfort those who had lost loved

The opening gates of heaven on the John C. Morrison stone. The icon was popularized by a trio of novels by the Spiritualist author Elizabeth Stuart Phelps, beginning with *The Gates Ajar* in 1868. *Beyond the Gates* followed in 1883 and *The Gates Between* in 1888.

ones in the Civil War. In the story, a young woman named Mary comes to realize that her brother Royal, who died in the conflict, is not lost to her. Under the tutelage of her aunt, she accepts the Spiritualist view that death is not the end but a "translation," as it was called, to another realm where the dead continue to watch over and interact with the living.

The bulk of the gates ajar tombstones began to appear after the publication in 1883 of the second book in the trilogy, *Beyond the Gates*. Even more explicit than the first novel, this one describes heaven in detail when another female protagonist, also named Mary, dies and goes to heaven. There she finds, not a nebulous "heavenly home," but a middle-class house, prepared especially for her and satisfying in every way down to the fine dog waiting on the front porch. She is greeted by young men who died in her care as a Civil War nurse. Heaven is a place where transformed human beings can walk on water and attend concerts featuring Beethoven's new oratorio and a Symphony of Color composed by artists such as Raphael and Leonardo.

By the time the third novel was published in 1888, Phelps' influence was established, and many Christians had embraced the idea that heaven—and the beloved dead—are accessible to the living. The gates ajar icon has never completely faded from popularity as an optimistic symbol that probably does not fare well when subjected to Christian doctrine. But it is normalized for Christians who, like Elizabeth Stuart Phelps' audience after the War, take no comfort in the believing that some people are destined for heaven and others are not.

According to Helen Sootin Smith, Mark Twain (Samuel Clemens) was not impressed with *The Gates Ajar*, describing Phelps' idea of the afterlife sarcastically as "a mean little ten-cent heaven about the size of Rhode Island." In 1909 he published a hilarious send-up of Phelps' work called "Captain Stormfield Visits Heaven." He delayed its publication for several years, partly because Mrs. Clemens did not recommend making fun of such popular books. Gates ajar icons can be found in many American cemeteries, but few people have even heard of Captain Stormfield. Like Attie Bostick's enduring reputation as a female missionary, it was the female version of Christianity that won out in the end.

Emma Virginia Frick (1871–1928)
Ora Brewster Eskridge (1885–1928)

Joe: Danger stalked two Shelby women on the eve of the Great Depression. The year 1928 had started with a bitter cold wave, but Emma Frick and Ora Eskridge could handle that. What they couldn't foresee or control was their destinies. Both would die in separate disasters within six months of each other on opposite sides of the same Shelby street.

Emma went first, in May, from injuries she suffered in a February fire at the Central Hotel. Ora followed in August when the temporary building of the First National Bank collapsed, killing her and five others. Both Ora and Emma were the only women who lost their lives in the catastrophes. Emma was a native of Baltimore, Maryland, and Ora grew up in Shelby. They had witnessed the town's steady growth and as adults made positive contributions to the community.

Shelby was fortunate to have good citizens like Emma and Ora. And then they were gone. Many in town might have reflected on the mysterious workings of fate.

How was Emma to know it wasn't safe to be in her hotel room on the early morning of February 23? And why didn't Ora take a day off instead of reporting to work on time at the First National Bank the morning of August 28?

Ora and Emma might have married and lived to ripe old ages. But the two friends had no idea of the lurking danger or that Sunset Cemetery was already whispering their names.

Emma

She came into the world when fire streaked the sky. A thunderstorm hit Baltimore with near hurricane force late on July, 4, 1871—the day of Emma Virginia Frick's birth in the city.

By nightfall, the heavy rain and lightning had subsided and Baltimore's big Independence Day fireworks display went on as planned. The *Baltimore Sun* described how the night sky turned into a colorful tapestry of exploding rockets, Chinese fans, revolving wheels, and dancing devils.

Emma wouldn't remember her first July fourth, but she likely accumulated memories of the city up until 1885 when her father, Englehart, died at age 54. Then 14-year-old Emma relocated to Shelby with her mother, Cecilia, and older sister, Rachel. Emma's brothers, George and Charles, were already in Shelby where they co-edited the *New Era*, a smartly written newspaper that promoted the local economic boom.

Two years after patriarch Englehart Fricks's demise, tragedy struck the family again in their new home of Shelby. The *New Era* ran this item on August 31, 1887: "Miss Rachel Shower Frick, the elder of the two sisters of Messrs. George A. and C.E. Frick, the editors of the *New Era*, died suddenly at the residence of her brothers on Thursday at a quarter before nine o'clock. Miss Frick, about a week before she died, began to complain of feeling unwell, but neither she nor any of her family thought that anything serious was the matter, nor would she have a physician summoned. The night of last Monday she passed uneasily and Dr. Victor McBrayer was called and pronounced her disease typhoid fever. She continued to grow worse until Wednesday night when her condition was apparently so much better that it was believed the progress of the disease had stopped. About five o'clock on Thursday morning, however, she passed into a comatose condition and continued gradually to sink until she died at the hour stated."

Born and educated in Baltimore, Rachel was 18 years, 7 months, and 21 days old. The obituary, probably co-written by George and Charles, stated that Rachel had made many friends in Shelby and was a "girl of fine promise, being possessed of a most amiable disposition, considerable personal attraction, a decided artistic talent and, for one so young, of excellent literary taste. Dutiful, loving and kind, her distinguishing characteristic was devotion to the members of her family whose home was drearily darkened when the light of her life went out."

An Episcopalian minister from Lincolnton conducted the funeral service at the home of a brother. A stone in the shape of a cross marked the grave of the teenaged girl, the first Frick family member buried in Sunset Cemetery.

Just a few weeks later, in mid–September, the Fricks had another scare—this time with young Emma. From the *New Era* on September 14: "Miss Emma V. Frick, sister of the editors of *The New Era*, is suffering from typhoid fever, but she is not thought to be dangerously ill." Typhoid fever had taken her sister, Rachel away, just a month earlier. Even though it appeared Emma was in no danger, family members still were probably on edge and taking nothing for granted.

But Emma recovered, and life went on in Shelby. Shortly afterwards, the *New Era* shut down, and the Frick brothers sold the equipment. Shelby had not appreciated their brand of outspoken journalism, they complained in the paper. The town had shown them no support and they had never made any money. Shelby was to blame for their failure and they were leaving—for good. George returned to Baltimore, opened a law office, and was elected to the Maryland State Legislature. Charles moved to Charlotte, where he worked in real estate and hotel management. Emma and her mother stayed in Shelby and lived the life of leisure. They took trips together, spending the summer in Black Mountain and Blowing Rock. They were members of Shelby's small Episcopal Church of the Redeemer, where Emma organized and taught the first Sunday school classes.

Emma's name appeared most frequently in the social columns of the *Cleveland Star*. By the early 1920s, she and her mother lived in an apartment in the Central Hotel above the First National Bank on West Warren Street. In the hotel parlor, lavishly decorated with fresh flowers, Emma hosted literary clubs such as the 20th Century and Chicora clubs. Emma loved literature and the arts. The *Cleveland Star* reported that at one club meeting she read a paper on English poet Algernon Charles Swinburne and at another gave a program on the celebrated English actress Ellen Terry.

She hosted progressive Flinch parties and Chafing dish parties, visited with her brothers when they passed through town, and took out-of-town day

Marker for staunch Episcopalian Emma Virginia Frick. Catholics and Episcopalians are more likely to use plain crosses as gravemarkers than non–Catholics or other Protestants, who typically combine the cross with other symbols such as a crown.

trips with friends. But Emma always made time for church work and during World War I helped with the local war bonds drive. As a volunteer social worker, she counseled struggling young mothers in Shelby's textile mill villages. Emma's mother, Cecilia, died on July 26, 1926, at 93 and joined her oldest daughter, Rachel, in Sunset Cemetery.

Emma kept the third-floor apartment in the Central Hotel. On February 28, 1928, around 5:30 a.m., a hotel clerk pounded on her door yelling that the hotel was on fire. Newspaper accounts would tell how Emma ran into the hall and got a fire extinguisher by breaking protective glass. She fought her way to safety, but discovered she had suffered severe cuts from the broken glass.

In Shelby Hospital, she continued to fight for her life as Shelby kept vigil. Long ago, Emma had beaten typhoid fever—surely she could survive this. Months passed by, and she held on. In the end, blood poisoning took her away. Fire had heralded her birth on July 4, 1871; fire marked her exit from life on May 5, 1928. A third stone cross went up where the Frick women rested in Sunset Cemetery.

Ora

Ora Brewster Eskridge first saw the light of day on September 16, 1885. That was the same year Emma Frick and her family moved to Shelby. And a little over two months before the birth of Ora Eskridge, Ora Brewster of Sweetwater, Tennessee, married Shelby native Charles Coleman Blanton. Ora and Charles had met when she taught music at the Shelby Female Academy. The Blanton and the Eskridge families were related and the new baby Eskridge was named after the new bride of Charles Blanton. Ora Eskridge probably had few if any memories of her namesake because Ora Blanton died in 1890 at the age of 31.

But memories of that first Ora stayed alive in Shelby for years. The youthful Ora Eskridge likely listened to recollections about the brilliant music teacher who made such a name for herself in town. Ora Eskridge also made a name for herself. People liked her, and she liked people. The doors at her home on West Marion Street, "The Oaks," were always open to visitors. Her name regularly popped up in the social columns of the *Cleveland Star*: Ora helping with a spring party of the Tongues and Needles Club or presiding over a punch bowl at a reception.

For all her socializing, Ora was also a working woman. Early on, she had taught in a rural school, then moved on to secretarial jobs, and in the early 1920s joined the staff at First National Bank. In time, she would rise to the post of head clerk. The Roaring '20s rushed by. And then it was January 28, 1928. As usual, Ora went to work at the bank which had been temporarily quartered in the McKnight across West Warren Street as renovation work continued at the Central Hotel, heavily damaged by fire in February. Ora had lost a friend, Emma Frick, as a result of that fire; Emma, the mainstay of Shelby's Episcopal Church, was probably never far from Ora's mind.

The bank doors opened at 9:00 a.m. on Tuesday, January 28, customers entered the building, and business transactions begin. Construction sounds drifted in from the hotel across the street and the basement of the McKnight building where excavation prepared the space for use as a pool hall. All the while, the clock kept ticking.

Years later, a bank employee would recall for a local reporter how shortly after 9:00 the building began to tremble slightly. That was the only warning anybody got. In the next instant, the roof collapsed, tumbling down on Ora's desk. She lived for a few minutes after rescuers pulled her from the rubble.

Five others died in the collapse of the bank building. Businesses closed the day of Ora's funeral at Shelby's First Baptist Church. Hundreds lined the city streets as a hearse carried her to Sunset Cemetery, where an even bigger crowd awaited. Ora was already in the ground before Atlanta musician Dan Hornsby wrote and recorded "The Shelby Disaster." Future visitors standing by Ora's grave may have quietly recited some of Hornsby's lyrics about the day of Shelby's stricken heart. And if they listened closely, they may have heard Ora singing along.

Mimi Elliott Hirsch and the Making of a Marker

June: The pre-need marker for Mimi Elliott Hirsch sits snugly between those for her parents and her brother. She explains that her mother bought six plots in 1945. Her maternal grandparents—Samuel and Jemima Elizabeth ("Mamie") Parker—and her mother's brother, Archie Parker, rest together in the family plot with her own parents and brother. Since the plot could not accommodate another

A grouping of family markers for John Wesley Elliott; Mildred Parker Elliott; John Wesley Elliott, Jr.; and Mimi Elliott Hirsch. These markers are notable for carefully chosen epitaphs that include poetry, a philosophical aphorism, and a popular hymn. The epitaphs and icons reflect the personalities and occupations of the four people memorialized.

burial, her stone will some day become a cenotaph, a memorial marker with no body. But her ashes will be scattered in Sunset.

Ms. Hirsch's marker offers insight into what happens when people choose what will go on their monuments and how they choose epitaphs and icons for their family members. Her marker itself is a simple rectangular block of marble with a classical urn on top. The words and symbols are what tell us how she wishes to be remembered. Aside from identifying her by name and dates, they fall into the common categories of

- family relationships,
- spirituality/religion, and
- philosophy of life.

Other common choices include

- occupation
- affiliation with an organization
- personality revelation

Mimi Elliott Hirsch's marker, which includes a statement about important relationships, an aphorism attributed to Ralph Waldo Emerson, and a symbol of Celtic origin called a triquetra. The triquetra has many meanings, including the never-ending cycle of life and death and the three ages of women.

Fitting the complexity of a human life onto a stone in letters large enough to be read at a glance is a tall order. Some people simply throw up their hands at this impossible task and provide only the most basic information—names and dates—leaving the rest to the imagination of the viewer once they no longer exist in living or written memory.

Mimi Hirsch is leaving nothing to chance by exerting her own agency over how she will be remembered. Family relationships come first. After her name and birth date, the inscription identifies Mimi Hirsch as a "Grateful Daughter" and "Loving Mother." She describes her childhood as idyllic. Her father ran the power plant for the Lily Mill Company at Stice Shoals near her home and was always close by. Her mother was a church pianist and organist, and the family would gather in the evening to sing hymns and secular songs after supper. Both her parents were musical, and her father played the guitar for these musical evenings. Ms. Hirsch grew up supported and "pushed 'gently' to use [her] abilities to make the world a better place and to strive for excellence."

She taught school for a few years after her marriage, but then chose to create a similar childhood for her children by devoting herself to being a stay-at-home mother. Her three children and seven grandchildren are her pride and joy, her "magnum opus," as she puts it, quoting Rose Kennedy. Daughter Miriam is a neurosurgical nurse who works with movement disorder patients. Miriam's sister, Melissa, is a family counselor, and their brother, Jonathan, is a veterinarian. "Grateful Daughter" and "Loving Mother" are very condensed indicators of the quality of her family relationships.

The marker also includes a triquetra, a triangular figure comprising three interlaced arcs, often looped, as in this case, through a circle. Ms. Hirsch likes this symbol because it is Celtic and thus reflects her family origins. She also likes it because it is spiritual but not specifically religious. Raised a Protestant Christian, she converted to Judaism upon her marriage and now considers herself a "Unitarian with a humanism component." While organized religion is an important part of many people's identity, the triquetra suggests a broader view of spiritual commitment than one bounded by creeds and doctrines. As Carol Ochs puts it in *Women and Spirituality*, "Spirituality is the process of coming into relationship with reality…, that which is larger than our experiences and our consciousness." The infinite loops of the triquetra suggest the never-ending process of life, death, and rebirth. They also refer to the stages of a woman's life in pagan religions: maid, mother, crone. Ms. Hirsch likes the idea that the triquetra can symbolize female empowerment.

The quotation at the bottom of the stone is attributed to Ralph Waldo Emerson: "The purpose of life is/ To be useful,/ To be honorable and/ To be compassionate." Ms. Hirsch remembers a father who loved Emerson and hopes that these words will make the cemetery visitor pause and reflect. It is a more humanist directive than the common colonial admonition to "Remember, friends, as you pass by, as you are now, so once was I. As I am now, so you shall be. So think of death and follow me." It is less clearly religious than the innumerable nineteenth-century hands pointing the viewer to heaven or the hand of God coming down to break a chain or pluck a flower. At the same time, it reflects Ms. Hirsch's view that her most important role was as a mother. The quotation gently urges all of us to live well by adopting values that contribute to the culture as a whole. Usefulness, honor, and compassion are not glamorous, self-serving values. They are simply the values that create harmony among human beings—and the memory of a life well lived.

With its emphasis on relationships and maternal values, Ms. Hirsch's future cenotaph is clearly gendered female. Her brother's tombstone is just as clearly gendered male with its emphasis on his career and accomplishments. After attending Gardner-Webb College and completing a degree at the University of North Carolina, John Wesley Elliott, Jr., earned a master's degree and doctorate at Harvard, thus the Harvard University seal on his tombstone. His mother and sister also chose a quotation from William Wordsworth for his tombstone because he eventually went to Columbia University to earn another doctorate, specializing in British Romantic poetry. He could "quote Wordsworth's poetry by pages," according to his sister. After a career teaching British literature at Fairleigh Dickinson University, he died in hope of "liv[ing] in peace eternal," as the epitaph puts it, a reflection of the orthodox Christian faith he inherited from his mother.

The markers for John Wesley Elliott, Sr., and Mildred Parker Elliott show a similar level of care in crafting memories that reflect lives that were useful, honorable, and compassionate. Mr. Elliott's memory prompts are a Masonic symbol and a quotation from Shakespeare's *Julius Caesar*. The symbol and epitaph identify him by affiliation with an organization and, more unusually, by an attempt to capture his personality in an apt quote. Ms. Hirsch describes her father as a Renaissance man who was a well-known beekeeper, a musician, a woodworker. He was also an autodidact who did not attend college but became a voracious reader. He loved Elbert Hubbard's fourteen-volume *Little Journeys to the Homes of the Great*, Spinoza, and Henry David Thoreau's *Walden*. He was a joyful man who could be "the life of the party," but he was also "troubled by the human condition witnessing poverty, ignorance, and prejudice."

When John Wesley Elliott, Sr., died in 1981, his wife, son, and daughter chose a quotation that evokes the memory of a complex man with Antony's description of Brutus as a man who, though flawed and human, was yet noble, "and the elements so mixed in him that Nature might stand up and say to all the world, 'This was a man.'" Perhaps Mr. Elliott would be pleased to be described as a "man" in the Emersonian sense of a fully realized human being. The words might remind him of Emerson's description of the American scholar as "Man thinking" rather than simply "thinking Man." As "Man thinking," Mr. Elliott was a well-rounded person enmeshed in nature (those bees!), who worked with his hands and who read the timeless ideas of others but maintained his own originality. He was more than just a bookworm.

Mildred Parker Elliott, according to her daughter, was a woman of "rock-solid faith," who read the Bible to her children every day. She was the organist and pianist at Zoar Baptist Church before becoming a founding member of John Knox Presbyterian, where she was also the organist and pianist as well as a deacon and elder. Her inscription is the last verse of "Amazing Grace," which Mimi Hirsch describes as "our family's favorite hymn," noting that "its message of redemption and hope [was] a perfect illustration for my mother." Although the story of John Newton, the reformed slave trader who wrote the original six verses of "Amazing Grace," is well known and widely loved, the verse that appears on Mrs. Elliott's gravestone—the one that begins "When we've been there ten thousand years"—is not by Newton. According to hymnologist William J. Reynolds, it is the final verse of a different hymn, "Jerusalem, My Happy Home," which appeared in many nineteenth-century hymnals and eventually was incorporated into "Amazing Grace."

"Amazing Grace" is, perhaps, the most beloved hymn in American history, sung by people of all faiths and no particular faith for hope and comfort. It is also an especially apt choice for a grave in Cleveland County, North Carolina. The man who joined the text "Amazing Grace" to "New Britain," the hymn tune to which the Elliotts would have sung it, was William "Singing Billy" Walker of Spartanburg, South Carolina, around 35 miles from Shelby. Reynolds identifies "New Britain" as an American melody whose composer is unknown. It was certainly a staple of the singing schools common in early twentieth-century Cleveland County. Mrs. Elliott was a trained musician, and she grew up in an area of the country that valued singing in harmony, both to promote human fellowship and to teach cultural/religious values.

The August 16, 1905, edition of the *Cleveland* Star, for example, reported that a Reverend Blanton from Caroleen had conducted a successful singing school for several weeks at Sandy Plains Church and had recently held a similar school at another area church. Singing schools taught untrained musicians to read music by assigning specific shapes to the different notes of the scale. The singing masters used for their textbooks shape-note tune books such as William Walker's *The Christian Harmony*, first published in 1866. Like other tune books—the most famous of which was one edited by Walker's brother-in-law called *The Sacred Harp*—*The Christian Harmony* emphasized the music over the words. As a result, each entry is titled by tune rather than by text. Walker's book, which is still in use, includes the tune "New Britain" with three verses of "Amazing Grace." An annual memorial "singing" celebrating the life of William Walker held in Spartanburg each spring ends with singing "Amazing Grace" to the tune "New Britain" in four-part harmony at his grave site.

Memories such as singing "Amazing Grace" at home in the evening after supper may seem embedded in time and place, but the work of a well-chosen epitaph or icon can transcend those limitations to create durable memories. The memorial window clings available from online businesses and the memorial tattoos that have become common seem poor substitutes for the care and attention that went into choosing the memorials for Mimi Hirsch's family. The information that appears on tombstones may seem boring or inconsequential to cemetery visitors. But, properly chosen, it can condense the most valued elements of human identity into words and symbols that keep memories alive.

Betty Singleton Holdridge, "The Fat Lady" (1910–1954)

Joe: Under a sideshow tent, gobs of flesh rippled in the pale afternoon light. A flimsy costume exposed the Fat Lady's 600 pounds as a magnificent moving mountain for all to see. But only Valda Hord witnessed the spectacle one cold, rainy autumn afternoon in 1954, and many years later told a *Charlotte Observer* reporter about what happened that day. Bad weather kept many dedicated Cleveland County Fair goers at home, but not Valda. Nothing could stop her from coming to this once-a-year event.

At the last fair, she had stood in the tent at this same spot and spoken to the Fat

Lady. The sideshow attraction had been happy then. Now, on a chilly October afternoon in 1954, something had changed. Valda approached the woman who stood forlornly on a raised platform, and saw clearly a flushed face, tears, and extreme misery. The woman recognized Valda and smiled. "What's wrong, honey?" Valda asked.

The Fat Lady replied that she had fallen and hurt herself, then took Valda's hand and squeezed it tightly. That confirmed what Valda had already been thinking: this person needed help. And the Fat Lady got help, thanks to her friend. Before long, emergency workers arrived and hoisted the woman into an ambulance, transported her to the Shelby Hospital. Staff had to rig two beds together to accommodate the huge patient. It didn't take long for word about the hospitalized Fat Lady to get out around town. The local paper ran a story, and cards and letters from well-wishers poured in.

Valda dropped by for a visit and thought the Fat Lady showed signs of improvement. But on October 7, pneumonia and the injuries took her away. The carnival paid for a special wooden coffin to hold the remains. Valda and five other people, including the carnival owners and the Fat Lady's husband, attended a graveside service for her in Sunset Cemetery. Two bouquets, including chrysanthemums from Valda, marked the spot. The carnival left town, the bouquets faded, but no tombstone went up to remind people the Fat Lady ever existed or had a name. She came to town a sideshow freak and never left, sleeping nameless and mostly forgotten on a hillside in Sunset Cemetery.

The Betty Singleton Holdridge stone donated by a local monument company after her friend Valda Hord kept the story of the "Fat Lady" alive.

But Valda didn't forget. She knew the location of the Fat Lady's grave and went there with flowers every Christmas. Flowers ignored by passers-by on the cemetery road beside the spot. Flowers the elements would destroy. New flowers faithfully provided by Valda year after year.

What was it that stirred her memories of the Fat Lady when the Cleveland County Fair came to town in the fall of 1990? Valda shared the story, it got into the newspapers, and interest in the nameless Fat Lady gripped imaginations. A search for her name began, and after much digging finally scored a success: Betty Singleton Holdridge, born August 17, 1910, in Rochester, New York. A death certificate revealed she had broken a shoulder in a fall six weeks before arriving in Shelby. For six weeks she had traveled the carnival circuit in pain—the pain Valda had seen on Betty's face that afternoon in 1954.

A Shelby monument company offered to provide a tombstone for Betty, and Valda picked it out. And she came up with an inscription: "She came to Shelby a simple Fat Lady in the fair. She left this earth as our friend."

If there had been any music at the installation of the monument, it might have been an unlikely hit song from Germany in 1954, the year of Betty's death: "The Happy Wanderer" by the Oberkirchen Children's Choir that includes the word "Valda." The Fat Lady would have liked that.

Caring for the Dead

June: The body of Betty Singleton Holdridge was prepared for burial and interred at Sunset Cemetery in the conventional way. Her body was embalmed, placed in a casket, and buried by professionals. The only thing out of the ordinary was that her casket was wooden and custom-made in a time when mass-produced caskets, often of metal, had become popular.

The late George Clay, a local funeral home director and former mayor of Shelby, explained to a class of students studying death in American culture at Gardner-Webb University years ago before his death that Ms. Holdridge's casket had to be specially made to accommodate her size—and that he had to remove the doors to the back of the funeral home to maneuver it into the establishment. He joked that her husband whispered to him very seriously that "the carnival advertised that she weighed 625 pounds, but it's not true. She really weighed only 600 pounds!" Black humor was a staple for purveyors of "the dismal trade" by 1954 when Betty Singleton Holdridge died, and caring for dead bodies had been completely professionalized by then. Those who died a century earlier would have been shocked.

In all parts of the country, loved ones cared for their dead at home. Family members—almost always women—washed and dressed the body for burial. It was then laid out at home for visitation in most cases. Neighbors brought food to the home, and the men of the family constructed wooden coffins or found a local cabinet maker to assume the task. In some cases, pre-made coffins could be purchased at a local general store.

Friends and family dug the grave and buried the body of their loved one. Belonging to a church made the task easier. The church records of Boiling Springs Baptist Church, around ten miles from Sunset Cemetery, show that the church maintained a box of supplies for this purpose. In a business meeting on June 2, 1894, for example, the minutes show that "the Internal Improvement Committee were [sic] authorized to purchase two Shovels, ax, hoe, have picks repaired and purchase any other tool necessary to be used at the grave-yard." On February 6, 1897, the church purchased ropes "for the benefit of the Grave-Yard." As late as November 3, 1906, the church purchased "a broad hoe and webbing [for lowering coffins]" to be used by the sexton at burials.

In other words, burying a body was a community affair. Family members were hands-on participants in all stages of the process. We can imagine coffins carried into Sunset on wagons using the narrow carriage roads in the oldest part of the cemetery. Once there, they were carefully unloaded, perhaps by men sweating in their Sunday clothes, and lowered into a grave prepared the day before by people who actually knew the deceased.

The Civil War began the change to outsourcing all of these services to professional undertakers or, to use the more modern term, "funeral home directors." The immediate issue was sending bodies home from the battlefield in good enough shape to allow family and friends to view their dead before burial. The historian and former president of Harvard University Drew Gilpin Faust describes what happened in *This Republic of Suffering: Death and the American Civil War*. In a frantic effort to return bodies to their homes for burial, some families employed so-called "ice coffins" offered by transportation companies who sent the dead home via train or horse-drawn carriage.

At the same time, embalmers began traveling with armies, offering their services to those who could afford them. Embalming the body of a private soldier cost about $5 but embalming the body of a colonel might fetch $100 and a brigadier general $200. $100 in the 1860s would be the equivalent of over $3,000 today. Though embalmers were often viewed as ghoulish opportunists, anxious families still scraped together the money to buy their services when they could. And eventually embalming became the conventional way to care for a dead body. As Faust observes:

> In the 1850s embalming had been chiefly used not to prepare bodies for funerals but to contribute to the study of anatomy and pathology by providing cadavers preserved for dissection. It was during the war that embalming first became more widely practiced, not just generating a transformation in physical treatment of the dead but establishing a procedure that would serve as a foundation for the emergence of the funeral industry and the professionalization of the undertaker.

By 1880, the first convention of funeral directors took place in Michigan, and the National Funeral Directors' Association drafted its constitution in 1882. And thus began the professionalization of the funeral industry. By the time Betty Singleton Holdridge died in 1954, bodies were routinely embalmed, buried in caskets from the Batesville Casket Company or another manufacturer, and buried in graves dug by professionals and lined with sturdy vaults that do not allow the earth to settle over a grave. Cremations without funerals, delaying the publication of obituaries, and holding memorial services without the deceased long after a death mean that people no longer have to deal openly with bodies and the painful reality of death. At the cemetery, mourners are shielded from acknowledging death by astroturf covering the raw earth and a mechanical device to lower the casket into the ground. Workers fill the hole after the mourners leave. During the coronavirus pandemic, Zoom funerals allowed even more detachment from the dead.

It all seems very … civilized, but the emotional and spiritual toll this lack of time-honored rituals has taken may be larger than we realize. Both Thomas Lynch in *The Good Funeral* and Suzanne Kelly in *Greening Death* observe that popular entertainment—novels, TV shows, movies, videogames—have become obsessed with dead bodies in the form of zombies and vampires.

One response has been the Green or Natural Burial Movement, which encourages resuming the practice of traditional burial practices. In addition, home funeral organizations such as Crossings teach people to care for the dead at home, as we once did. Dr. Billy Campbell, the founder with his wife Kimberley Campbell of Ramsey Creek Preserve in Westminster, South Carolina, explains that neo-traditional burials are exactly what people have done for most of human history. What is new is Ramsey Creek's mission to reclaim the earth. It is the first conservation burial ground in the United States.

At Ramsey Creek, established in 1996, people bury their dead in biodegradable containers such as wooden coffins, simple shrouds, wicker baskets, or handmade quilts. Loved ones in some cases prepare their dead for burial in the old way by washing and dressing them but without embalming. Some people bury the ashes—cremains—of their dead. Ramsey Creek does not allow burial vaults or elaborate tombstones. Instead, graves might be marked by plantings or by simple indigenous stones that include only names, dates, and perhaps a very brief epitaph or icon. Ramsey Creek Preserve

A natural/green burial at Ramsey Creek Preserve in Westminster, South Carolina. Ramsey Creek is the first conservation burial ground in the United States (photograph by June Hadden Hobbs).

can locate all the graves, whether they are marked or not, using GPS coordinates.

In 2020, the United States had around 100 registered green burial sites. The closest one to Shelby is Carolina Memorial Sanctuary near Asheville, North Carolina. Some of these sites are also, like Ramsey Creek Preserve, conservation burial grounds, meant to conserve land that has been overworked or might be appropriated for commercial purposes. Honey Creek Woodlands, owned by the Monastery of the Holy Spirit in Conyers, Georgia, is one of these. And some conventional cemeteries are self-proclaimed "hybrids" because they now include sections devoted to neo-traditional as well as conventional burials. Even Mount Auburn Cemetery, the first rural/garden cemetery, now advertises itself as a hybrid.

In truth, Sunset Cemetery—like most cemeteries whose burials span the turn of the twentieth century—is already a hybrid. The burials in the oldest sections are "natural" in that bodies are buried by hand without embalming in biodegradable containers while newer burials are more conventional. Some people find the older practices ecologically responsible as a way to preserve the earth. As Mark Harris points out in *Grave Matters*, a ten-acre conventional cemetery "contains enough coffin wood to construct more than forty houses, nine hundred-plus tons of casket steel, and another twenty thousands tons of vault concrete. To that add a volume of formalin [a biocide and carcinogen used in embalming] sufficient to fill a small backyard swimming pool."

But perhaps conservation of the earth and doing things by hand again is the province of those whose identities are well represented in written records in Cleveland County. The bodies of middle-class white people who dominate Sunset Cemetery have usually been treated respectfully at all seasons in their lives. In contrast, the anonymous burials in the "colored" section of Sunset, the empty field on the west end of the old section, are a way of saying that Black bodies don't matter. They don't even deserve the dignity of recorded names and dates.

One reaction to such a tragedy, as Suzanne Kelly points out, is "extreme embalming—where bodies are superpreserved and then posed with props." The funeral in 2018 of the late Aretha Franklin, is an excellent example. During the four days leading up to her funeral, Franklin was arrayed as the diva she was in costumes that were changed out daily. The first involved a ruby-red cocktail dress and Christian Louboutin stilettos with five-inch heels. It was a send-off suitable for the Queen of Soul and a way of giving her the respect so often denied Black people in America, even in the cemetery.

The Presbyterian minister Thomas G. Long reminds us that "human beings are ultimately incarnate and social creatures. We are not people who happen to have bodies; we are, rather, *embodied* beings." How we care for those bodies in the end is crucial to maintaining our humanity.

III

Guys Your Mother Wouldn't Let You Sit With in Church

Rafe King (1891–1949)

Joe: The 1929 stock market crash monopolized most news outlets, but Rafe made headlines, too.

His name was splashed across front pages of newspapers all over America. A country music duo recorded a song about him. *True Detective* magazine chronicled his alleged misdeeds in its pages. Readers couldn't get enough about Rafe King of Shelby, North Carolina, accused of killing his wife at their South Carolina home. Rafe denied it and held firm all the way through two trials. Both juries didn't buy his story and found him guilty.

Rafe King dodged the electric chair. Instead, he got life with the possibility of parole. During 18 years behind bars, he never stopped trying to get that parole. He probably never considered all the shame and dishonor he had brought on his family and community and whether Shelby would welcome him back. In fact, most of Shelby probably tried to forget Rafe. It hadn't always been that way.

Born in Shelby on November 2, 1891, Rafe came from a prominent and well-respected family. He had a winning personality that made him popular around town, as reflected in news items that appeared in the *Cleveland Star*. As an adult, Rafe ran a service station and swimming pool on East Marion Street. But few people likely knew about his darker side. That wouldn't come out until the murder trials. In the late 1920s, Rafe married high school French teacher Faye Wilson of Kings Mountain, who also came from a well-known family. After a honeymoon at Chimney Rock/Lake Lure, the couple settled in Shelby. It wasn't long until Faye discovered something sickening about her new husband.

The Kings moved to Sharon, South Carolina, when Faye inherited property, and they lived in a small, one-story cottage on the edge of the village. Faye taught French part-time at Sharon High School. On Friday, January 26, 1929, around 11:00 a.m., Faye visited a neighbor, borrowed a jar of milk, then chatted a while before leaving. This was likely the last time she was seen alive.

Meanwhile, shortly after nightfall, Rafe pounded on a neighbor's door, crying out that his wife hadn't returned from the high school that afternoon. Wondering if neighbors had seen her, Rafe explained that he had been sick in bed sick all day and

was worried about her. A search party set out and found Faye's body in an outbuild-
ing near the main house. Lying on a pile of walnuts with one arm upraised, her other
hand was near a bottle of what might be poison. Blood on her body was apparently
caused by the fall.

Rafe explained she had been depressed about discovering she was pregnant.
Twice, she had tried to kill herself by taking poison, he claimed. Now Rafe believed
she had finally succeeded. Neighbors were horrified at the sudden death of a young
wife and teacher. While women washed the blood off Faye's body, the men sat in the
kitchen, talking and chewing tobacco. When someone spat into the fire place there
was a sizzle as tobacco juice hit the coals.

Talk ceased. All eyes shifted to the fire place. Something peculiar was going
on. Rafe had just told the men he had been in bed all day and that his wife had left
work at noon. So if nobody had been up and around, why were there still live coals
in the fireplace? The men took a closer look around and observed the kitchen had
been freshly scrubbed. A cloud of suspicion began hanging over Rafe in the minds
of some. But after an autopsy, the county coroner ruled death by drinking poison.
The Rev. Eb Hunter of Sharon was at the King home making arrangements for Faye's
funeral when he noticed something had been burned in the fireplace. Later, it would
be revealed that Rafe had dumped some of his wife's clothing in the fire.

Faye was buried at Mountain Rest Cemetery in Kings Mountain, but the case
didn't end there. Investigators kept probing the King home. Eventually, they found
what was believed to be blood spots in various locations in the house. They found
underwear with blood spots stuffed in a trunk. More doubts were raised. A second autopsy was ordered and Faye's body exhumed. Bruises were discovered on her
throat. She wasn't pregnant and there was no poison in her stomach. The investigation intensified, and authorities found a bundle of Rafe's clothes with blood on them.

In the end, Rafe was charged with murder and pled not guilty. At the first trial in
Chester, South Carolina, testimony revealed Rafe had contracted syphilis and passed
it on to Faye shortly after their marriage. On top of that, their finances were a mess,
and he had taken out a large life insurance policy on her, naming himself beneficiary.
Rafe didn't testify during the two-day trial. The jury took only 45 minutes to find him
guilty and made no recommendation for mercy. Rafe was sentenced to death in the
electric chair.

An appeal was filed and Rafe's family hired a new legal team which included
Shelby's silver-tongued attorney, Clyde Hoey. The team's arguments for a new trial
resulted in a judge granting one. The second trial was moved to Lancaster, and 700
people jammed a courtroom that seated 350. Rafe gained entrance by using a ladder.
He didn't take the witness stand, but results were the same: Guilty, except this time
he got life.

Rafe went to Columbia's formidable Central Correction Institution, where huge
granite and brick buildings housed some of South Carolina's most vicious criminals
and killers. Among the toughest, meanest, most depraved inmates on the planet, Rafe
held his own. The Great Depression came and went; World War II gave way to the
Atomic Age and the Cold War.

All the while, Rafe King, who had been so tight-lipped during the trials, kept repeating to visitors and in letters to lawyers, court officials, family members, media representatives, and preachers, anybody who would listen: "I didn't kill my wife. I didn't kill my wife."

In early June of 1949. Rafe made headlines again in some papers (not the *Shelby Daily Star*) when he came home for good. But home this time wasn't the King place he grew up in on Sumter Street. It was just down Sumter Street in Sunset Cemetery. By then, RCA Victor's 1931 record "The Rafe King Murder Case," cut in Charlotte by the Stapleton Brothers, was a largely forgotten antique from the Great Depression. Post-World-War-II Americans had moved on. The Rafe King Murder Case resided in the dust bin of history even if it had been one of the most notorious cases in the annals of South Carolina crime. The last verse of "The Rafe King Murder Case" went like this:

> Just how it all happened, God only knows.
> King must have been guilty by the blood on his clothes
> He was then tried in Lancaster for killing his wife
> King was convicted and sentenced to life.

If people remembered the case, they may have stood by Rafe's grave and imagined his endless pleadings that he didn't so it. And wondered: Did he really do it?

Edwin Chambers Dodson, Jr. (1949–2003)

This was the epitaph Eddie probably wanted on his gravestone: World's greatest bank robber.

Except he would have expressed it differently, maybe in off-color language. In the end, though, Eddie got just the basics: full name, dates of birth and death. His gravesite in Sunset Cemetery rests on a slight incline and heavy precipitation pushes mud over his marker. Mother Nature may be making a statement. How Eddie muddied his own life and those of others.

Still, there's no denying it: this Shelby boy set records as a bank robber. A *Charlotte Observer* article covered the details of his life in 2014, the year a biographical movie about Eddie, *Electric Slide*, appeared in theaters with the role of Eddie played by English actor/singer-songwriter Jim Sturgess. A $1,000-a-day heroin habit drove him to crime in 1983. He had once made good money running a fancy antique shop in Los Angeles,

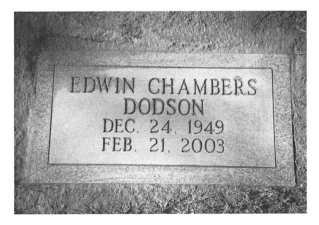

Tombstone for Eddie Chambers Dodson, Jr., the "Yankee Bandit" who grew up in Shelby but robbed banks in Los Angeles. The FBI named him the most prolific bank robber of all time.

but that business went bust. With the legal cash flow gone, Eddie started robbing banks. He had always liked nice clothes and dressed up for the bank capers: expensive suit, shirt and tie. At first glance, he might have been mistaken for an executive. But he topped off the outfit with a New York Yankees ball cap—a touch that earned him the nickname "Yankee Bandit." Eddie didn't mean to hurt anybody and carried a toy pistol inside in a Gucci bag. Handsome and full of charm, he sweet-talked female tellers and left them swooning. Eddie made his getaways in a restored 1965 black Lincoln. The media loved this classy bank robber with an uncanny ability to outfox the law. One day he robbed six banks and got away clean and easy. Nobody could touch the Bandit. Or so it seemed.

Sixty-four bank robberies and $280,000 later, a bank teller followed the bandit and called police. In 1984, Eddie went to prison. If Eddie had been the type given to reflection, he might have used the ten years behind bars to reflect on how he had gotten into such a mess. Things had started badly for him. Eddie was only two months old when his father died of a heart attack. An only child, he grew up in the care of a doting mother and grandmother. Bernice Dodson worked two jobs so her precious baby got anything he wanted. Deeply religious, she took him to church, but Eddie's mind probably focused on girls and rock music. Mick Jagger and the Rolling Stones, especially. To Eddie, they personified coolness. He cultivated that quality, along with a natural charm.

And so it went: Eddie a typical teen in Shelby. In Charlotte, he was in college and something of a hippy, dabbling in drugs and running into minor trouble with authorities. When the trouble turned serious, he left the West Coast with a buddy. And there, in Los Angeles, everything came together for Eddie. He acquired a pricey furniture store on Melrose Drive and catered to the cream of Hollywood celebrities such as movie stars Jack Nicholson and John Belushi. The drugs flowed as Eddie hobnobbed with the rich and famous. He dated beautiful women and drove fancy cars. On furniture buying trips to England, he kept partying hard. Somewhere along the line in this glitzy whirlwind, he graduated from cocaine to black tar heroin. And that would bring him down. Eddie unraveled. During the ten years he spent in prison, he may have thought about the long journey that led to his downfall.

Because when he got out, he stayed clean. For about four years. But the heroin monkey had never really gotten off his back: In 1999, he relapsed into drugs and robbed eight banks before his arrest. The Yankee Bandit no long looked cool and debonair. He looked like a junkie.

Sentenced to 48 months, Eddie served three years and was released early because of poor health. He died February 21, 2003, of liver failure related to hepatitis C. Eddie was 54.

The FBI had ranked him the most prolific bank robber of all time. When all was said and done, this was the mark Eddie Dodson had made on the world. He took pride in the accomplishment and asked that it be mentioned in the program at his memorial service in Los Angeles. He had invited a few friends, including the chief of the LA FBI unit that had caught him in his bank-robbing days. The program for the service had a few Eddie proclamations: "My God—I sure do have a long trip back to myself"; "But I've had a picaresque education in life, haven't I?"; "Thanks for the ride, Pard"; "World's Greatest Bank Robber."

In Sunset Cemetery, there's nothing about bank robbery on Eddie's plain marker near his mother. Just the basics for all to see—when mud doesn't cover them up. What tune played for this wayward soul in the nearby trees? Maybe "Whispering Hope" from the year of Eddie's birth on Christmas Eve, 1949. He wouldn't have cared for it, but his mother would: On the back page of his memorial service program, Eddie added this comment: "And one more thing—let's get it on." This could have been a message to all the women he had charmed and possibly loved, framed in the lyrics of Marvin Gaye's 1973 hit, "Let's Get It On."

Tombstones and Virtual Memory

June: Eddie Dodson's tombstone, like Rafe King's, gives us very little information about one of the most colorful figures buried in Sunset Cemetery. It's almost as if it is deliberately hiding his identity in the guise of briefly identifying the person buried on that hill. Still, having his full name and dates gives curious viewers plenty to go on. They can always start with Findagrave.com. In fact, if you google "Edwin Chambers Dodson, Jr.," the first hit is his Findagrave page.

Findagrave.com is a huge online data-collection site owned by Ancestry.com. Friends and loved ones can use it to identify where a person is buried and post pictures and biographical information about the dead. Eddie Dodson's Findagrave page is bare bones, but it does give additional information about his parents (including pictures of their gravestones), his immediate survivors, and the time and place when his funeral was held. It also includes a picture of a handsome young Eddie, his long hair swept back from his face and sporting a natty boutonniere. He seems to be seated before a dessert plate at a fancy restaurant. It's probably just how he could like to be remembered.

Judith Parker-Proctor, who posted the picture, adds this memorial in the section where viewers can leave virtual "flowers": "Rest peacefully just doesn't fit for someone who was racing through this life with all the gusto he could muster. May your rest be glorious Eddie, you will be long remembered…." But that memory will not be based on the tombstone, which practically begs the viewer to connect to the Internet in order to find out anything at all about who Eddie was. To put it bluntly, Eddie Dodson's tombstone either leaves his memory a blank or outsources memory to cyberspace, a common modern phenomenon. In fact, it's quite easy to whip out a smart phone and google his name right there at the gravesite. Very few people go to a cemetery without that sophisticated little computer that keeps us all connected to the virtual world.

Some tombstone makers, such as Quiring Monuments of Seattle, Washington, take advantage of this technology by creating what they call "Living Headstones." (You can easily google them!) These headstones allow immediate connection to the Internet with the aid of what is called a QR code, a small symbol that encodes information to lead the viewer directly to a website when they take a picture of it with their smartphone camera. Quiring affixes the QR code to the gravestone, but some historic sites such as Congressional Cemetery in Washington, D.C., simply put them on small, impermanent markers at gravesites. On the website created by Quiring for the deceased as part of a "living headstone," family and friends have posted obituaries, pictures, memories, and tributes to the dead person that create a fuller picture of the person buried there. It is the funerary equivalent of Facebook but with fewer updates. The Quiring website features pictures of a family at a gravesite clustered around an iPad or other tablet, presumably enjoying the memories accessed via a QR code.

QR (quick response or quick read) codes on gravemarkers are a growing trend in the UK, the US, Denmark, Japan, and several other countries. Given that Facebook is free but QR markers cost around $75 and require additional fees to secure the website in perpetuity, why would anyone bother with a QR code that might be outdated technology in a few years or that might not last on a tombstone once the stone itself begins to deteriorate? Possible answers to these questions suggest that we inhabitants of the modern world view ourselves and death itself very differently from the way people did even a century and perhaps even a generation ago. Like those people who get memorial tattoos because they think of them as more "permanent" than tombstones, QR codes on tombstones suggest that modern people have difficulty conceiving of a time when they do not exist or when they did not exist.

Internet sites of memory in virtual space are a way to link the body in the cemetery to a new site where s/he lives on. *ICCFA Magazine*, published by the International Cemetery, Cremation, and Funeral Association, calls the product "storytelling from beyond the grave." Mark C. Taylor has observed that "the graveyard is where we keep the dead alive as dead," and that observation can apply to a virtual site assigned to memory as well. The virtual site also limits what can be remembered once individual personal memory is gone. It is an ultimate act of control over what is worthy to remember and what is unworthy to remember. Eddie Dodson's page on Findagrave.com omits the facts that he was a bank robber and a drug addict. It focuses on the positives, or at least on neutral information about him.

Facebook offers a less-restrictive version of memory control by allowing a designated "legacy contact" to maintain a Facebook page as a memorial to a deceased person. The dead person's pictures and posts remain, but the legacy contact can change profile and cover photos, add information about the funeral, and invite friends to post memories. The deceased person's name is preceded by the word "Remembering" at the top of the page. As Facebook legacy pages demonstrate, having a memory website does not require a QR code. Scott Neal of Paradise Pictures, producer of a memory site called Admired Life, points out that the webpage is the point, not the method of access. Admired Life, in fact, accesses its memorial pages via GPS coordinates for the gravesite. Facial recognition of a picture on a gravestone is another option.

Should allowing a website to control memory of a human being cause us alarm? Some people might object, for example, to the fact that QR codes can be used to generate income for commercial entities even as they give family and friends a way to create and protect sacred memories. After all, they are used for advertising purposes on everything from bottles of salad dressing to the covers of textbooks. In fact, *ICCFA Magazine* points out that "since the codes can be retrofitted onto existing monuments, they offer cemeteries a potential source of new revenue." And, as a recent article in the magazine emphasizes to those in the death care industry, "Younger generations, and a growing number of baby boomers have smartphones glued to their hands. If you want to attract them to your business, focus on their phones." So much for sacred memories.

And what of memory itself? Cemeteries and conventional tombstones/memorials do a great job of prompting natural memory. Mourners are reminded by favorite icons or epitaphs of shared values or precious memories of those they loved. Other visitors can let what is on the gravestone itself or in the cemetery design and its natural features provoke imaginative recreations of the dead or, indeed, of a whole culture.

Popular author Nicholas Carr warns in *The Shallows: What the Internet Is Doing to Our Brains* that "the Web is a technology of forgetfulness" because it diverts our attention from consolidating and enriching memories to simple data collection. When the Internet takes over memory, it does more than just store information; it replaces human memory functions, including contributing to our rich fund of cultural memories. Carr's chapter on memory ends with this dire warning: "Outsource memory, and culture withers." To put that point into context, though, it's worth remembering that Socrates, according to his student Plato, was skeptical of the technology of writing. He feared reading would make us all lazy and ruin the ability to think and analyze because no one would have to remember anything any more.

Robert E. Harrill (1893–1972)

Joe: Robert Harrill—the Fort Fisher Hermit—was buried in Sunset Cemetery twice at the same spot before he was hauled off to the North Carolina coast. The Shelby native's plain grave marker rested on a northwest-facing hill until his remains were exhumed and sent to the State Medical Examiner in Chapel Hill to determine, if possible, the cause of his death. About ten years earlier, the Hermit's lifeless body had been found in an abandoned World War II bunker on a lonely stretch of beach near Wilmington. There was no autopsy, and the cause of death was ruled a heart attack. Still, questions had lingered about the mysterious circumstances.

But too much time had passed to say how the old man had died, the Medical Examiner concluded. Harrill's body was shipped back to Shelby and reburied in Sunset Cemetery. It would be a short stay; a son who had raised the issue that his dad hadn't died of natural causes reached the conclusion that the Fort Fisher Hermit should be buried near Fort Fisher. Here, on the coast, Harrill had come into his own. It happened like this, according to a feature article on the Hermit that appeared in the *Shelby Star*: One day in 1955 the 62-year-old Harrill took a long walk. He traveled more than 250 miles from the North Carolina foothills to land's end. Crawling into the big concrete shell, he might have found a certain amount of solace from his business failures and broken marriage.

Harrill grew a beard, let his hair sprout and tromped around in a straw hat and bathing suit. Cats prowled his junk heap of a bunker where, amid the gloom, dozens of skulking cats, and rusty old typewriters, he banged away at a "common sense" book of philosophy aimed at saving society. Curious beachgoers began calling the strange little guy the "Fort Fisher Hermit" because he lived near the historic fort. About 17,000 visitors a year stopped to hear him espouse "hermit wisdom," sign his guest register, and leave cash donations in an old frying pan.

Hundreds of magazines and newspapers ran articles on the "hermit" and also published his letters taking potshots at crooked politicians, cops, and rich folks. Harrill, who looked a little like Ernest Hemingway, became North Carolina's Old Man of the Sea. In another time, he might have been a Martha Stewart–type entrepreneur with his own "hermit" brand of bathing wear, bottled water, and cookbooks.

He was the subject of at least two books and a documentary that aired over North Carolina PBS stations. A Hermit Society is dedicated to his life and spirit and his letters and other writings are available to researchers at East Carolina University's Joyner Library. The self-styled guru of "common sense" now rests near the coast and his grave marker reads: "Robert E. Harrill, the Fort Fisher Hermit. He made people think." At the original burial site in Shelby, it's easy to imagine the sound of waves above the voice of an old man babbling a strange philosophy that makes no sense.

IV

Gone Too Soon

Laurens McGowan (1853–1873)

Joe: Fingers of light reached into crevices on the stone and plucked out the young man's name—Laurens McGowan. The light also revealed the inscription explaining how he came to be in Shelby's silent city: "Born in Cross Hills, S.C. on October 17, 1853, died April 4, 1873 in Shelby while a student at the high school of Dr. D. McNeill Turner, DD. In death separated from near relatives his soul took its flight to God in whom he trusted. Laid here by his devoted friends, his body shall rest until the resurrection."

Laurens was named after his home county in South Carolina which, in turn, was named after Revolutionary War leader Henry Laurens (1724–1792). Young Laurens McGowan's father, John Jackson McGowan had left the security of his family's farm in 1836 to join the U.S. Army and serve in Florida during the second Seminole War. In 1861, he left again, this time as a Confederate soldier during the Civil War. He would live almost until the turn of the century, dying in 1896 at the age of 78. After 1873, did his thoughts often turn to his young son buried in a Shelby cemetery?

Dr. D. McNeill Turner was the reason Laurens came to the village. His father likely knew or knew of the nationally known educator and Presbyterian minister. A native of Charleston, South Carolina, he traveled all over North and South Carolina, helping establish new churches and opening private high schools. He stayed in a town a few years, then moved on, as if stirred by a strange restlessness. In September 1872, he was in Transylvania County, North Carolina, when he ran an advertisement in the Raleigh-based *Southern Home* newspaper announcing his plans to open the McNeill Turner High School in Shelby.

"Good news for young men!" it proclaimed. The spring session would open on February 14, 1873, and the fall session on September 14. Terms included "board, with tuition in English, German, French, Spanish, Latin, Greek, pure mathematics, surveying, leveling (with field practice), short hand, writing (Prussian system), bookkeeping (Bryant and Stratton system), topographical drawing, fencing and gymnastics, commercial calculations and commercial law."

The cost per scholastic year of 42 weeks was $140. Vacation of eight weeks in the summer and two weeks at Christmas. McNeill declared that he had 40 years of experience as a teacher and "I employ none but thoroughly qualified assistance." One assistant would be his son, Stringfellow.

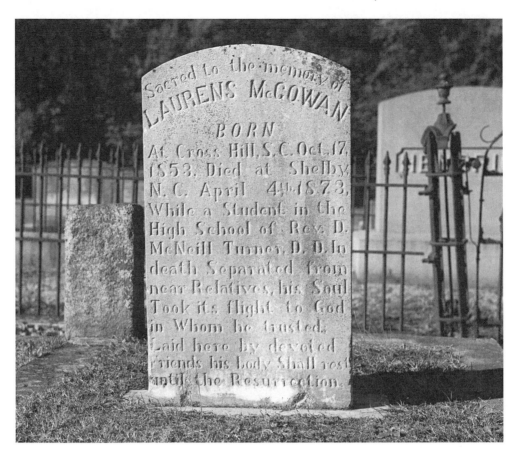

The hand-carved Laurens McGowan stone with a summary of his short life. The epitaph describes him as a high school student of Dr. D. McNeill Turner, who established a school for boys in the era before free public high schools were common.

Later that same month, McNeill ran this ad in the *Raleigh Christian Advocate*:

> Proclaim it from Dan to Beersheba. Thorough Education at Small Cost. McNeill Turner High School, Shelby, Cleveland County, North Carolina. Pretty village, fine climate, mineral springs, daily mails, railroad connections, four churches, good society, six teachers. Young men prepared for the University or to become teachers, surveyors, book-keepers, or musician. Tuition: $25 per session, payable in advance … board in private residences. More than 100 pupils in attendance. Spring session.

The location was the former Female Seminary on the grounds of Cleveland Springs, two miles east of Shelby. Laurens McGowan arrived in February for the spring session. In early March of that year, a writer with the *Southern Home*, a Charlotte-based newspaper, wrote an article about a trip to Shelby with his son, who was entering the McNeill High School. From Charlotte, they took the W.C. & R. train to the railroad's closest point to Shelby—a spot east of the village known as Buffalo. Here was the site of several old paper mills that

> employ about 50 hands, many of whom are women and boys and require about 2,000 pounds of rags per day, and it when manufactured into paper, weighs about 1,500 pounds having lost one quarter in its manufacture.

The paper sells, on an average, at 1 cents per pound; the rags themselves being worth 3½ cents at the mills. They manufacture all kinds of wrapping paper, newspaper and book paper. I saw several bundles of this paper marked to purchasers in New York City. The thought occurred to me that probably this very paper is first shipped North and then bought by Southern publishers and re-shipped South, thereby incurring double freight. Is this the fault of the publishers, or is it because the proprietors of the paper mills discriminate against home publishers and sell at such heavy discounts to large Northern dealers as to enable them, after paying double freight, to sell to southern buyers at a better rate than they can buy it at home? I know nothing of this matter and merely make the enquiry.

The writer and his son climbed into a two-horse hack and headed to Shelby, a few miles distant. The trip was "very tedious and unpleasant," he wrote. No place along the way where travelers could buy a meal, decent or otherwise. But when he got there he found Shelby, population about 600, a "very pretty, cleanly and sociable town." There were three churches—Baptist, Methodist and Episcopalian—with plans to build a Presbyterian house of worship. Shelby had a foundry, steam planing mill, machine shop, tobacco factory, twelve dry goods stores, two drug stores, one hotel run by J. Borders, and two carriage shops. The writer continues,

Their court house is entirely worthy of the noble county and be it said to their credit, there is not a single criminal in the county jail; and the court does not usually hold more than three or four days in the week. This fact will not seem to strange when it is known that there is but one single grog shop in Shelby, and that representatives from the county had a law passed at the session of the legislature which has just closed, entirely prohibiting the sale of ardent spirits within the town for a certain distance within the corporation.

Only one grog shop: a big change since the early days of the village. Twenty years ago, ardent spirits were everywhere to be had in tiny Shelby. The main reason for the writer's trip to Shelby "was to place my son under the tuition of Rev. D. McNeill Turner, who has just opened a high school there. The school really opened on February 14, just one month ago, and now they have in the preparatory department and school proper about 105 students."

These students came from Alabama, Mississippi, Florida, South Carolina, Georgia, and eastern North Carolina:

The boys present a fine appearance and seem to be young men of refinement…. His (Dr. Turner's) plan is to prepare young men for practical life rather than as mere literary drones, who never turn their fine classical education to anything practical. Sometime last summer or fall, Dr. Turner visited Shelby on a kind of prospective tour and found the present academical building idle and ready for sale. He bought it at nearly half its original cost.

The *Southern Home* writer devoted considerable attention to the vineyard of W.P. Wells and Dr. Gidney, located just south of Shelby. In 1872, they made 700 gallons of good wine from 1,300 Concord grape vines grown on two acres, worth, at least, $2 per gallon. In addition,

They also made 100 gallons of the finest vinegar I ever tasted and might have made 200 gallons more. Besides, they sold $400 worth of grapes. The excellency of the wine I can testify to from actual experiment, for they not only kindly furnished me with a sample there, but generously presented me with a bottle to bring home, which I did and turned it over to Dr. P. whose taste is superior to mine, and he pronounces it number one.

In time, Wells and Gidney planned to have a 15-acre vineyard. They had already hired a Mr. Paganstecker of Germany at a salary of $600 a week to run the wine-making operation. His assistant got $300 a week. The writer wished them well: "I say success to all such enterprises and enterprising men as Messrs. Wells and Gidney." The writer concluded with an observation about Shelby's cemetery. It was "about a quarter of a mile distant and northwest of the public square, but owning to the purity of the water and salubrity of the climate and scarcity of the medical profession, the 'city of the dead' is but sparsely populated."

Before leaving Shelby, the *Southern Home*'s reporter bade an "affectionate adieu to my host, Dr. W.J.T. Miller, Cleveland and Gaston's worthy senator and family whose hospitality I can never forget." A prominent doctor like W.J.T. Miller probably knew the distinguished Rev. D. McNeill Turner and was present when high school student Laurens McGowan was laid to rest. If family or friends ever stood by the young man's grave in the Shelby cemetery, perhaps they remembered the words to a hymn written by Fanny J. Crosby the year Laurens died:

> Blessed assurance, Jesus is mine!
> O what a foretaste of glory divine.
> Heir of salvation, purchase of God
> Born of His Spirit, washed in His blood.

"Safe in the Arms of Jesus" and Other Hymns on Tombstones

June: Evangelical Christians such as the members of First Baptist Church of Shelby do not endorse formal written creeds or require their children to memorize catechisms. This is not to say that Baptists and other evangelicals lack bedrock convictions. But the tenets of their faith are more often memorized as hymns than as, say, the Apostle's Creed. That is why hymns on tombstones are crucial to understanding the people buried in Sunset Cemetery.

Hymns appeared on tombstones before the nineteenth century, when Sunset was founded. Take for example, one that appears on the double gravestone for Christina and Evert Arser, who died at 17 and 22 years old. The Arser siblings died a month apart in 1765. They are buried in Sleepy Hollow Cemetery in New York, the cemetery that became part of Washington Irving's "The Legend of Sleepy Hollow." The words (with modernized spelling) are by Isaac Watts, the Father of English Hymnody. Watts is best known today for writing the Christmas carol "Joy to the World," which is markedly different from these lines:

> Hark! From the tomb a doleful sound,
> My ears, attend the cry.
> Ye living men, come view the ground
> Where ye shall shortly lie.

Clearly, the words on this tombstone are meant to confront, not console the visitor.

As attitudes toward death and cemeteries changed in the nineteenth century, however, hymns used as epitaphs begin to deliver more optimistic messages.

The Christina and Evert Arser stone in Sleepy Hollow Cemetery of Sleepy Hollow, New York. The siblings are remembered after their death in 1765 with a long epitaph that concludes on the bottom right half of the stone with lines from a hymn by Isaac Watts, the Father of English Hymnody. Watts' hymn reminds viewers of their mortality (photograph by June Hadden Hobbs).

One is British writer Thomas Moore's "Come, Ye Disconsolate," which appears on at least one tombstone in Sunset Cemetery. The title sounds like language from the King James version of the Bible, and few people sing it today. Still, it has one line that provides a balm to grief: "Earth has no sorrow that heav'n cannot heal." Another comforting hymn is "Asleep in Jesus," written in 1832 by the Scottish hymnist Margaret MacKay. The idea that the dead are sleeping peacefully as they await the resurrection accounts for the shift in language from referring to places for burying the dead as "graveyards" to calling them "cemeteries," or "sleeping places" in the Greek. It also accounts for the popularity of what were called "grave cradles" that look like beds as tombstones. Usually tombstones use only the title of "Asleep in Jesus" for an epitaph, but some include the whole first verse:

"Earth hath no sorrow that heaven cannot heal" from Thomas Moore's hymn "Come, Ye Disconsolate."

A popular nineteenth-century grave marker called a grave cradle. This one was carved by local artist L.H. Harrill, who signed the stone. These markers are visual representations of the comforting idea that the dead are asleep awaiting the Resurrection.

Asleep, in Jesus! Blessed sleep,
From which none ever wakes to weep;
A calm and undisturbed repose,
Unbroken by the last of foes.

The most unusual use of "Asleep in Jesus" in Sunset Cemetery is on the gravestone for Addie Williams McAfee, who died November 19, 1888. She is remembered as the "relic of the late Col. Lee M. McAfee." "Relic" or, more commonly, "relict" is an archaic term that means "widow." Underneath this basic information is the last verse of "Asleep in Jesus":

Asleep in Jesus! far from thee
Thy kindred and their graves may be;
But thine is still a blessed sleep,
From which none ever wakes to weep.

Mrs. McAfee's husband, Confederate Col. Leroy Mangum McAfee, died in 1873 at only 35 years old. He is buried in a Rose Hill Cemetery in York County, South Carolina. Because this particular verse of "Asleep in Jesus" is frequently omitted from hymnals of the time, it must have been chosen

The Addie McAfee stone includes the last stanza of Margaret MacKay's 1832 hymn "Asleep in Jesus." Many tombstones of the era use the title of the hymn as an epitaph.

quite deliberately. It is a poignant reminder that Addie McAfee, though buried with some of her family in a plot enclosed by concrete coping, is far from others.

Far more common in Sunset is Fanny Crosby's "Safe in the Arms of Jesus," published in 1869 and set to a tune by William H. Doane. It is a standard feature of hymnals published before World War II, and then it abruptly disappears. Hymnologists distinguish between the word "hymn," which refers to the lyrics, and the "hymn tune," which refers to the music. Any particular hymn can and often is sung to a number of hymn tunes. So we would be correct in calling Crosby the "hymnist" and Doane the "composer."

Edith L. Blumhofer tells the story of Crosby and Doane's collaboration:

Late in April 1868, as he often did, [William H.] Doane wrote a melody on the train [while on a business trip]. When he reached New York, he hurried to Crosby's apartment to hum his new tune and beg her for appropriate lyrics. Crosby had been thinking about "the sweet sense of security felt by the soul that puts its whole trust in Jesus," and now her thoughts rapidly took on metrical form. After twenty minutes of concentrated effort, Crosby recited the words known since as "Safe in the Arms of Jesus." She insisted: "I sat down with a melody in my heart. I didn't know what happened. The Spirit wrote it. I do not want to take the praise for it." Doane took the words down himself and hurried off. That night he introduced the song to a rapt audience at a religious gathering in the parlor of New York's fashionable St. Denis Hotel at Broadway and Eleventh Street.

Apparently Crosby, who is credited with writing from 3,000–9,000 hymns, frequently composed in a similar fashion. Another oft-told story is about "Blessed Assurance, Jesus Is Mine." As William J. Reynolds and others tell it, Crosby was summoned to the home of her friend Phoebe Palmer Knapp in 1873 to hear a new tune Mrs. Knapp had written. When asked what words should go with the tune, Fanny Crosby immediately quoted the first verse to the hymn. "Blessed

A line from Fanny Crosby's 1869 hymn "Safe in the Arms of Jesus" on the marble grave cradle of little Jane Webb. "Safe in the Arms of Jesus" was Crosby's most popular hymn in her own time.

Assurance" is one of the few numbers in many Protestant hymnals with both a female hymnist and a female composer.

Would the composition stories have mattered to people of the time? Probably they would have. People knew that Crosby was blind, which endeared her to people who liked the idea that she was a literal representation of someone who walked "by faith, not by sight," as II Corinthians 5:7 puts it. But more than that, her composition narratives emphasize the notion that she was divinely inspired, an idea that became even more popular as the Higher Criticism of the Bible became a divisive element in American Protestantism. Higher Criticism requires analyzing the social and cultural conditions under which books of the Bible came to be written. Many evangelicals reject this approach even today for implying that the Bible is not divinely inspired.

That fact that "Safe in the Arms of Jesus" was written just four years after the end of the Civil War was also probably a factor in its popularity. At a time when the whole nation was still in mourning, the idea that lost husbands, sons, and brothers were finally "safe" was comforting indeed. It was the Christian version of Walt

Whitman's vision in "When Lilacs Last in the Dooryard Bloom'd," published just four years earlier. In his long poem of consolation for the nation after the death of President Lincoln and all those who died in the war, Whitman imagines the horrors of battlefields covered with the dead but assures the nation that the dead "were fully at rest, they suffer'd not," even though "the living remain'd and suffer'd."

Edith Blumhofer maintains that Fanny Crosby never intended for "Safe in the Arms of Jesus" to become a funeral hymn, but that is how it has been categorized in hymnals, and most people think of it as being about the fate of the soul after death. The hymn compares the safety and peace of heaven to being clasped in the arms of Jesus:

> Safe in the arms of Jesus,
> Safe on his gentle breast,
> There by his loved o'ershaded
> Sweetly my soul shall rest.

The intimacy of the scene probably accounts for the popularity of the image. This Jesus is not the terrifying God of the Old Testament waiting to visit judgment on the sinful. He is not the Lord of a heaven that is reserved only for the elect. Instead, Jesus in this hymn could be a loving father, a gentle lover, a bosom companion. Even today the words are calming. No wonder Fanny Crosby's hymn is the choice of so many grieving families who laid their loved ones to rest in the old section of Sunset Cemetery.

Wade Stough Lattimore (1877–1896)

Joe: He woke up on a bright spring morning, possibly from a dream about water. This was the day—April 25, 1896—that 18-year-old Stough Lattimore walked with friends along the banks of the First Broad River at a place called Stice's Shoals. Water strummed the rocks and made them sing. Stough heard this music as sunlight washed the forest, and he kept listening when he went into the water seining for fish. It was a joyful day at the river, and Stough had been looking forward to it for a long time.

After breakfast, he hurried to the court square where he joined 15 friends from Shelby First Baptist Church and other churches around town for a five-mile buggy ride to the shoals. The somewhat peculiar name of Stice came from an early settler who operated a grist mill on the river. It was a favorite getaway spot for Shelby's young people. Tucked away from prying adult eyes, the shoals offered a charmingly sylvan setting for picnics, fishing, woodland hikes, and courting.

Seven years before Stough's group left on their outing, Shelby's *New Era* newspaper ran a tongue-in-cheek account of an Easter picnic at Stice's Shoals, involving 30 "fun-loving young people." The writer, who identified himself only as "one of the party," began by noting that "the forenoon was spent in visiting the natural 'house of rock,' fishing and gathering wild flowers along the banks of the First Broad River." He continued "As the rays of the mid-day sun began to throw forth their heat, the party slowly gathered at the residence of Mr. and Mrs. R.S. Jones. After a short rest from the fatigue of the long tramp, the young ladies, looking prettier and happier and feeling hungrier than before," prepared a meal that included 31 pounds of fish freshly caught in the First Broad River.

The food was spread out under huge shade trees, and the feasting began. Caught up in the spirit of the moment, did anyone remember a lyric from "The Picnic," a popular song from the 1880s?

> A Picnic we must have right soon
> From early morn till rise of moon.
> It must be near the water
> In a grove near the water.

"Everyone ate until his heart was content (as far as eating was concerned) and still there were fish on the plates," wrote the *New Era* correspondent, who apparently had his eye on a certain young lady in the picnic party.

That afternoon, the young folk roamed the woods, gathered wildflowers and used them to decorate their buggies. As the sun headed downward, they climbed into the buggies and departed on an around-about journey home that took them past Patterson Springs and Cleveland Springs. It was during this leisurely ride, according to the *New Era*, that at least one young man made "an unsuccessful attempt at fishing on dry land." As the weary party neared their homes "all were of the opinion that it was the most successful and unsuccessful fishing party that ever went out of Shelby."

On April 25, 1896, the 15 teenagers leaving the court square in Shelby had probably been to Stice's Shoals many times before and knew how much fun awaited them there. As their buggies rolled down Lafayette Street, twenty-one-year-old Miss Ollie Hamrick watched the group pass by her home. She recognized many of them: her sister, Beuna Hamrick, and brother, Olan Hamrick; Mamie Cabaniss; Lillian McQueen; Blume Kendall; Stough Lattimore and his brothers, E.B. and Josh. The Lattimore boys' parents were prominent Shelby figures and among the earliest members of Shelby First Baptist Church, the largest church in town. Their father, Thomas D. Lattimore, was Clerk of Cleveland County Superior Court. Their mother, Matilda Beam Lattimore, was the sister of Hattie Beam Jenkins, widow of Jesse Jenkins, founder of Shelby's first bank. Everybody in town knew the colorful, irrepressible Hattie. The Lattimore brothers would probably feel pride in their attachment to a local legend like her.

April 25, 1896: Ollie Hamrick still remembered that fateful day when she was 94 years. A group of picnickers in buggies passed her house. And she waved to them. Miss Ollie waved, and the buggies faded from sight on Lafayette Street, drawing closer to Stice's Shoals, where destiny waited for one of their party. Newspapers all over North Carolina told about what happened on the river that day.

The *Morganton Herald* reported that four boys went into the First Broad with a net to seine for fish around a rock: Fairley Tiddy, Harry Sullivan, Blume Kendall and Stough Lattimore.

The boys came to the only deep place that had a swift, circling current: a dangerous suck hole. Fairley Tiddy got caught in it, and the current sucked him under. Stough saw his friend go down and went to the rescue. He managed to reach Fairley and push him toward to the east bank where, drenched and gagging, he scrambled to safety, having just escaped what the newspaper called a "watery grave."

But Stough wasn't as fortunate. The killer current now had him and fetched him down into the deep water. A mile away from Stice's Shoals, searchers would pull his lifeless body from the First Broad River. "He rescued his comrade and for his chivalric deed he forfeited his own life," the *Morganton Herald* reported in a story headed "He Died a Hero."

Stough got a hero's send off at First Baptist Church, where future Congressman E.Y. Webb gave an eloquent eulogy, as quoted in *The History of the Shelby First Baptist Church*, edited by Grace Hamrick:

> On the 26th of April, 1891, he was baptized into this church, and since that time he has lived a beautiful, consistent Christian life; performing at all times for the church such duties as were placed upon him and always serving his Master by kind words, example, and in every way his good heart prompted him to act. No eulogy at our hands is necessary to fix his virtues in the hearts of those who knew him. His own honest, guileless life wove itself into our heart-strings without any effort on his part—and when his death was announced, all hearts who loved him … and all loved him … were torn and lacerated and cast in gloom.

Webb's eloquence kept gaining momentum:

> It seems to us finite beings who grieve for him that such a genteel sunshiny life should have had a less tragic close, but without murmuring we remember that God doeth all things well, and paraphrasing a stanza of "The Eternal Goodness" by Whittier, we have our feelings expressed:

> > We long for household voices gone
> > For vanished smiles we long
> > But God hath led our dear one on
> > And he can do no wrong.

In the church, on the playground, everywhere he was one of nature's young noblemen. With sympathies with the bereaved parents, he was their son but our Stough. And though it was just five years from the time he was buried in baptism to the time earth opened to receive him, it is beautiful and consoling, though to his mother and father, that they had such a lovely flower to bloom on earth and so soon to be transplanted to adorn the garden of Paradise.

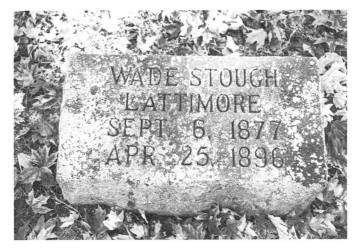

The Wade Stough Lattimore stone. This simple stone memorializes a young man who drowned in the First Broad River after saving a friend who was also seining for fish during a picnic. Sunset Cemetery reminds the visitor that the mortality rate for babies, children, and young people was higher than for the elderly in the nineteenth century.

Webb said much more. And then Stough, the town hero, went to Shelby Cemetery, and sleeps forever, dreaming of water.

Robert Olney Kerr (1895–1905)

Noon on May 16, 1905: classes in South Shelby's Belmont Chapel School recessed for lunch.

Three boys—all under the age of 12—darted toward Little Hickory Creek for a quick dip before classes resumed in an hour. Most probably lived in the village that sprawled around Belmont Cotton Mill. This big brick building had the distinction of being Shelby's first steam textile plant when it opened in 1887, made with brick from local craftsman Charles H. Fromm.

When classes were in session, the hum of machinery could probably be heard by students in Belmont Chapel School. The three boys scampering toward Little Hickory Creek that noon day in 1905 possibly detected distant machine-made melodies and were reminded how much the workings of that big cotton factory meant to the welfare of their families. Parents worked in the mill, they lived in mill houses, bought food at the company store. Mill children went to the mill school.

Belmont Cotton Mill was their lifeblood and guardian. But on May 26, 1905, 10-year-old Olney Kerr slipped outside the boundaries of that guardianship. He heard mill music for the last time at the old swimming hole on Little Hickory Creek. Olney was the oldest of the three boys and went in the water first, according to newspaper accounts. He and the others had been here often and knew the creek was shallow at this spot. What he didn't take into account was that recent rains had washed out the swimming hole until it was at least five feet deep. Olney and none of the others knew how to swim.

The moment he jumped into the creek, he went down. In a panic, his friends ran for help. The first person they met was a man named Luther Beam, who hurried back to the creek with them. Beam removed his clothes and waded-waist deep into the water. Feeling around with his feet, he touched something at the bottom. He had found drowned Olney Kerr.

"Just in budding childhood and snatched away in the most lovable period of life, his sudden and horrible death is almost unbearable by his mother and father," the *Cleveland Star* reported the tragic story. "Olney was next to the oldest child and was sweet and kind always. Like all boys he liked fun and outdoor sport. He was lively and cheerful, and his vacant place in the family will be a source of sadness to all. The whole community sympathizes with Mr. and Mrs. Kerr and hopes they will find some consolation in the love and wisdom of God who doeth all things well."

From classroom to creek to eternity: Olney's journey, all on a fine day in May. The words spoken at Olney's funeral aren't recorded, but what a character said in Shakespeare's "Romeo and Juliet" might apply:

> When he shall die,
> Take him and cut him out in little stars,
> And he will make the face of heaven so fine
> That all the world will be in love with night
> And pay no worship to the garish sun.

Little Georgie Rebecca Clower (1873–1878)

The people who knew 5-year-old Little Georgie are long gone and she lies forgotten in her hometown. Because of accumulating lichen and grime, cemetery visitors can overlook her small gravestone. But caring people like the Conservation Team of the Association for Gravestone Studies have cleaned it, and the images came easily into view: a hand clutching a ribbon with the words "Gone Home" with the index finger pointed skyward. An inscription on the stone tells us that Little Georgie "budded on earth, to bloom in heaven."

What was she like? Did the little girl play on the streets of Shelby and did her laughter charm the locals? What did the future hold for her as an adult? Few would think about these things as time wore one. Little Georgie's parents, H.L. and Georgie Clower, had left Shelby. Memories faded.

Only the gravestone remained. So, passing pilgrim, if you're curious about Little Georgie, you'll have to imagine her as a child and adult. She has just one message, for now and forever, etched on her gravestone: "Gone Home," with an index finger showing you where.

Burying the Young

June: The statistics from government and academic sources tell pretty much the same story. Until some time in the twentieth century, approximately ¼ of infants in the United States died by their first birthdays and ½ before they lived to reproduce. One model from the University of Pennsylvania reports that in 1900 about the half of the deaths in the United States were of infants and children. The deaths of citizens over 65 accounted for less than ⅕.

Today we regard the death of a baby or a young adult as an unaccountable and completely unexpected tragedy. But it was not so at the turn of the twentieth century when Laurens McGowan, Wade Stough Lattimore, Robert Olney Kerr, Georgie Clower, and others died. Babies, children, and young people died more often than the elderly. And these young people were all white. The death rates among young black and brown people were likely higher. How did people cope? The epitaphs and icons on the tombstones of the young give us some idea, as does popular literature such as newspaper obituaries and magazines.

The Home Monthly, a family magazine published in Boston and, according to the title page, "devoted to home education, literature, and religion" is a good example. The issues published in 1863 at the height of the Civil War illustrate what captured the public attention. Heart-wrenching poems such as "The Soldier to His Mother" about death on the battlefield remind readers of an inescapable truth: the nation was at war. But the magazine seems equally focused on the constant loss of babies and children. A poem titled "The Angel's Visit" describes the angel of death coming to take three of "our precious flowers." "To That Mourning Mother" sympathizes as "a mother lays her spring-bud low/ With grief, that *mothers only know*."

We commonly associate flowers with funerals and mourning for a very good reason. Flowers are the generally beautiful but short-lived products of a plant, and they remind us of both the beauty and the brevity of life. The idea that babies and children were like flowers plucked prematurely makes the notion even more poignant. E.Y. Webb picks up on this figure of speech when he says young Stough Lattimore's parents can take comfort in thinking of him as "a lovely flower to bloom on earth and so soon to be transplanted to adorn the garden of Paradise." Ten-year-old Olney Kerr is described as being "in budding childhood."

The tombstone for Little Georgie Rebecca Clower, a five-year-old girl buried in Sunset who died in 1878, reflects this notion in one of the most common epitaphs of the nineteenth- and early twentieth centuries: "Budded on Earth to Bloom in Heaven." Her epitaph was so popular by 1906, when the Sears Roebuck Company began publishing a separate "Tombstones and Monuments" catalog, that it is offered as one of the standard epitaphs available for inscription on mail-order tombstones. The tombstone generally cost around $30. The epitaph added as little as $.70 to the cost. No wonder it can be found from coast to coast.

Describing the young as flowers budded on earth to bloom in heaven is more than a simple expression of profound grief. It also suggests the consoling thought that the little "buds" that have not yet reached maturity will never have the opportunity to sin. They will grow up in heaven, ever pure and happy. To a mourning mother or father who might have buried several children, that thought could be sustaining. "To My Baby in Heaven," a long sentimental poem by "Mabelle" in *The Home Monthly* puts it this way: "And there's no room for sadness,/ For you are my baby now,/ Where no sin will stain your garments,/ Where no thorns can pierce your brow."

The idea of the Grim Reaper as an angel come to collect flower buds for heaven was popularized in Henry Wadsworth Longfellow's 1839 poem "The Reaper and the Flowers." It was included in *McGuffey's Fifth Eclectic Reader* and almost certainly memorized by many nineteenth-century children. It describes a "Reaper, whose name is Death" coming to earth to gather both "the bearded grain" and "the flowers that grow between." He then takes the children to heaven to wait safely for their broken-hearted mothers to join them. The last verse recharacterizes the reaper as an angel:

> Oh, not in cruelty, not in wrath,
> The Reaper came that day;
> 'Twas an angel visited the green earth,
> And took the flowers away.

The last two lines of the poem—"'Twas an angel visited the green earth, and took the flowers away"—also became a popular nineteenth-century epitaph for children's tombstones.

It was, of course, unnecessary to add that dead children went directly to heaven. The Calvinists who dominated colonial New England, including the Puritans and the Separatists we call the Pilgrims, would not have bought this idea for a minute. Their strict interpretation of the doctrine of election left choosing who would

This side of the Hudson family marker uses a slightly revised version of Fanny Crosby's "Safe in the Arms of Jesus" to memorialize 8-year-old Vernia Lee Hudson, who died in 1885. The last line has been changed from imagining the arms of Jesus as a place where "sweetly my soul shall rest" to one where "sweetly our darling rests."

be predestined for salvation and heaven squarely in the hands of an unfathomable God. Even babies could go to hell if they were not among the elect. Those old Calvinists referred to them as "reprobate babes."

But by the nineteenth century, all of that had changed, partly through the influence of evangelical hymnists such as Fanny Jane Crosby, Queen of the Gospel Song, who could blithely assume with "blessed assurance" that "Jesus is mine." A stanza from her most popular hymn among her contemporaries, "Safe in the Arms of Jesus" (1869), is on the nearby tombstone of eight-year-old Vernia Lee Hudson, who died in 1885. It echoes the comforting idea that a dead child is a "safe child" who will neither sin nor experience pain because she is "safe in the arms of Jesus." The epitaph is a tender memorial for a child her mother mourned for thirty years before her own death.

It was also common by this time to imagine that dead children were not only safely waiting in another realm but somehow transformed into heavenly beings trained for Providential purposes. The Rev. M. Blake's "The Service of Babes in Heaven" in *The Home Monthly* speculates that dead children will comfort lonely parents who arrive in heaven leaving their own little ones behind. His essay begins by stating the sad fact about youth mortality that begins this discussion: "It is a striking and deeply affecting fact, which infallible figures prove, that full one-half of the human family finish their earthly being before they pass three years of age." The Reverend Blake struggles to come to grips with the fact that God would create so many immortal souls on earth just to take them away to heaven months after their births.

Another popular notion was that the dead—including dead babies and children—continue caring about and interacting with the living. The Spiritualist movement, which began in 1848 and was full-blown by the time of the Civil War, promoted this very view. It was not Christian, but it became so entwined with Christian doctrine that many people in our own time believe dead people turn into angels and watch over them from the heavenly realm.

However, they comforted themselves, most parents struggled with the loss of their children. Today, parents might hope to have two or three children. In a time before antibiotics and vaccinations, the hope was to keep two or three children. Popular culture echoes the themes of "household voices lost," as Whittier put it and of the vacant chair or bed, which in some nineteenth-century cemeteries is symbolized by small marble chairs or beds engraved with the names of dead children. Sunset has a few grave cradles, which also emphasize a household loss. As a popular verse that appears with small variations on tombstones from coast to coast puts it,

> A precious one from us has gone,
> A voice we loved is stilled.
> A place is empty in our home
> Which never can be filled.

The loss of young people and children such as Laurens McGowan, Stough Lattimore, Olney Kerr, Georgie Clower, and others was heartbreaking, but perhaps in their willingness to face death directly, our ancestors were better equipped to handle it than their death-avoiding twenty-first-century descendants.

Emmett Nelson (1882–1902)

Joe: He loved trains. As a boy, he watched them come and go in Shelby and dreamed of the day he could work for a railroad. That day came when Emmett Nelson was still in his teens. He got a job as baggage master on the Seaboard Line and must have felt he had arrived at last. Much as he enjoyed working for Seaboard, ambition stirred in his soul and Emmett resigned for a better position with the Southern Railroad. He had work as a flagman with a good chance of getting a promotion at an early date. Emmett was 19 years old in April 1902, when he worked aboard a train in Old Fort near Asheville. Newspaper accounts of what happened gave no details of what caused him to slip and fall. Just that he fell, and that the train ran over his legs, cutting them off.

Anxious railway workers hoisted Emmett's bleeding body back onto the train which sped away toward the hospital in Salisbury. Did the broken railroad man realize this might be his last ride? In fact, it was. Emmett died before the train reached Salisbury. A Southern Railway train carried him back to Shelby where, on a bright spring afternoon, a large crowd of family and friends gathered around Emmett's grave.

The *Cleveland Star* described the departed as "a warm-hearted generous young man and had many friends in Shelby. His whole life was full of good deeds and rich in all that goes to ennoble character and elevate manhood." Railroading could be dangerous—the proud young flagman surely knew that. An unfortunate accident had cruelly snatched him away. But Emmett likely bore no malice toward railroading. If you stood by his grave and listened to the wind, you might hear him declaring: I loved trains.

Annie Wray (1883–1902)

"Death, the reaper, is no respecter of persons," began the *Cleveland Star*'s obituary for Annie Wray in 1902. "He visits the homes of the great and the humble cottages of the poor; he stalks through palaces and claims kings and queens as his victims."

The messenger of death had entered the happy home of Mr. George W. Wray, one of Shelby's most prominent citizens, and

> wafted away to the spirit land the pure soul of Miss Annie Wray, the idol of the family and a bright, soft sweet light in the home.
>
> Miss Annie was just blooming into a beautiful womanhood, educated, refined and possessed of a genial disposition and gracious manner. She numbered her friends by the extent of her acquaintance. She had been sick for several weeks and the sad end was not unexpected. The deceased was a graduate of Converse College, not quite 20 years of age, a member of the Baptist church and a lovable Christian young lady.

Hundreds came to the funeral at Shelby First Baptist Church. Then they all marched out to Sunset Cemetery where Miss Annie's remains "were tenderly laid to rest and the grave hid beneath a wealth of handsome floral offerings, the cut flowers ordered by friends from Charlotte being particularly beautiful."

A dozen or so young women dressed in white, all friends of the deceased, acted as honorary pallbearers. And so another young person of promise came to rest in Sunset Cemetery. Perhaps Miss Annie had a sweetheart or secret admirer who visited her grave in coming years. Standing there, they might have remembered sentimental songs from the early 1900s like "Bye and Bye You Will Forget Me."

> Bye and bye you will forget me
> When my face is far from thee
> And the day when you first met me
> Only lives in memory.
>
> For 'mid other scenes and pleasures
> Nearer joys my heart shall sway
> And my love like childish measures
> Will be tossed and thrown away.

Robert Cone Elliott (1890–1921)

A Christmas Day trip from Columbia, South Carolina, had delivered the grocery man to Sunset Cemetery. Could even he have explained what really happened that morning he wrecked on the highway?

Robert Cone Elliott was probably exhausted. According to newspaper accounts, he had worked all day Christmas Eve at his wholesale grocery business in Columbia. Around midnight, he got behind the wheel of his Ford roundabout and headed toward Cleveland County, North Carolina, to spend the holidays with his parents. On the highway early that Christmas morning, Cone Elliott probably looked forward to reuniting with his family in a few hours. But those thoughts were cut short by something that remains a mystery because there were no eyewitnesses. About five miles from Chester, South Carolina, Cone's vehicle ran off the highway, down an embankment and overturned.

The exact time was never determined but investigators would later figure it was around 7:00 a.m. Around 8:00 a.m., Charlie Kennedy, a Columbia resident who was also headed to Shelby, spotted a wrecked car by the roadside with its lights still on. Kennedy pulled over and found Cone's lifeless body pinned under the Ford. The windshield was shattered and the steering wheel badly damaged. Most would agree that Cone probably fell asleep at the wheel. But almost immediately a rumor began to circulate that someone might have run into Cone's car, despite the fact neither the front nor back of the Ford showed signs of being struck.

The mystery lingered as a quiet Christmas morning turned into a tragedy for the Elliott family. Instead of holiday festivities, they had to plan a funeral. The service was held at the Waco Baptist Church where Cone had been a member since 1906, when he was 16. The *Cleveland Star* wrote: "The church was filled with sorrowing friends and relatives and the floral designs were numerous and beautiful and were carried by six young ladies, cousins of the deceased, while six young cousins served as pallbearers." The newspaper described Cone, who had served overseas in the famed 81st Infantry Division during World War I, as "a young man of noble character and a dutiful son and loving brother."

V

Rebels and Revisionists

Harvey Dekalb Cabaniss (1826–1904)
Aurelia Ann Otterson Cabaniss (1822–1899)

Joe: July 17, 1864: Another day in the stinking trenches. Sporadic cannon fire rumbled around Petersburg, Virginia, as Harvey Cabaniss wrote a letter to his family in Shelby, North Carolina. Harvey was stuck in what will go down as the longest siege in American history.

Every bitter day, he probably missed his wife, Aurelia; his sons, Davis and George; and daughter, Ida; he missed their tranquil life together in the Carolina foothills. Perhaps, on this evening, as he gathered pen and paper, Harvey hummed a tune that was popular with soldiers on both sides of the American Civil War, "Lorena":

> Oh, the years creep slowly by, Lorena,
> The snow is on the grass again.
> The sun's low down the sky, Lorena,
> The frost gleams where the flow'rs have been.
>
> But the heart beats on warmly now,
> As when the summer days were nigh.
> Oh, the sun can never dip so low
> A-down affection's cloudless sky.

Thinking of home, he began writing. On the eve of the national bicentennial in 1976, a *Shelby Star* reporter would find Harvey's Civil War letters in a cache given to him by a Cabaniss family member. The letters eventually became part of *Our Heritage*, a Cleveland County history published by the *Shelby Star*. From Petersburg, Harvey wrote to Aurelia: "Glad to hear from you and the children, yet there comes with the pleasure pain and sorrow from the hard conditions of living for you and the children. The time was when we lived well, yet could not be satisfied. How changed the times. But enough of this. So you have been on a regular country visit. I was truly glad to know that you had such a visit and that you enjoyed it for I know you are lonely."

To Davis and George: "Are you trying to help your mother while I am away? Do you have a great many peaches and apples to eat? I wish I could get some to eat for I haven't had one this year. They sell here for four or five dollars a dozen and I have no money to buy."

To Ida: "You must study all you can and recite lessons to your mother every day and help her all you can and be a good and obedient girl for your mother has a hard time now with nobody to help her to do anything while your father is away being shot at by the bad and wicked Yankees. While I am writing they are shooting bombs over me and I reckon 20 have busted close to me in 20 minutes, but none have hit me."

Will the awful war ever end? And will he survive and go home to his family and law practice? The questions probably weighed heavy on Harvey while he rotted in the trenches at Petersburg. But the day he dreamed about finally came, and the fighting ended. Harvey went home, but the war had taken a toll on his health. He was never quite the same. The law career restarted, but his income dwindled. The family broke up as his sons moved to Georgia and Texas. Only Ida stayed behind with her parents.

Life was hard during Reconstruction. The Cabaniss family somehow managed to keep their West Warren Street home. Then the letters began to arrive, bearing postmarks from Belize, British Honduras. Often, they were stamped "via Jamaica mail." These letters, which remained in the possession of the Cabaniss family, came from Aurelia's two sisters, who lived in Mississippi but removed to Central America during Reconstruction.

They had gone there with hundreds of other ex–Confederates looking to recreate a Little Dixie in the jungles. The British Honduran government offered cheap land in the southern part of the country where immigrants could start sugar cane plantations. Aurelia's sisters and their husbands named their spread Big Hill. The two women begged Aurelia to quit Shelby and join them in the jungle. But Harvey wasn't up to it. Aurelia stayed home to look after him. Shelby photographer W.E. McArthur made a portrait of the couple in December 1889. Aurelia struck an almost regal pose beside her husband, who is seated. Glassy eyed, leather-faced, Harvey appeared feeble. But Aurelia died first, on August 22, 1899.

"Mrs. Cabaniss was the daughter of the late Dr. Samuel Otterson who lived at Limestone Springs and was born near Pickney in Union County in 1822," the *Gaffney Ledger* reported, continuing,

> She was of one of the most prominent families in the upper portion of this state and was herself a good Christian woman of more than ordinary sense and was highly cultivated.
>
> She was a lady of refinement and culture, gifted with rare intellectual traits; a charming companion and delightful conversationalist. She was held in loving esteem by a wide circle of acquaintances. With a rich store of varied knowledge, she dispensed sunshine and happiness with that ease and grace so characteristic of the ideal ante-bellum Southern matron.

Three years later, Harvey slipped on ice, took a hard fall, and was laid up for weeks. He returned to work but was even more limited. The *Cleveland Star* wished him well.

Harvey was tougher than he appeared. He had beaten the odds in the bloody trench warfare in Petersburg that foreshadowed World War I. He had survived Reconstruction and kept working. But in 1904 the old soldier answered the last bugle call and joined Aurelia in Sunset Cemetery. The pitifully small gravestones of Harvey and Aurelia were stark evidence of post-war economic plight. Decades later, a relative from Texas, erected more fitting markers.

Harvey and Aurelia: caught in a world of great war and oppressive peace—and survived.

From the Petersburg encampment in '64 the final verse of "Lorena" drifted down to Sunset:

Maj. Harvey Cabaniss' original stone next to a government-issued marker identifying him as a Confederate officer. Confederate markers are distinguished from Union markers by the pointed tops that caused Confederate veterans to joke they were designed to keep the Yankees from sitting on their gravestones.

> The past is in the eternal past;
> Our heads will soon lie low, Lorena.
> Life's tide is ebbing out so fast.
> There is a Future! O, thank God!
>
> Of life this is so small a part!
> 'Tis dust to dust beneath the sod;
> But there, up there, 'tis heart to heart.

Harvey and Aurelia: heart to heart.

Micajah Durham (1804–1864)
Plato Durham (1840–1875)
Robert Lee Durham (1870–1949)

They all loved the Old South and mourned its passing. Only Robert Lee Durham lived for long in the New South, but he never quite embraced it. His views on race remained unchanged over the years and he knew that his grandfather, Micajah, and father, Plato, smiled with approval from somewhere out in the cosmos. They made their marks in many fields, these Durhams clustered together in a Sunset Cemetery plot.

Micajah's remains actually rest in a nameless grave near Fredericksburg, Virginia, where he died fighting in the Battle of the Wilderness in the spring of 1864. A bronze plaque on the Sunset Cemetery marker reveals that Micajah, a States Rights man, joined the Confederate army although beyond the age of military service. He was brave and true to the South. A lover of books and "things of the spirit." And most remarkable: In the year 1850 he rode horseback from rural Rutherford County all the way to New York City and then again down to Charleston for the sole purpose of hearing soprano Jenny Lind sing.

That feat alone should have made him a legendary figure. The rock-star–like Swedish Nightingale began touring America that year courtesy of impresario extraordinaire Phineas T. Barnum. The talented and beautiful Miss Lind caused quite a stir, especially with the male segment of the population. A fellow who had seen her perform in Philadelphia wrote to the editor of the *Richmond Enquirer* that when Jenny appeared in that "godly city … perhaps no cause could create the sensation that she does if Abraham, Isaac and Jacob should for 24 hours ride up and down Chestnut Street, in the chariot which bore Elijah to Heaven, attended by all the music that was ever heard in King David's day and generation."

Jenny gave two concerts in Charleston in late December 1850, and the *Charleston Mercury* commented on the

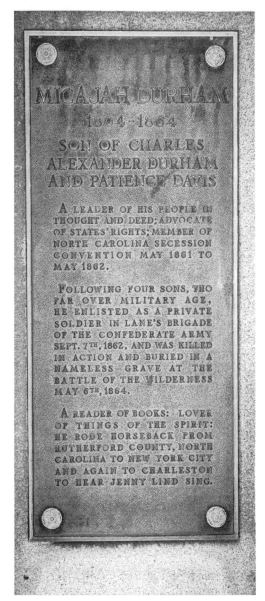

The cenotaph (marker without a body) for Micajah Durham, whose body lies in an unmarked grave where he died in the Bottle of the Wilderness. The epitaph describes him as a "lover of things of the spirit." Such a description is consistent with Lost Cause ideology, a revisionist version of history that made the Civil War a fight to maintain an aristocratic way of life.

"exquisite sweetness and tenderness with which she gave expression to the sentiment of her songs. In the song of 'Home Sweet Home' which seems to be as great a favorite with her as with the audience, she poured forth her feelings with a fervor and pathos beyond the reach of mere art, and with her glowing and animated countenance, radiant with smiles, she seemed with impersonation of all that was requisite to make Home a paradise."

Micajah Durham probably sat in a Charleston concert hall packed with other slack-jawed, awestruck men transfixed by The Nightingale's radiant rendition of "Home Sweet Home." After the show, Micajah rode the nearly 250 miles back home with a head likely filled with visions of the divine Miss Lind. Over the years, perhaps he talked about her, even as the nation began tearing itself apart in earnest. The Secession movement sucked him in and spit him out into the Confederate army after Fort Sumter fell. As Micajah marched off to war, did he remember the songs Jenny Lind sang in Charleston that night way back in 1850? Maybe her voice came to him as he sat around a camp fire with other soldiers, thinking of home.

> Mid pleasures and palaces though we may roam
> Be it ever so humble, there's no place like home.
> A charm from the skies seems to hallow us there
> Which, seek through the world, is ne'er met with elsewhere.
> Home, home, sweet sweet home.
>
> An exile from Home Splendor dazzles in vain
> Oh, give me my lowly thatched cottage again.
> The birds singing gaily that came to my call.
> Give me them with the peace of mind dearer to all.
> Home, home, sweet sweet home.
> There's no place like home, there's no place like home.

Gravestones can't tell the whole story of a life. But Micajah's tells all we need to know: that a backwoods Carolina farmer made two epic journeys to hear the fabulous Swedish Nightingale. Jenny Lind's voice probably stuck with him until the day he died in the Wilderness.

Micajah's son, Plato, followed his father off to war. With the Confederate army on the battlefields of Virginia, Plato rose from the rank of private to captain. He saw almost continuous action right up until the surrender at Appomattox. Durham's company claimed to have fired the last shots of that climatic battle. His cool performance in the thick of the fight didn't go unnoticed by his superior officers. Gen Robert E. Lee would one day comment: "Captain (Plato) Durham was the bravest man I ever knew."

After the Civil War, Plato attended the University of North Carolina at Chapel Hill, got a license to practice law, and opened an office in Shelby. He quickly rose to prominence, not only in the legal profession but as a legislator and political leader during Reconstruction. A co-founder of the Shelby chapter of the Ku Klux Klan, Plato soon became disenchanted with its violent methods and tried to stop it. Yet he held on to his white supremacist views.

In May 1870, Plato welcomed a new son, Robert Lee Durham, named after Gen. Robert E. Lee. Six months later, the son's legendary namesake died at the age of 63 in Lexington, Virginia.

Five years later, 35-year-old Plato Durham died of pneumonia. The *Shelby Aurora* reported that "a dark gloom was spread over our community by the death of

Capt. Plato Durham. He was a man of generous impulses, of large sympathies for his fellow citizens, and devoted much of his time, talent and property for the promotion of the public good."

Like his white supremacist cousin Thomas Dixon, Jr., Robert Lee deplored miscegenation.

He felt so strongly against so-called race mixing that he wrote a long novel, *The Call of the South*, on the subject. Published in 1908, the book's intricate plot had a simple message: Nobody, white or black, comes out a winner in an interracial marriage. Many critics referred to it simply a novel about "the race problem" without going into details. The *Baltimore Sun* got more specific:

> *The Call of the South* is a clarion note in the form of a novel bidding the public stop, look and listen while the writer flings upon the screen of the future the appalling picture of consequences that menace the American nation from the increasing miscegenation of the white and black races, resulting from the encouragement toward social equality given to the negro race by those in high places of authority.

While one critic favorably compared Durham's novel to the writings of Count Leo Tolstoy, the reviewer for the *Times Dispatch* of Richmond, Virginia, had a different view:

> The mischief done by such misleading books as *Uncle Tom's Cabin*, rightly estimated as one of the fruitful causes of the War Between the States, might be many times repeated, if such present works of fiction as *The Call of the South* should go abroad in the land to inflame the minds and pervert the judgment of those unacquainted with the actual conditions which the nation is facing.

Durham practiced law, became politically active, serving on the North Carolina Democratic Committee. Then he took up teaching. After teaching posts at Davenport Female College in Lenoir and Centenary College-Conservatory in Cleveland, Tennessee, he became dean of faculty at Martha Washington College in Abingdon, Virginia. Later, Durham was principal and president of Southern Seminary and Junior College in Buena Vista, Virginia. Durham, who had earned a B.S. degree in civil engineering from Trinity College (later Duke University) used his training as an engineer to patent inventions ranging from a self-closing gate for livestock to resilient tires. According to "A Lifetime of Change: Robert Lee Durham and the New South," a 2011 thesis written by William Allen Hunt, Durham's family, friends and students remembered him as a "man of science and educator, but primarily as a southerner."

In late 1944, when Durham suffered from serious health issues, a cousin tried to get him to repent and change his attitude toward African-Americans. Durham's response led his biographer to write that

> good southern men credited Durham with addressing the "negro question" 30 years earlier. His father and grandfather understood the proper relationship between the races and were committed to carrying that legacy. The irony was that Durham openly admitted to hostile feelings towards African Americans founded in his father's animosity towards them, but there are no African Americans in *Since I Was Born* (Durham's memoir). Durham obviously considered his racial attitude as an inheritance and a responsibility, but he also understood that he could not pass that element of his character down to his grandchildren.

Robert Lee, Plato, Micajah Durham: unreconstructed sons of the Old South.

The Lost Cause

June: The monuments for Micajah, Plato, and Robert Lee Durham are examples of a distinctive feature of Southern cemeteries: romanticizing the War between the States as The Lost Cause. During the half century following the end of the conflict that Southerners sometimes still refer to as "The War of Northern Aggression," white, mostly middle-class Southern women became the custodians of public memory. During this period they engaged in what the eminent historian Eric Hobsbawm has called "the invention of tradition."

As Hobsbawm explains, traditions assumed to be longstanding and rooted in ancient history are quite often relatively new and invented because they serve a need. A good example would be the Scottish Highland "traditions" of wearing kilts and playing bagpipes. According to Hugh Trevor-Roper, these practices were the result of a deliberate effort to separate the entwined histories of Scotland and Ireland by appropriating some Irish legends and customs and inventing others as distinctively Scots during the late-eighteenth and early nineteenth centuries. The whole project came to fruition in 1822 when King George IV, on a state visit to Edinburgh, was treated to a Highland pageant featuring men in kilts and newly created clan tartans. The master of ceremonies was Sir Walter Scott.

Similarly, after the Civil War, the Daughters of the Confederacy and other women's memorial associations began the work of erecting public monuments to glorify the Confederate dead and inventing traditions such as Confederate Memorial Day. These invented traditions promoted a version of the war that ignored the issue of slavery almost completely and portrayed the South as the refuge of European aristocrats who continued an Old-World legacy of genteel living devoted to the finer things of life: literature, music, and art. This mythology of an aristocratic heritage had already sparked the imagination of Confederate poets such as Francis Orray Tickor and Henry Timrod, who borrowed the mythology of the King Arthur legends for their pro–Confederate odes and calls to arms. Ticknor's "The Virginians of the Valley," for example, lauds Confederate sympathizers in Virginia:

> We thought they slept! the sons who kept
> The names of noble sires,
> And slumbered while the darkness crept
> Around their vigil fires;
> But aye the "Golden Horseshoe" knights
> Their old Dominion keep,
> Whose foes have found enchanted ground,
> But not a knight asleep.

In contrast, Northern poets such as Julia Ward Howe and Henry Wadsworth Longfellow typically cited Biblical justifications for the Union cause. Howe's reference to the "grapes of wrath" in "The Battle Hymn of the Republic" references Revelation 14: 19–20.

In the Lost Cause view of things, the war was a noble, even spiritual endeavor, that should not be dismissed simply because the better side "lost." As the inscriptions on benches within the open-sided "House of Memory" in Raleigh's Oakwood

Cemetery proclaim: "'Tis the cause/ That is glorious./ Not the fate of the cause."
The Ladies Memorial Association of Raleigh proudly designed and raised funds for
the cemetery as a shrine to the Lost Cause.

The same sort of thing happened in Shelby though on a smaller scale suited
to a smaller community. At the Confederate Memorial Day celebration organized
by the Daughters of the Confederacy in Shelby on May 10, 1905, a lawyer from
Charlotte named Cameron Morrison delivered a stirring ceremonial oration that
"imparted truths and high ideals which are lasting," according to the *Cleveland Star.*
Morrison "showed that on constitutional grounds the south was eternally right."
After ceremonies at the courthouse, which was adorned with Confederate flags and
wreaths of flowers, women and children repaired to Sunset Cemetery to decorate
the graves of Confederate soldiers.

Micajah Durham's cenotaph—the correct term for a memorial marker without
a body under it—is a perfect example of this Lost Cause version of the war. After
extolling his sacrifice and the noble humility of going to war "as a private soldier"
and "far over military age" at 60 years old, the monument encourages the reader
to remember Durham as living the very life the Lost Cause version of the War was
supposed to protect. He was "a reader of books: lover of things of the spirit: he rode
horseback from Rutherford County, North Carolina, to New York City and again
to Charleston to hear Jenny Lind sing." A modern-day GPS identifies the distance
from Shelby, North Carolina—which was part of Rutherford County before Cleveland County was created in 1841—to New York City as 669 miles. Micajah Durham
was so passionately devoted to "things of the spirit" that he undertook spiritual pil-
grimages to feed his soul and, the marker implies, died a martyr to his cause.

His son Plato, commemorated with a brass plaque on the other side of
the monument, was given a classical name associating him with the glories of
fifth-century Greece and an epitaph that again hints at glorious tradition in the Old
World. It is a "Welsh Triad" that, we must assume, describes this honorable man:

> Three things, if possessed
> by a man, entitle him to be
> called a chief of his kindred:
> That he speak on behalf of
> his kin and be listened to;
> That he fight on behalf of his kin and be feared;
> And that he offer himself as pledge for his kin and
> be accepted.

A historical plaque in downtown Shelby honors Plato Durham more prosaically as a
"Confederate captain; legislator; member of conventions of 1868, '75; conservative
leader in Reconstruction period" and identifies the location of his home. The plaque
omits the fact that he was a co-founder of the Ku Klux Klan in Shelby. But his gravestone turns him into a "chief" of a "clan," whose memory must be preserved as part
of the Lost Cause.

And then there is Robert Lee Durham, whose name is itself a tribute to the
greatest Confederate general. The inscription on his modest marker also identifies him as one who honors the tradition of a "reader of books" and "lover of things

of the spirit." It is a quotation from Robert Browning's poem "Epilogue":

One who never turned his back but
   marched breast forward,
Never doubted clouds would break,
Never dreamed, though right were
   worsted, wrong would triumph,
Held we fall to rise, are baffled to
   fight better,
Sleep to wake.

Durham was an unreconstructed son of the Old South, but the "Home, Sweet Home" this epitaph imagines is not the literal homeland of the antebellum South. If that had been the case, poetry by Francis Orray Ticknor; Henry Timrod, the "Poet Laureate of the Confederacy"; or Sidney Lanier would have been more appropriate for his memorial. Instead, the lines are associated with England and Victorian poetry, symbols of a place and era his father and grandfather would have known and loved.

A bronze memorial plaque for Capt. Plato Durham, Confederate officer and co-founder of the Shelby chapter of the Ku Klux Klan.

And where are the sacred memories of the enslaved people liberated by that conflict and their descendants? Sadly, African Americans usually lacked the financial and political resources to erect monuments and invent traditions set in stone in the decades after the war. Instead, they watched in the 1920s as the United Daughters of the Confederacy petitioned the U.S. Senate to grant land for a monument celebrating "the faithful colored mammies of the South" in the nation's capital, a proposal that died after a flood of protests. The traditions from this era mostly survive in events such as Juneteenth celebrations.

Material memories of the War from the perspective of enslaved people are emerging slowly. In Arlington, Virginia, for example, the Contraband [escaped slaves] and Freedmen's Memorial now marks the final resting place of enslaved men, women, and children who escaped to Arlington and of "colored" troops who died in the city near the end of the Civil War. Their graves were desecrated when roads and a gas station were built over them, but in the last decade they have been excavated and properly marked with a gut-wrenching memorial created by the artist

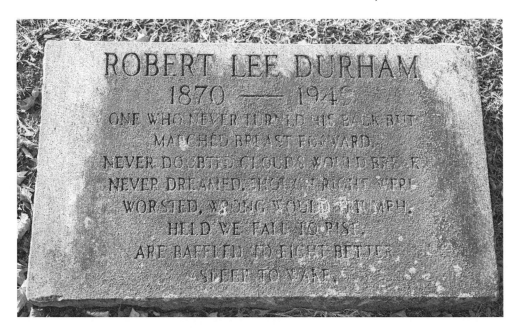

A memorial stone for Robert Lee Durham, son of Plato and grandson of Micajah Durham. The quotation is from Robert Browning's "Epilogue."

Mario Chiodo. Titled "The Path of Thorns and Roses," this bronze sculpture depicts emaciated and exhausted people climbing up to freedom through rose vines with huge prominent thorns, symbols of the cause that was not lost.

Thomas Dixon, Jr. (1864–1946)

Joe: Almost everything that fed his melodramatic imagination had its origin on the Shelby court square. In *Southern Horizons*, an autobiography Thomas Dixon, Jr., penned in his old age, he recalled how as a little boy he peeked out the window of the family home at Warren and Lafayette streets, watching high drama unfold in those toxic days of Reconstruction.

Born in 1864, he remembered nothing of the Civil War although the final months tainted his soul. What blazed so fiercely in his memory led him toward international fame and fortune unequaled by anyone in his generation. Tom agreed with critics that his bestselling novels had no literary merit. But that meant nothing to a fiery propagandist preaching white supremacy. Tom's spin on Reconstruction history also made him one of the nation's most vilified figures and it eventually caught up with him. All those romantic moonlight-and-magnolia novels became fodder for scholars probing the mind of an American racist. And not just any racist. *The* American racist—with no apologies.

The Rev. Thomas Dixon, Jr., glorified the original Ku Klux Klansmen as heroes and railed against miscegenation in such books as *The Sins of the Fathers*. He wrote *The Clansman: A Historical Romance of the Ku Klux Klan*, basis for director D.W. Griffin's 1915 silent film, *The Birth of a Nation*. This blockbuster feature not only made history for making money and cinematic innovation, but for controversy and racial unrest. The NAACP boycotted theaters nationwide where the film was being shown, and riots broke out in protest.

None of this bothered Tom Dixon; he laughed all the way to the bank. The sights and sounds he had soaked up as a child in Shelby were blended into what one critic called his "luxuriant" imagination that produced stories—seemingly authoritative, always emotionally overwrought.

In *Southern Horizons*, he recalled one moonlit night when he heard the eerie sound of horses' hoofs thundering down the streets of Shelby:

> In a moment they flashed into full view riding four abreast. Tonight the wild music of the beat of more than 5,000 hoofs wakes every sleeper in town. The ghostlike white columns moved slowly with the consciousness of resistless power. The scarlet circle on their breast I could see plainly in the moonlight, and the big letters K.K.K. stood out alive on each horse's flank.
>
> In the center of the line hung from a spear the battle flag of the Klan. As they passed the lamp at our corner I saw it plainly, a huge black dragon with flaming eyes and tongue that seemed a living thing crawling over a scarlet tipped yellow cloud. They rode slowly around the square until they completely enveloped it, twelve deep, filling the streets a solid white and scarlet mass from curb to curb.
>
> A group of them massed around a tree in the square.

Tom recalled that he yelled, "Look, Ma. They are hanging something on the limb of that tree."

His mother didn't reply but watched intently. As Tom observed in *Southern Horizons*,

> It was quick work. When the group moved back in a line a dark figure swayed from a limb. A whistle rang its shrill cry over the square and a volley from 200 carbines and revolvers roared. I saw the dark object on the limb jump and sway and swing back and forth. Every bullet had ripped through it.
>
> There were 1,500 white robed horsemen in the streets. I thought there were 15,000.

What Tom saw swinging from the limb was a black man convicted of raping a white woman and recently pardoned by Gov. W.W. Holden. Somehow, he had fallen into the hands of the KKK. When the governor's men cut the body down from the limb they found a piece of paper with these words written on it: "The answer of the Klan to the challenge of our civilization."

As Tom would tell the story, the original Klan counted among its membership the best people of the community—including his father, Tom Sr., and uncle, Col. LeRoy McAfee. When the riffraff took over the organization, the quality folks dropped out. Tom's take on this original Klan formed the foundation of his early literary successes—all at the expense of African Americans. The movie director Griffin stuck to Dixon's version in *The Birth of a Nation*.

Prominent black leaders such as W.E.B. DuBois and poet James Weldon Johnson spoke out against Dixon and the movie. In September 1915, a Black viewer of *The Birth of a Nation* responded to the *Los Angeles Times*' editorial favorable to the author of *The Clansman*:

> I must say that I am very much surprised to know that you could praise a man who has done more perhaps than any one man in America to try and crush the hopes of a mistreated and

misrepresented race, nevertheless a peaceable and law abiding race; one who had made more rapid strides along the lines of progress than any other race in history. Mr. Dixon has not been a good citizen, let alone a minister of the gospel. His whole aim seems to be to cater to prejudice in order to make money. He knows as well as you do that the worst crimes in the history of this country have been made by members of his own race.

Thomas Dixon, Jr., probably didn't care what this man or any other thought of him. "I had a message," he always said. "I told it like I saw it." Tom remained a lifelong white supremacist, unrepentant and proud.

There was more to him than that. At one time or another, he preached the Social Gospel, ran a law office, served in the North Carolina House of Representatives, wrote plays and movie scenarios, and headed his own movie production company, the Dixon Studios on Sunset Boulevard in Hollywood. Dixon wanted to make a feature film epic like *Birth of a Nation* so he cranked out *The Fall of a Nation*, a plea for American preparedness as World War I raged in Europe.

Always thinking big, Dixon hired American composer Victor Herbert of *Babes in Toyland* fame to write what is probably the first original score for a feature film. *Fall of a Nation* got several good reviews and strong box office initially but couldn't sustain the momentum. The movie disappeared, and Tom sold the studio property. He soldiered on—more books, plays, scenarios, more get-rich schemes. His last visionary concept was for an artist colony in western North Carolina—a sprawling campus with stone dormitories and classrooms and a five-star hotel, catering to all the arts. He called it Wildacres, and it might have pulled it off if the Great Depression hadn't killed the project.

A friend came to the aid of the nearly penniless Tom and got him a job as federal court clerk in Raleigh. Clerking was his day job. His heart went into the writing a novel called *The Flaming Sword*, a melodrama about Communists duping Blacks into waging war against the federal government. Dixon predicted this magnum opus would be his biggest bestseller, but that didn't happen. His health declined and Tom died from a cerebral hemorrhage in 1946.

Shelby friends passed the hat and erected a gravestone for him in Sunset Cemetery. He's buried there on a hillside with his second wife, Madelyn Donovan, who died in 1975. Madelyn had acted in some movies Tom had penned and stayed with him as a secretary. She married him three years after his first wife, Harriett, died. Harriett Bussey Dixon (1863–1937) is buried in a Raleigh cemetery. By then, Tom was a bedridden and Madelyn became his nurse. She remained loyal until the end—and beyond.

Standing by their joint grave, one can imagine appropriate music, perhaps "The Perfect Song" love theme from *The Birth of a Nation*. No mention of the KKK or miscegenation; no flaming swords or hangmen's nooses. Just love, along with a little melodrama.

> The day is grey
> And all the way is drear and lonely
> Though together, side by side
> Through life we go.
> Without the light of love
> To shine up on our path
> We cannot know a friend from foe

Where all is dark.
And yet, amid the throngs
That pass and mingle
Are hearts that ache
For sympathy and love.
A look perchance
A word of tender meaning
Lo! Two happy hearts are one.
Perfect song of loving hearts united
Golden dream of heaven
Melting in today!
Perfect love of hearts forever plighted!
Joy with summer blends
And winter ends
In perfect love's June day!

People strolling through Sunset Cemetery might have recognized Tom's name on the stone and paused to denounce the man's literary output and what he stood for. But if Tom could respond, it might be like this: "I don't care!"

The Memory of Heroes

June: An important tenet of the Rural/Garden Cemetery Movement was promoting the public veneration of heroes. The nineteenth-century poet and novelist Lydia Maria Child—the woman who penned "Over the River and Through the Woods to Grandfather's House We Go"—also wrote advice books, a profitable venture in the nineteenth century. In *The Mother's Book*, she explained that taking young children to cemeteries was a solemn responsibility for parents. How else were they to learn the values of their culture and be inspired by its heroes?

One of the first cemeteries in the Western world to promote the idea of using memorial markers to identify and honor cultural heroes was Père Lachaise in Paris, which opened in 1804. Until the late eighteenth century, Parisians were buried in the Cimetière des Innocents in the center of the city. But, according to David Charles Sloane, as the cemetery became overfilled with bodies, many buried in mass graves, trouble was brewing. The graveyard could no longer contain its dead. As the boundaries of mass graves broke down, "carnal matter" flooded the basements of nearby neighborhoods. It was time for a change. Change came in the founding of a new kind of necropolis, a "garden of graves" in a rural setting, where Parisians could stroll among beautiful markers and lovely trees and flowers. Père Lachaise became the prototype for the rural/garden cemeteries of the United States, beginning with Mount Auburn in Cambridge in 1831 and including Sunset Cemetery ten years later.

The idea of burying their dead in a remote municipal cemetery unblessed by the Catholic Church caught on slowly among Parisians until the cemetery's administrators came up with the idea of using the burial grounds to promote a "cult of heroes." Writers Jean de La Fontaine and Molière were moved to the cemetery. In 1817, the purported remains of doomed lovers Abélard and Héloïse were added

under a roofed memorial covering their reclining statues. Polish composer and pianist Frédéric Chopin joined them in 1849. Père Lachaise became THE fashionable
resting place for the permanent Parisians.

Thomas Dixon, Jr., grew up in the time when cemeteries such as Sunset readily accepted the responsibility of preserving the memory of heroes as the many
elaborate memorials to Civil War heroes in the older sections demonstrate. But he
died when attitudes were beginning to change. We can tell this because his imposing monument is made of granite, not marble or indigenous materials such as
gneiss, soapstone, sandstone, or slate.

When he was born in 1864, white marble had become all the rage for tombstones. In keeping with the idealized moonlight-and-magnolia ethos of a Southern
garden cemetery, the newly popular white marble glowed in the sunlight. Its almost
otherworldly beauty was meant to inspire reverence for the finer things in life,
including classical statuary. Nineteenth-century marble tombstones differed markedly from colonial markers of slate or other dark stones. These could be as inherently depressing in appearance as the winged skulls that so frequently adorned
them. In contrast, the nineteenth-century ideal was optimism. Death was a transition to heaven, not a terrifying encounter with judgment. Cemeteries like Sunset
feature distinctive gates at their entrances, not as a way to keep people out after
hours, but as a way to separate the cemetery from the soul-destroying world of
commerce and industry. The cemetery became a place for rest and refreshment, a
place to imbibe the truths to be learned from nature and the work of human artists
that create communal memory.

In many cemeteries, those truths are embodied in larger-than-life statues such
as the Sphinx of Mount Auburn Cemetery in Cambridge, Massachusetts, or its
Southern counterpart, the Lion of Atlanta in Oakland Cemetery. The Sphinx, completed in 1872, is a tribute to those who gave their lives for the Northern cause. The
inscription on it reads:

> American Union Preserved
> African Slavery Destroyed
> By the Uprising of a Great People
> By the Blood of Fallen Heroes

The Sphinx itself is associated with ancient Greece. In the story of Oedipus, the hero
must answer a riddle set by the sphinx before he can move on to the future. As the
historian Blanche M.G. Linden has written in *Silent City on a Hill*, "Likewise, Americans emerging from the Civil War with the Union intact could turn away from the divisive past and a pessimistic view of a cyclical history ending in disaster toward a new
belief in future progress." The Sphinx was carved by Martin Milmore from a large
block of granite, the durable, almost-indestructible material that gained popularity
for tombstones in the late-nineteenth century when the pneumatic tools necessary
to carve it became available. Granite is a forward-looking stone, suitable for a strong
nation that has come into its own after the horror of the Civil War.

In contrast, The Lion of Atlanta, erected in 1894 to commemorate the Confederate dead buried in Oakland Cemetery of Atlanta, Georgia, is a throwback to

The Sphinx, Martin Milmore's monument to the Union dead, in Mount Auburn Cemetery, Cambridge, Massachusetts. The Sphinx is an allusion to the story of Oedipus, who must solve a riddle involving an unthinkable transgression before he can move forward into the future (photograph by June Hadden Hobbs).

a version of the past that dictates its material form. T.M. Brady carved it from the largest block of marble ever quarried in Georgia at that time. The carving depicts a larger-than-life king of beasts in its death throes, falling on a Confederate battle flag, muskets, and mini balls. It is modeled on the Lion of Lucerne, a monument to another romantically hopeless cause: the defense of Queen Marie Antoinette by the Swiss Guards. Instead of looking forward to an optimistic future, the Lion of Atlanta symbolizes a culture looking to the past. In classical mythology, lion cubs are

The Lion of Atlanta, a memorial for the Confederate dead, in Oakland Cemetery of Atlanta, Georgia. The monument suggests that, like mythological lions, the South shall rise again (photograph by June Hadden Hobbs).

believed to be born dead. They do not live until the third day when their sire comes to breathe life into them. Similarly, Jesus, the Lion of Judah, rose from the tomb after three days. The implicit message of the Lion of Atlanta is abundantly clear: "The South shall rise again."

The words and the icon of an old-fashioned quill pen with an ink bottle and book on Tom Dixon's large, impressive tombstone endorse the heroic model of an earlier day. He is to be remembered as the traditional man of letters who exemplifies the values of the Old South. We cannot imagine that such a man would ever have used a typewriter. If he had died in 1864 instead of being born that year, his monument would have been in shining marble, and we could write him off as a quaint throw-back. But he died during World War II, and it's hard to imagine why he was not, by then, ashamed of the racist book that inspired *Birth of a Nation*. The words and picture on his stone are at odds with the modern granite on which they are inscribed. The shock value of this clash works subtly on any viewer who knows Dixon's story. Instead of inspiring reverence, it provokes soul searching about a culture that even in the twentieth century could condone enslaving and killing human beings because of the color of their skin.

The granite tombstone for Thomas Dixon, author of *The Clansman* and *The Leopard's Spots*, novels that were adapted to create the silent film *Birth of a Nation*. A book, quill pen, and ink bottle at the top of the stone suggest that Dixon was an old-fashioned Southern gentleman writer, but he is remembered today for his racist depictions of the Old South.

Wilbur Joseph "W. J." Cash (1900–1941)

Joe: Three months before W.J. Cash hanged himself with a necktie in a Mexico City hotel room, he wrote to his friend *Cleveland Star* staffer Erma Drum explaining why he had canceled a talk at her Shelby book club. It boiled down to bronchitis and booze, the author of the recently published *The Mind of the South* explained.

When Wilbur wrote Erma in April 1941, the once-obscure North Carolina news-paperman had been transformed into a national figure with the February publication of his personal examination of Southern culture. Critical acclaim, including a full-page story in the *New York Times Book Review*, kept pouring in. *Time* magazine commented, "Anything written about the South henceforth must start where he [Cash] left off." The droopy-eyed fellow known to some as "Sleepy Cash" now had earned a little respect. Shelby didn't quite embrace this oddball with an acid pen or present him the Key to the City. But with Wilbur becoming a star, interest in him moved up a few notches. He had been awarded a Guggenheim Fellowship and would be leaving soon for Mexico City to work on a novel about a Southern textile family. Erma invited the great local author to speak at her book club. Wilbur accepted, backed out at the last minute, and made excuses:

> I was genuinely upset about having to wire you Monday night that I couldn't make it Tuesday. I knew you already had your arrangements made, and if I had thought there was any way out of it I would not have upset them for the world. I have been bothered by chronic bronchitis all winter and have just about coughed myself to death on many occasions. However, I thought I was pretty well over it at the time I agreed to come up to Shelby. Then Sunday night we went out to see some friends, were plied with Scotch, and I drank too much. I coughed all day Monday and Monday night. I saw no hope of it letting up. It did let up sometime Tuesday morning, and I could have made it—though as a miserable wretch—if I had known, but of course I didn't.
>
> I have been candid about this because I want you to know that I would not promise to do something for you and then break the promise for trivial reasons, such as mere stage fright at appearing in Shelby. If I thought it would make amends, I'd offer to come at any other time between now and the time we leave, but I'm afraid that it would not fit with your own wishes and that of the club. At any rate, I do want to see you before we go. We'll probably spend a few days in Shelby before leaving.
>
> Mary joins me in her regrets over the way things turned out. Both of us have worried about it.

After Erma's death in 1999, that letter, along with clippings and reviews relating to *Mind of the South*, went on display at Cleveland County Memorial Library in Shelby. Wilbur, or Jack to his friends, had struggled for years to finish his first book. *The Mind of the South* originated with an article of the same name that appeared in 1929 in *The American Mercury*. Under the editorship of the legendary H.L. Mencken and theatre critic George Jean Nathan, the *Mercury* published work by some of the most important writers of the 1920s and '30s; any newcomer appearing in its pages immediately got the attention of sophisticated readers throughout the country.

After landing a book deal with one of the nation's most prestigious publishers, Alfred A. Knopf, an overjoyed Wilbur went to work as Mr. Knopf waited on the results. By 1936, it appeared that Wilbur might be headed toward the finish line. An article in the *Charlotte News* that June announced: "W.J. Cash's Book Will be Printed Soon": "Mr. Cash, who lives in Shelby, was formerly on the city staff of The News and was a frequent contributor to The American Mercury.... He has been working on his book, which is long and covers the South from early colonial days to the industrial present, for several years. In Charlotte yesterday, he said he had completed the work save for the two final chapters."

Just two chapters left to write. Weeks passed, but still no completed book. Wilbur paid the bills with freelance work. That slowed things down. But he plugged away at it, working in locales scattered from the old Boiling Springs post office to Shelby, always a perfectionist. Erma Drum helped her old friend by typing the manuscript of *The Mind of the South*. In the evenings, she sneaked her Underwood typewriter out of the *Cleveland Star* newsroom and lugged it home. Erma, who was married to the *Star*'s editor Renn Drum, wore many hats at the paper—from writing society news to far-ranging columns and book reviews. She followed Wilbur's career from start to finish.

Later in the 1930s, Wilbur returned to the *Charlotte News*, writing editorials and book reviews. His new obsession: the rise of fascism in Europe. Hitler and Mussolini were the monsters he went after with a vengeance. With a loud voice, he cried out to readers: Can't you see what's happening? Can't you understand? Don't you care? (One day, after Wilbur's death, a *Charlotte News* editorial writer would observe: "It is peculiarly tragic that this eloquent and tortured man could not have lived a few more months, long enough to see the mighty spectacle of the decent people of the world aroused at last against his enemies, long enough to understand that he had earned a place in the little group of dedicated men who fought fascism with words and insured its ultimate destruction by those who fought with guns.")

Back in the 1930s, Wilbur's fixation on a world falling apart clouded his mind, making it hard to concentrate on writing about the South. Alcohol helped him relax. Especially on weekends. He had time to write then, but instead he drank and listened to music—nodding off, falling asleep as the same recording spinned over and over, according to Bruce Clayton's biography of Cash.

Co-workers could see the evidence of Wilbur's lost weekends on his face when he slunk into the newsroom on Monday. He was hung over and still in a fog. But the fog cleared when he started writing about those fascist dogs, Hitler and Mussolini.

1936 came and went and no Book. The same for 1937. In 1938, Cameron Shipp with the *Charlotte News* organized a four-day Carolinas Book Fair in Charlotte and invited his friend Wilbur to attend. Shipp was former editor of the *Cleveland Star*, which had then changed its name to the *Shelby Daily Star*. While Wilbur was at the book fair, Shipp introduced him to a 32-year-old woman interested in writing by the name of Mary Bagley Ross Northrop. Mary was recovering from tuberculosis in a Charlotte sanitarium. She was a divorcee who smoked, drank, talked a lot and loudly. She and Wilbur appeared to be opposites, but they were still attracted. That same year, 1938, Wilbur wrote to Alfred Knopf, confident *The Mind of the South* would be ready by January 1, 1939. But its wasn't. Wilbur made excuses. "Chronic bronchitis" was one of them. He failed to mention he was drinking more and more. Meanwhile, Alfred Knopf's patience was wearing thin. Finally, he told Wilbur *The Mind of the South* was going on the company's fall list, published in whatever form the author had completed by that time. Take it or leave it. That declaration did the trick. Wilbur buckled down and handed in the completed manuscript in July 1940.

Early on Christmas Day 1940, Wilbur and Mary were married by a justice of the peace in York, South Carolina. *The Mind of the South* was published in February 1941. Wilbur went on the lecture and book signing circuit. He and Mary hobnobbed with other writers such as Margaret Mitchell of *Gone with the Wind* fame. Then he was awarded a $2,400 Guggenheim Fellowship for a year of uninterrupted work. In May, he and Mary headed to Mexico City, where he planned to write a Southern textile saga. (Wilbur always considered himself better at writing fiction. As a student at Wake Forest College, he edited the weekly *Old Gold and Black* paper and won a prize as the college's best short story writer.)

Before leaving for Mexico, there were more signings and lectures and interviews. Erma Drum invited him over to her Shelby book club. Going home as a married man was a little touchy: Wilbur's parents, devout Baptists, didn't care much for Mary, her being a divorcee and all.

Hopefully, that situation would improve in time. Meanwhile, the future looked bright for Wilbur, at long last.

Mexico: living in a tiny apartment, coming down with Montezuma's revenge. Altitude dizziness. Oppressive heat. Wilbur had writer's block and seemed depressed, according to Clayton's biography. Wilbur heard voices outside the apartment: Nazis plotting to kill the two Americans inside, he claimed. Things got even worse: Wilbur grabbing and waving a knife; Mary dragging him to a psychiatrist; moving out of the apartment and into the Hotel Geneve. Then Wilbur disappeared. A police dragnet. Mary hysterical. Then the call to come to the La Reforma Hotel where a man named Cash had checked in. Wilbur was found hanging by his necktie on the bathroom door. It was July 1, 1941. Did Nazi agents get him? The official verdict was suicide. At least one North Carolina newspaper reported Wilbur suffered from nervous exhaustion brought on by over work. Mary had him cremated and brought home to Shelby where his parents insisted their non-church going son get a traditional funeral at First Baptist Church. The preacher's remarks about suicide offended Mary.

Wilbur's ashes were buried in Sunset Cemetery within sight of the grave of Thomas Dixon a writer he detested. The Cash family stone bears these words from Isaiah: "The Morning Cometh." The brief inscription on his marker calls him a scholar who "loved the South with intensity." But no mention of The Book. The Book he poured his life into. The Book that would never go out of print and be his greatest legacy. In the fall of 1941, an African American student at Johnson C. Smith University, sent the *Charlotte News* a versified tribute to Cash. The words hint at another legacy and might have been music to Wilbur's ears:

> Cash. Thou hath gone!
> But thy work still liveth
> In the hearts of the countrymen
> Though goeth thou to Him that giveth,
> Thy works shall be an inspiration
> Yes, a light and a lamp
> To the comrades you left behind
> To the soldiers and to the tramps
> Many eyes shall be opened
> And great things they will behold
> For your works shall be a revelation
> To a color-blinded soul.
> The wise will see a thing or two.
> And Adam's race will advance
> Avenues of thought will've been opened.

The footstone for W.J. Cash, author of *The Mind of the South*, a book both widely celebrated and widely panned for its unflattering portrayal of Southern culture. The first line of the poetry in the bottom half of his epitaph ("God's finger touched him and he slept") is from Alfred, Lord Tennyson's "In Memoriam A.H.H." The second sentence is a quotation from James Russell Lowell's poem "The Present Crisis," which the Cash family probably knew from its adaptation as the hymn "Once to Every Man and Nation."

> And every one given a chance.
> Yes, you have crossed the bar
> The way that we all must go.
> But you have left your mark behind,
> To be remembered forever more.

D.J. Hamrick, Local Stonecarver

June: The tombstone for W.J. Cash is a typical example of a memorial manufactured in the twentieth century. Most customers today order tombstones and other memorials from businesses that allow the customer to choose from a variety of lettering styles, icons, epitaphs, and stones (generally different colors and qualities of granite). Technology makes sandblasting or laser etching the stone a fairly quick, routine process with consistency guaranteed. Modern stones usually emphasize the individuality of the person memorialized, not the artistry or execution of the tombstone design. But it was not always this way.

Well into the beginning of the twentieth century, most gravestones were carved by hand, usually from locally available materials such as soapstone, limestone, or slate, or from materials that could be shipped in once American railroads were up and running. In some places in colonial America or later, a "family" of carvers established a stone carving business that devoted itself to nothing else. The John Stevens Shop in Newport, Rhode Island, one of the oldest continuously operating shops in the United States, is an example. Founded in 1705, the Stevens Shop, known for its beautiful colonial-era stones, is still famous. The work of its current owner, Nicholas Benson, is represented on the memorial for President John F. Kennedy in Arlington National Cemetery and for the Civil Rights Memorial in Montgomery, Alabama.

Closer to home, the Bigham Family carvers of Charlotte, North Carolina—as described in the "Tombstones and Cemeteries 101" section—produced unique works of art installed in cemeteries such as the one belonging to Steele Creek Presbyterian Church in Charlotte. Although no longer in operation, the Bigham shop employed both members of the family and other artisans who learned the distinctive lettering and carving styles associated with the Bighams. The Bigham family was part of the eighteenth-century migration of Scotch Irish immigrants who came on the "Great Wagon Road" from Pennsylvania to settle in this area.

So was the family of Drury Joseph Hamrick, whose Hamrick clan settled in the Boiling Springs area in the 1760s. Born in 1851, D.J. Hamrick is a good example of the typical small-town stone carver who saw an opportunity to make money after the Civil War in Cleveland County. He combined stone carving with his other work as a boarding-house proprietor, farmer, and owner of a general store. One job would never have been enough to support his family, which included his wife, Lizzie, six living children of the eight she bore him, and the three grandchildren who came to live with them.

D.J. was known as a man who walked very fast, so fast that someone following him would continuously see the soles of his shoes, according to family stories recorded by his great-granddaughter, Caroline Greene Hamrick. Apparently, he had to move quickly to keep up with everything he wanted to do. In addition to joining a failed attempt to establish a cotton mill and serving as a bulwark of Boiling Springs Baptist Church, he became the first mayor of Boiling Springs, North Carolina, when the town was incorporated in 1911. The burning issue that year was whether to allow Coca Cola sales in this small town just a few miles away from Shelby. Prof. J.D. Huggins, principal of Boiling Springs High School and Hamrick's opponent in the mayoral race, frowned on allowing this dangerous drink in his town because it was widely believed to contain cocaine. Hamrick won handily.

D.J.'s great-granddaughter, Maida Scruggs, believes that he was self taught and created his designs free-hand rather than using a pattern book. All of them were carved with a mallet and chisel. His ledger, rescued from a mud puddle when his wife broke up housekeeping after his death, includes careful plans for stones in both North and South Carolina. The family of Paul Hamrick, who died after a few weeks of life in 1891, for example, asked for a carving of the popular "gates ajar" motif depicting the opening gates of heaven. The small (2.0 × 0.8 × 02) slab inscribed for the baby daughter of J.D. Wilkins from Pacolet, South Carolina, included the common epitaph "Budded on earth to bloom in heaven." It cost $5.00. A more elaborate monument for several members of the A.L. and Julia Hamrick family, including a longish epitaph, cost $65 with "an extra one cent per letter for [the] verse." A tombstone with a "short verse" for a Lipscomb child cost the family $17.50. It was good money. D.J. Hamrick's kinsman, S.C. Jones, observes in his family memoir *The Hamrick Generations* that a day's pay in 1881 was fifty cents, a pair of shoes cost $2 to $3, and a "suit of clothes" was priced at $8 to $12.

A grainy photograph of D.J. Hamrick's stonecarving shop between what is now the Methodist Church and Oak Street in Boiling Springs, shows several men standing in front of a wooden structure behind a yard covered with "blanks," pre-cut tombstones ready for additional shaping, artistic designs, names, birth and death dates, and epitaphs. Based on his signed stones, D.J. seems to have worked almost entirely in marble, the trendy material of the mid- to late nineteenth century. The source of his marble could have been the Georgia Marble Company of Tate, Georgia, established in 1884. It was just over 200 miles away. *Our*

The F.A. Andrews stone hand carved by D.J. Hamrick, a local artist. Hamrick, who was also mayor of nearby Boiling Springs, has a number of signed stones in Sunset Cemetery.

Heritage: A History of Cleveland County, published by the *Shelby Daily Star*, notes that the railroad was running through the area by 1885, so goods could have been hauled from the station in Lattimore "by wagon or ox cart." Since Carolina Greene Hamrick's memoir includes reference to at least one "Italian marble" monument, it is possible that D.J. occasionally ordered his marble from abroad to suit the tastes of a particular client.

By the time D.J. Hamrick died in 1926, the day of hand-cut tombstones made to order was giving way to sturdier granite stones that required pneumatic tools

D.J. Hamrick's signature on a tombstone in Sunset Cemetery. Other signed D.J. Hamrick stones are in Sunset, nearby Boiling Springs, and other area graveyards.

for lettering and designs. It is still possible today to commission one-of-a-kind, hand-carved memorials from shops such as Karin Sprague Stone Carvers in North Scituate, Rhode Island, but these exquisite works of art are often very expensive. People today are much more likely to patronize the local monument dealer who can work with wide range of budgets. Even relatively modest memorials such as those produced by D.J. Hamrick would be out of range for most Cleveland County folks today because they were hand carved. Still, his "D.J. Hamrick, Boiling Springs" signature marks the base of many gravestones in Sunset and other cemeteries in the area and demonstrates that he rendered an invaluable service to his fellow citizens. They deserve a second look in an age of mass production, as do the progressive ideas of the man who authored *The Mind of the South*, D.J. Hamrick's grandson W.J. Cash.

VI

Law and Lynchings
in the Jim Crow South

Police Chiefs: Robert Shelton Jones (1860–1901)
Edgar Hamrick (1868–1904)

Joe: Two nights in August, two police chiefs dead. Gunshots rang out in 1901 and 1904, heralding twin seasons of violence in the village of Shelby. The first to die was 40-year-old chief Robert Shelton Jones; three years later, Chief Edgar Hamrick, 36, joined his fellow police officer in Sunset Cemetery. On their gravestones were no mention of the shocking circumstances that put them there. But what happened to the two chiefs was etched into the community's memory for decades.

Robert Shelton Jones had started his law enforcement career early in life. In 1887, at the age of 27, he was a deputy marshal who helped confiscate property seized for violating the Internal Review Law. A wagon, harness, and other accessories were taken near Ellis Ferry down on the main Broad River. That same year, his wife, Catherine, was seriously ill and spent a month recovering at the country home of her father, John T. Bailey.

Jones became Shelby Police Chief around 1889. An additional responsibility came with the law enforcement job: collecting taxes. But Jones apparently balanced both jobs well and got along with people. Shelby at the turn of the twentieth century had emerged, along with small towns around Piedmont North Carolina, as a burgeoning textile town. New fortunes were being made. But while Shelby pulsed with a new industrial current, it still embraced a cultural heritage that had set it apart from other small towns. The Blanton Opera House on the court square continued to bring in quality speakers and performers. The Cleveland Springs Hotel still had a regular flow of customers from around the South stopping there for months at a time to take the mineral water cure. Many of these visitors took an interest in the arts. But like all towns, Shelby had a criminal element. Keeping watch on that segment of society fell to the police chief and his officers. Most of the time the town was quiet and law abiding. But Jones would have known all too well how danger often appeared from nowhere. Around 3:00 a.m., on August 1901, Chief Jones and Officer S.M. Ford raided a suspected gambling house.

Ford stood outside an open window while Jones opened the door. That's when an African American man named James Lowry fired a pistol at both officers, emptying

The tombstone for Police Chief Robert Shelton Jones, who was killed in the line of duty. His stone identifies him only by name, date, and affiliation with the Masons. He shares the stone with William W. Jones, whose name is below the fraternal symbol for the Independent Order of Odd Fellows (I.O.O.F.). The logo comprises three linked circles with the letter F, L, and T for friendship, love, and truth.

two chambers and hitting Jones in the stomach and heart. Despite his wounds, Jones grappled with Lowry and tried to hold on, but he broke loose and bolted from the house. Jones fired three shots at the fleeing shooter, but he got away. Twenty minutes later, Jones lay dead. Bloodhounds followed Lowry's trail for a short distance, but lost the scent. A posse of 75 armed men were still combing the countryside when the *Charlotte Observer*'s latest edition appeared with this comment about what would happen if Lowry was captured: "He hardly will be brought to trial."

Feelings were running high against Lowry. And it was a well-known fact that Judge Lynch, the personification of lynch law, had held court in North Carolina before. One of Cleveland County's most gruesome lynchings happened in 1888. An African American by the name of Van Canady was convicted of killing white farmer James Philbeck at his home. Shelby's *New Era* newspaper reported that the lynch party gathered west of Shelby and rode into the village along Morgan Street to Marion Street, opposite Wray & Suttle's stable. There they dismounted and walked to the jail, which was at the corner of East Warren and DeKalb streets. Another group joined the main body of men, and together they rushed the jail, opened the door, and put out the light. When they demanded keys to the cells, the sheriff and jailer both refused. But the crowd had come prepared. They used sledgehammers to break the lock to the cage holding Canady and five other prisoners. Canady had been asleep when the mob broke into the jail, and the other prisoners tossed him out of the cage, fearing they might get hauled out by mistake.

The mob tied a half-inch cotton rope around Canady's neck, fastened his hands, and shoved him out of the jail onto the street. There began a torch-lit *danse macabre*. The crowd had swelled to more than 300, some of them mere spectators. With their bound captive in tow, they headed toward a secluded wooded spot called Flat Rock on the eastern edge of town. Canady dodged a barrage of questions about the shooting. In time, he kept telling the mob. "Just wait, in time I'll make a full confession."

The mob marched along dirt streets, past darkened houses, where at least some residents probably peered from windows at the strange shadows outside. When the procession reached Flat Rock, Canady kept his word and told the story of his life in brief: He had been born in Mecklenburg County and was now nearly 23 years old; he had been convicted of stealing a saddle in Iredell County and sent to jail; he had served less than two years of his sentence and escaped; he had drifted to Cleveland County, picked cotton on Philbeck's Mooresboro farm, and gotten crazy notions in his head. Canady claimed he had gone to Philbeck's house that night intending only to rob the farmer. Instead, he killed a man. Canady admitted he had been drinking whiskey.

That was it—what the mob wanted: a confession. But they had another question for Canady: What did he think of the punishment he was about to receive without a legal trial? The *New Era*'s reporter either heard it from someone present that night at Flat Rock or heard it himself while standing in the crowd. The newspaper's version of Canady's answer to the question about punishment was this: It was not only merited, but it was an honor to the county for the mob to hang him.

An honor to hang: Maybe Canady said it; maybe not. The mob gave him time to pray and then chose a tree limb to support the hangman's rope. However, Canady begged his captors to let him make the selection and he settled for a limb on a big oak tree. With the noose around his neck, Canady probably looked out at dozens of torches staring at him like mysterious eyes in the darkness. The *New Era* reporter painted a vivid scene:

His hands and feet were tied, the rope around his neck tightened and tied to the tree, he was placed on a small claybank horse which was driven from under him at 1:15, just as three magnificent meteors fell across the eastern sky. The body twitched but little, and in a few moments the crowd began to disperse. Canady acted throughout the lynching with great coolness and spoke with remarkably firm voice.

Magnificent meteors had punctuated the night's cruel work.

Most of Sunday the body dangled from the oak limb as hundreds of gawking spectators filed by. Finally, at 2:30 p.m., Coroner Hopper held an inquest—strictly a formality since everybody already knew what the outcome would be. And they were right. Four witnesses were examined, but nobody had recognized a single face in the lynch mob. The jury brought in a swift verdict: Canady had died of strangulation by the hands of parties unknown. Canady's body was placed a plain pine coffin and hauled east of town to the spot on Hickory Creek where convicted murderer Henry Roberts had been buried in 1878. He, too, had swung from the gallows.

Thirteen years after the lynching of Van Canady, rumors of another possible lynching circulated after the murder of the Shelby Police Chief. But this time cooler heads prevailed. Community leaders urged the public to remain calm and let the wheels of justice take care of things. Shelby Aldermen offered a $200 reward for Lowry's capture, and North Carolina Gov. Charles Aycock added another $200. Lowry sightings began cropping up. In October, Lowry and another man were spotted on the court square in Shelby. Both appeared to be drunk. When police officer Edgar Hamrick spoke to them, Lowry shot at him and ran. Hamrick fired five times but missed Lowry, who kept running and made it out of town. About 10:00 p.m., bloodhounds trailed him back to Shelby but lost the track. Authorities learned Lowry had traveled widely around West Virginia before returning to Shelby, the scene of his crime. He had gotten off a train at Kings Mountain on a Sunday night and walked to Shelby, arriving about 1:00 a.m. Monday. And there he encountered the police officers, exchanged gunfire, and disappeared again.

Did Lowry enjoy tempting fate? Later, a suspect arrested in Suffolk, Virginia, matched Lowry's description, but dental records showed that he wasn't the wanted man. An unfounded rumor circulated that Lowry had been shot and killed in Charleston, South Carolina. But it proved false as did many other sightings that surfaced over the years. Then they stopped. The man who had brought down Shelby Police Chief R.S. Jones got away with murder. Shelby aldermen had already named Edgar Hamrick the new police chief. An experienced lawman, he had the reputation for being cool and courageous. A newspaperman would write of Hamrick, "He never flinched."

Overseeing the task of policing a small Southern town put Hamrick on a path that would take him to Saturday, August 28, 1904. That was the day two African American men—Ben Clark and Randolph Davis—along with two unnamed white men, came to Shelby highly intoxicated. They had ridden a freight train up from Blacksburg, South Carolina, and were so unruly they were forced to ride in a box car, according to newspaper accounts. By the time they got to Shelby, even drunker and more disorderly, Chief Hamrick and Police Officer Joe Kennedy, with the help of some bystanders, arrested all four men and took them to the jail. The prisoners were placed in their cells, and when Hamrick and the others turned to go downstairs, Clark and Davis began cursing the officers. Hamrick went back in to quiet them down. That's when Clark whipped out a gun he had hidden away and shot the chief.

Hamrick sank to the floor in the arms of Charles Eskridge. As Clark ran away, he fired four shots, hitting Officer Kendrick, who returned fire and brought Clark down, but not fatally wounding him. The time was 7:20 p.m. Chief Hamrick, still conscious, lay bleeding on the jail floor. Fifty-four years later, the *Shelby Daily Star* publisher Lee B. Weathers would share a childhood memory of that day in his book *The Living Past of Cleveland County: A History*:

> Over at our home near the Seaboard depot, our front porch was a gathering place for men in the evenings and we boys loved to lie down on the porch and hear the adults discuss the events of the day. I shall never forget the night word came to the men that Police Chief Ed Hamrick had been shot by a Negro whom he had arrested. The men hurriedly gathered their firearms, telling us to stay at home. After they had gotten out of sight, we boys slipped off to the jail where the tragedy had occurred. I felt sure that there would be a lynching and I could not resist witnessing it. When I got to the jail, I climbed up to the iron-barred window and looked in. There on the floor lay the dying chief, with blood flowing from his chest. His wife had arrived in the meantime, and I shall never forget her agonizing prayers that he might live.

Doctors rushed to the jail and did what they could, but Hamrick knew he was finished. He called for his relatives, told them he was going to die and that he was ready. Then he asked that his two children, a 4-year-old boy and 18-month-old girl, be brought to him. When the children arrived and saw their father bleeding to death, what images might have lodged in their minds? Hamrick kissed the children and told them to meet him in heaven. Hamrick remained conscious until 20 minutes before he died at 3:15 Sunday morning. Businesses around town closed for his funeral. Mourners filled Shelby First Baptist Church for the service and then moved on to the next stop: Sunset Cemetery.

That October, a jury convicted Ben Clark of murder and sentenced him to hang. Sheriff Suttle didn't want the usual circus atmosphere that prevailed in town on public hanging days. Instead, he tried to keep the execution private and had a plank fence built around the jail yard as a screen. But it didn't work. Nearly 3,000 curiosity seekers still managed to watch Clark hang while gathered on hills and the tops of surrounding houses and barns.

Newspapers statewide ran accounts of the event. It was customary for condemned persons, if they wished, to make speeches before their executions. Usually, they exhorted those left behind to avoid alcohol and to walk the straight and narrow. The *Cleveland Star* quoted what Clark supposedly said:

> I am up here this eve on my last round, for committing a crime I am now sorry of. It had to come about and could not be helped. I thank the people all around for giving me a chance to meet my God in peace. We all got to die. We must die. We are all drawing nearer death every day, we all got to meet the same man. It don't worry me to die. God spared me and gave me a chance to prepare, I am satisfied. Friends and relatives, let this be a great blessing and warning to you all, liquor and bad company did it all, do not follow this, may God bless you all, white and colored. My time is near at hand when I must meet my God, I am just as well satisfied at this point of death as any man can feel.

Then he dropped. The *Star* reported "death was almost instantaneous. Clark's neck was broken. He never kicked or moved after the drop fell. In a few minutes Dr. B.H. Palmer, county physician, pronounced him dead. The body was given to his mother and she had it buried in Vestibule, colored cemetery."

Van Canady, Henry Roberts, and all the other lynching victims—summed up in a song written decades later to protest racism, lynching in particular:

> Southern trees bear a strange fruit
> Blood on the leaves and blood at the root
> Black bodies swinging in the southern breeze
> Strange fruit hanging from the poplar tree.
>
> Here is the fruit for the crows to pluck
> For the rain to gather, for the wind to suck
> For the sun to rot, for the trees to drop
> Here is a strange and bitter crop.

Families, white and black, torn apart by tragedy. And it wasn't over. Chief Hamrick's widow lived alone with her two little children and kept a pistol in her top bureau drawer. On January 2, 1906, little Edgar climbed into a chair and got the pistol while his mother was busy in another room. While standing in the chair, the boy tried to hand the pistol down to his four-year-old sister, Almira. But the gun went off, sending a bullet through the little girl's head. In the moment before death, did she hear the voice of her father, bleeding on the jail floor two years earlier—telling her they would meet again in heaven? Two nights in August, two lawmen killed, many broken hearts—all distilled into a single whisper in Sunset Cemetery.

The Jim Crow Monument

June: Tombstones in the older sections of Sunset Cemetery often reveal much more about the culture in which the deceased lived than about the person memorialized. But tombstones erected during the Jim Crow era in Shelby, which began at the turn of the twentieth century, sometimes hide more than they reveal. The appearance of the Robert Shelton Jones and Edgar Hamrick stones suggests only that they were respectable middle-class white men.

The monument that tells the real story is a couple of miles away from Sunset Cemetery on the old county courthouse square in Shelby. It is a bronze statue of a "common private soldier" cast for $2500 by the American Bronze Company of Bridgeport, Connecticut, according to *Documenting the American South*, a website maintained by the University of North Carolina. He stands over twenty feet in the air, rifle in hand, on a granite pedestal weighing around 18,000 pounds. This Confederate monument looks remarkably like other Civil War statues on both Southern and Northern states because, according to Marc Fisher, American Bronze was making a tidy profit using the same molds for statues both north and south of the Mason-Dixon line. Shelby's version has the slouch hat and short coat that eventually became associated with the Southern version, but all of the statues are very similar. What a Civil War memorial statue means is assigned rather than inherent.

The Confederate Memorial on the Courthouse Square in downtown Shelby, North Carolina. The memorial was erected in 1906 by the United Daughters of the Confederacy and dedicated on Confederate Memorial Day in 1907.

A general rule of thumb for memorial statues in the United States is that statues of men are usually historical while statues of women are usually allegorical. That is, statues of men are meant to represent actual men or groups of men, such as fire fighters or soldiers. Female statues, in contrast, usually represent abstract ideas such as faith, hope, or charity. The common statue of a female figure holding an anchor, for example, represents hope. It is a visual allusion to Hebrew 6:19, which speaks of the "hope we have as an anchor of the soul" in the King James Version of the Bible. In the case of Shelby's Confederate Monument, the statue represents a historical group of male human beings, but its meaning was assigned by a group of women, the United Daughters of the Confederate, who raised the money for the statue. The local chapter of the UDC is still active in Cleveland County and restored the original monument in 1991.

Six months before Robert Shelton Jones died in August 1901, Shelby's chapter of the United Daughters of the Confederacy was founded and named the "Cleveland Guards." As the journalist and Shelby native Jonathan Jones explains, "The group's title was a reference to the men from Cleveland County who served in the Civil War under the same name." One of the first initiatives of the Cleveland Guards chapter of the U.D.C. was raising money for a Confederate Memorial. Given that the War Between the States had been over for four decades, the timing is interesting. As Jones explains, the monument was planned just as Jim Crow laws began to suppress the civil rights of Black citizens. He calls it "Shelby's Monument to White Supremacy."

It is also a monument to a group of white women who would not earn the right to vote until 1920 but who had social power they would never have imagined before the war. The historian W. Fitzhugh Brundage explains that Southern women became the keepers of memory after the war. Many of the men were dead, of course, but it was more than that. As W.J. Cash famously observed, the Southern states had "an intense distrust of, and, indeed downright aversion to, any actual exercise of [governmental] authority beyond the barest minimum essential to the existence of the social organism." So, while the Federal government established the national cemetery system to honor the Union war dead, Southerners left similar efforts almost entirely in the hands of women.

Bronze plaque on the back of the Confederate Memorial in Shelby, North Carolina, marking its restoration by the United Daughters of the Confederacy in 1991. The Cleveland Guards chapter of the UDC takes its name from the regiment of Confederate soldiers from Cleveland County.

On February 2, 1905, the *Cleveland Star* ran a front-page news article announcing that the local chapter of the Daughters of the Confederacy was "instituting a campaign to be carried to every home, nook, and cranny of this county. This campaign has for its object the raising of a fund to build a monument in Shelby in honor of Cleveland County's Confederate Dead. The funds must be raised. The monument must be erected." While acknowledging that the funding drive was the work of the women, the article/editorial—perhaps written by future governor Clyde Hoey, who owned the paper at that time—admonished every man in the county to contribute. Miss Selma Eskridge, in the office of the register of deeds, was designated to receive subscriptions. The piece ends with a call to action: "Although it is true that the memory of the heroic deeds, unparalleled valor and devotion to duty, the chivalrous spirit, and the patriotic suffering of Cleveland's men who tramped to the Southern drum beat, is as deep-seated and lasting as it is sweet and soul-stirring, [we] will not show to the world how firmly fixed that memory is in our souls till we crown it with some outward sign." The article ends with a plea to give money in honor of the men who "died for our country."

By October 11, 1905, the women had raised $463.03, according to the *Star*, which began exerting pressure on Shelby's white citizens by reporting their subscriptions in the paper. By November 1, the fund had grown to $538.03. J.M. Roberts and R.S. Eskridge each contributed $1, which seems to have been the standard amount. Congressman E.Y. Webb made the magnificent contribution of $100 a week later. Finally, on November 16, 1906, the monument was delivered to

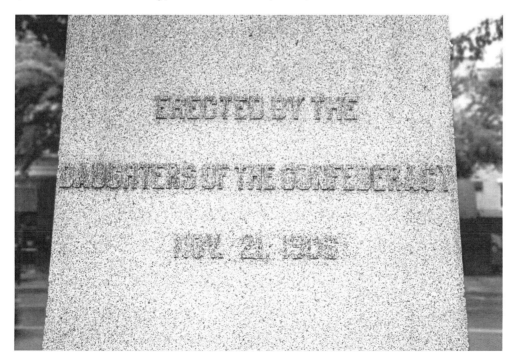

Carving on the base of the Confederate Memorial in Shelby, North Carolina, stating that it was erected by the United Daughters of the Confederacy.

Shelby. The base on which the statue was to rest was so heavy that ten mules were needed to pull the wagon "from the Southern depot to the court square." Shelby's Confederate Monument was dedicated on May 10, 1907, Confederate Memorial Day in North Carolina.

The resentments that catalyzed its installment had been brewing since the end of the war in 1865. During Reconstruction, Union soldiers were sent to camp on Shelby's courthouse square, where the monument now stands. According to O. Max Gardner III, they also commandeered the house that became Webbley, home of his grandparents, future Governor O. Max Gardner and his wife Fay Webb. Gardner was told that eleven Union soldiers died at the house, which was used as a hospital by the occupation forces. The Ku Klux Klan became active during the Reconstruction era, exacerbating the tension.

Meanwhile, Quartermaster General Montgomery C. Meigs was establishing the National Cemetery System to honor the Union dead throughout the nation and in ways that emphasized "the morality and righteousness of the Union victory," as Catherine W. Zipf puts it. Sometimes these burial grounds were established on land in existing Southern cemeteries, as happened in Cave Hill Cemetery of Louisville, Kentucky, and the large rural/garden cemetery in Lexington, Kentucky. During the same era, according to Zipf, the government erected new buildings to house the Departments of War, Navy, and State in Washington, D.C. These were designed in the then-modern Second Empire French style to distinguish them from the neo-classical architecture associated with the South. Gen. Meigs adopted the Second Empire style for the lodge houses in national cemeteries, thus placing what looked like miniature War Department buildings on the grounds. The cemetery superintendents, who lived on the grounds, were former Union soldiers.

The National Cemetery in Raleigh is an example of a Southern burial ground established specifically to honor the Union dead. In 1867, with the Southern states under military rule, Federal officers required the city to remove the Confederate bodies from a graveyard on Rock Quarry Road that had been designated a new national cemetery. Both Union and Confederate soldiers were buried on the property since it was near a Confederate war hospital. In a united effort, the city turned out to obey government orders and remove 400–500 bodies of Confederate soldiers to land donated for a new Confederate cemetery. The Ladies Memorial Association of Raleigh took the lead in establishing what would become Oakwood Cemetery in 1869.

Shelby, North Carolina, was spared all of this drama because there was no need for a national cemetery in a town far from the battlefields although a few unknown Union soldiers are buried among the Confederates in Sunset. The white establishment asserted itself in other ways during the years when the Daughters of the Confederacy were raising money for a monument to honor the Confederate dead. While every Confederate Memorial Day was lauded in the *Cleveland Star* for its patriotic fervor and beautiful tributes, adjoining articles typically describe "Negroes" as ignorant, prone to violence, and especially dangerous to white women. The Emancipation Day parade described on January 4, 1905, earned praise because the "dusky damsels and rollicking young colored bloods" who were "swarming the streets" did not disturb the white citizens beyond creating some picturesque moments of humor. A "race riot" in Atlanta required several articles in September 1906 to tell the story of how "a mob of 10,000 ruled the city for five hours" until heroic [white] policemen put down the riot, killing dozens of Black citizens in their efforts.

The phrase "social equality" appears frequently in the paper, usually as a term of derision. On September 6, 1905, a year before the story of the Atlanta riots, for example, the *Star* reprinted a story from the *Charlotte Observer* describing an occasion when Booker T. Washington escorted the married daughter of the businessman and Postmaster General John Wannamaker to dinner at a hotel in Saratoga. The *Observer* termed it a "nauseating incident" and berated Washington, probably the most influential African American educator of his day, for giving in to the blandishments of Northerners. In this atmosphere, the Confederate monument must have seemed just one more way to deny the power of the Fourteenth and Fifteenth Amendments to the Constitution. Erected on the courthouse square, it silently warned all who entered the courthouse that justice would never be blind to the color of those seeking equal treatment under the law.

With the passing of time, the racist attitudes of the early twentieth century have perhaps softened or at least become unacceptable to express in polite society. And people do change. Gov. Clyde R. Hoey, editor of the *Cleveland Star* during the Jim Crow era, directed funds to North Carolina Central University, one of the South's HBU's, to save the school during his tenure as governor although he did not support the Civil Rights Act. Hoey's sister-in-law and former First Lady of North Carolina, Fay Webb Gardner, also had a change of heart. O. Max Gardner III, her grandson, won a statewide contest sponsored by the United Daughters of the Confederacy as a seventh grader with a paper on the Battle of Gettysburg. "Mother Fay," as he called her, congratulated him and in the subsequent conversation admitted to having second thoughts about being one of the young women who raised money to build the Confederate monument. As she explained to him, "it was just not the right thing to do, and I regret it."

VII

Names You Might See
in the Newspaper

Oliver Max Gardner, Sr. (1882–1947)
Clyde Roark Hoey (1877–1954)
Lee Beam Weathers (1886–1958)
Frank Gladden (1882–1956)

Joe: A raging bull of a storm slammed Shelby when a jury got the murder case, the *Charlotte Observer* reported. To uneasy spectators, the ferocious afternoon wind probably seemed powerful enough to collapse the new brick courthouse. As thunder pounded and lightning flashed, one person in the Cleveland County courtroom that August day in 1912 remained calm: defendant Frank Gladden. The *Charlotte Observer* reported he "appeared to be the least perturbed of anyone."

The unflappable Gladden had been accused of taking an ax and beating to death a young mother named Clayton Dixon at her home the night of December 12, 1911. After pleading not guilty, Gladden offered an iron-clad alibi: His wife claimed her husband had been at home with her the night of the murder. An African American man, John Ross, had confessed to the slaying of Mrs. Dixon's farmer husband, John, that same evening. Ross, who had been sentenced to death, pointed the finger at Gladden, a white man, as Clayton Dixon's killer. Now, on this stormy afternoon in August, a jury considered Gladden's fate. With him in the court room sat three rising stars in the community:

- O. Max Gardner, North Carolina Senator and the lawyer representing defendant Gladden.
- Gardner's brother-in-law, Clyde R. Hoey, politician, lawyer, and part of the team prosecuting the accused.
- Lee Beam Weathers, the new editor and publisher of Shelby's newspaper, the *Cleveland Star*.

Weathers had purchased the *Star* from Clyde Hoey in January 1911. That same year, Weathers married. A hard worker, he had showed up early at the office one December morning and answered the phone, one of the few in Shelby. The caller explained that there had been a double murder in the Fallston community north of Shelby and that attempts to reach the sheriff's department had failed. The *Star* had a

The old Cleveland County Courthouse in Shelby, North Carolina, now the Earl Scruggs Center: Music & Stories from the American South.

phone, so the caller dialed that number. A prominent Fallston couple brutally murdered at their home; their unharmed 12-month-old daughter drenched in her own mother's blood: the biggest story of Weathers' career had just landed in his lap. When the dust would settle on this case in coming weeks, John Ross awaited death in the electric chair and Gladden waited in a courtroom on a jury's verdict.

Despite repeated claims of innocence, many doubted Gladden, including the father of murder victim John Dixon. Detectives were hired to look into the matter, and they dug up incriminating evidence against Gladden. Enough to convince North Carolina Gov. W.W. Kitchin to commute Ross' sentence to life in prison. So Frank Gladden went to trial. And after all the evidence was presented, he sat in a court room waiting on the jury's verdict. Had he ever read what newspapers papers said about him? For example, from the *Charlotte Observer*:

Frank Gladden, what of him? What of this factor in the finale of the tragedy about whom so little has been heard and so little written. Frank Gladden? They know him in Cleveland County. They know about the fickleness of his past, the shiftless spirit of his present and they prophesy the tragedy of his future. Gladden is a white man who has lived about Cleveland County for many years. He is a stalwart, raw-boned sort of a fellow with a reputation that will not bear scrutiny. He is a painter by trade. He had been painting the deceased [John] Dixon's house for some days before the murder. It was being said here today about the courthouse that he and Mr. Dixon had a "falling out," that Gladden asked Mr. Dixon to settle with him the evening before the murder and that Mr. Dixon had said he would pay him when the job was completed. To this Gladden replied, "You will settle with me tonight or I will settle with you." They did not settle that night so far as the evidence shows.

It took the jury about three hours to reach a decision. The foreman faced Judge F.A. Daniels and proclaimed: "Not guilty." Magic words to the defendant. For the first time, he showed emotion: unmitigated joy. Gladden began shaking hands—with lawyer Gardner, Judge Daniels, and each member of the jury. The jury had let Frank Gladden leave the courtroom a free man. But first the judge had a few words for the defendant:

> Frank Gladden, no mortal man, except yourself, will ever know what foundation there was for this crime to be charged to you. It was one of the most horrible crimes that has happened within the confines of our state. It shocks the highly civilized community like Cleveland County. The officers have done their duty in trying to ferret it out. There are better days in store for you, Mr. Gladden, if you live right. Although the jury has rendered a verdict of not guilty, you have proved to be a bad character. This ought to be a lesson to you and I hope you will turn over a new leaf.

Gladden stood and listened, and then left the court room. Some who watched him go may have wondered whether he would ever turn over a new leaf. Meanwhile, brothers-in-law Max Gardner and Clyde Hoey may have walked arm and arm back to their law offices as they often did. Working opposite sides of issues in court was nothing unusual for them. Max and Clyde were family. They shared bright prospects for the future: both would go on to become North Carolina governors, kingpins of the so-called Shelby Political Dynasty, and important national figures.

Weathers probably hurried back to write up the story about Frank Gladden's acquittal. Two years later, the *Star* ran a story about how John Ross, the convicted killer of John Dixon, escaped from prison and was never apprehended. Meanwhile, there were other stories to cover—local boys headed to a war overseas and local citizens fighting their own battles when the Spanish Influenza pandemic struck in 1918. The Twenties brought more waves of change as the Dixon murders became old news.

The *Star*, under the helm of publisher Lee B. Weathers, continued to document the rising careers of Gardner and Hoey; Gladden's once prominent name disappeared from the paper. One day, they all came together in the same place again: the silent city that asks no questions and makes no judgments: Sunset Cemetery.

Max Gardner

Young Max loved this place. His biographer wrote that Sunset Cemetery was a stone's throw from the boy's home on West Marion Street, and he went there often. Max may have paused in his rambles around Sunset and considered the sky. Around him rested characters from Shelby's past, including his mother, Margaret Young Gardner, who died in 1891 when Maxie was ten years old. He might have imagined her face smiling down from the sky, certain of the name her boy would make for himself.

Oliver Max Gardner, son of Dr. O.P. Gardner, probably had no inkling of what the future held for him. Many who knew him in those early days might have suspected this bright young fellow was destined for great things. Max was a hard worker. He earned $2 a week at a livery stable, sleeping in the office. In the summers, he held down jobs in area cotton mills. During the Spanish American War, 16-year-old Max Gardner signed on as a civilian teamster with an Army regiment in Florida. When Max completed Shelby High School, he won the only scholarship awarded by the state to North Carolina College of Agriculture and Mechanic Arts (now North Carolina State University).

January 3, 1900: Max arrived on campus and immediately began making a name for himself. The Shelby boy won every honor the college offered; he was captain of the football team and all-star player, manager of the baseball team, senior class president, commencement speaker. He graduated in 3½ years with a B.S. in chemistry and stayed on as an instructor in inorganic chemistry. But Max's career path eventually led to the University of North Carolina Law School and afterwards a distinguished legal practice and notable service in the political arena. In 1907, he married the dynamic Fay Webb (1885–1969) of Shelby. The *Charlotte News* reported on the wedding and reception afterwards at Fay's home: "The bride is the younger daughter of Judge and Mrs. Webb and is known not only in North Carolina, but very popular in Georgia. She is a graduate of the Lucy Cobb Institute and is one of the state's most beautiful women."

The *News* noted that Max "is a graduate of A & M Raleigh, where he taught for a year. He is a prominent athlete and is now practicing law, being a junior member of the firm of Anthony & Gardner, and is very popular." Fay would be with Max every step of their journey—from the North Carolina Governor's Mansion to Washington, D.C., where her husband had the ear of President Franklin Roosevelt. FDR didn't trust many people, but he trusted Max Gardner.

Max and Fay were benefactors of a tiny Baptist college in Boiling Springs, North Carolina, renamed in their honor: Gardner-Webb. Max and Fay: together in New York City's St. Regis Hotel on February 5, 1947, prior to setting sail the following day for England aboard the luxury ocean liner S.S. *America*. President Harry Truman had recently appointed Max Ambassador to the Court of St. James; he and Fay were off on another adventure. Worn out from friendly send-offs and trip preparations, Max went to bed at 10 p.m., probably looking forward to a prolonged rest aboard the S.S. *America*. Did Max, in the interval between 10:00 p.m. and 3:00 a.m. when he awoke to sharp chest pains, dream of his first Atlantic Ocean crossing in the summer of 1905? Max made that trip aboard a cattle boat, later telling friends he had acted as "chambermaid to 394 Montana steers."

Forty-two years later, as America's new ambassador to England, he would traverse the Atlantic on one of the last of the great ocean liners. But the stately S.S. *America* would depart without Max. He'd taken a different journey. It started with the pain at 3:00 a.m. and began in earnest at 8:25 a.m. when his heart stopped and launched him on the longest voyage.

On a cold, wind-swept afternoon, 64-year-old Max was laid to rest in his beloved Sunset Cemetery. Many dignitaries watched with thousands of others as his coffin was lowered into the grave. Standing in the crowd were North Carolina Gov. R. Gregg Cherry, Washington columnist Drew Pearson, and Ralph McGill, editor of the *Atlanta Constitution*. Twenty-two years later, Fay joined Max there in Sunset. Their last great adventure together had begun.

Clyde Hoey

The kid had printer's ink in his blood. Down at the *Shelby Review* newspaper, run by a fire-breathing editor Col. John C. Tipton, 12-year-old Clyde Hoey handled all the dirty work. The same way, more or less, as a young Ben Franklin had done in bygone days. Among many lowly tasks, a printer's devil sweated over a cauldron of molten lead used to create newspaper type. Clyde set all the type by hand and kept a dictionary nearby to ensure the proper spelling of words. Gradually, he built a vocabulary that served him well in the future as one of the South's best-known orators. All that dirty work in Tipton's shop added up to experience. When most boys Clyde's age still basked in extended idleness, Clyde was learning the operation of a small-town newspaper from top to bottom.

Working with Col. Tipton must have been an education, too. The colonel's biting editorials earned him many enemies, and circulation suffered. Clyde had moved on to the *Charlotte Observer* when he learned Tipton had offered the debt-written *Shelby Review* for sale. The colonel never stayed in one spot too long. Respiratory problems probably contributed to his restless spirit. By 1894, he'd had it with Shelby and Cleveland County and looked to Texas as a good place to start over. First, he had to unload the *Shelby Review*, not an easy task with creditors knocking at his door. Then young Clyde stepped forward with a bid. He'd had to borrow money, but his knowledge of newspapers, his reputation for reliability and hard work, along with a winning personality, opened doors for financing. At the age of 16, the former printer's devil became the editor and publisher of a small semi-weekly community newspaper. He immediately changed the name from the *Shelby Review* to the more inclusive *Cleveland Star*.

And he also set out to build circulation. Clyde rode a little "blue mule" around the county meeting folks and talking them into subscribing to the *Star*. That was one certain way to get your name in the paper. Clyde wrote stories like he talked—over the top. The *Star*'s young executive had entered a new phase in life and most likely felt comfortable there. Already he wore his signature outfit: swallowtail coat, wing collar, striped pants and high-topped shoes—all combined with long hair and a courtly manner. He became a familiar speaker at political rallies, schools, and churches. People began describing this colorful, effusive orator as "silver-tongued."

Clyde studied law, opened a practice and rose to prominence in the Democratic Party. At age 20, Clyde was elected to the General Assembly and from there rose steadily. In 1900, he married Bess Gardner, sister of O. Max Gardner, another up-and-coming young Shelbian. With a flourishing law practice and other demands, Clyde sold the *Cleveland Star* to Lee B. Weathers in 1911. The political path took Clyde to the office of North Carolina governor in 1937 and the U.S. Senate in 1944, two years after Bess died. On May 12, 1954, an assistant found Clyde slumped over a desk in his office, dead from a stroke at age 76. The Associated Press ran a story headed: "Red Carnation Put on Sen. Hoey's Desk":

> A single red carnation lay today on the Senate desk of late Sen. Clyde R. Hoey (D–NC) who always wore one during his 10 years in the Senate.
> The flower was placed there by Sen. Symington (D–Mo.) after tribute was paid to the North Carolinian who died suddenly yesterday.

Hoey told friends he always wore a red carnation in Washington and a red rose in Shelby, N.C. as memorials to his wife.

Later in May, Washington, D.C., syndicated columnist Drew Pearson, who served on a committee to present portraits of Hoey and his brother-in-law, Max Gardner, to the State of North Carolina, wrote about his two old friends: "Max Gardner was offered many high offices but turned most of them down. He loved people more than position. When he sat down for a visit, he wanted to know all about the other fellow's problems, never mentioned his own." To those in Washington who knew Hoey,

he is still famous for the fair and scholarly manner in which he conducted investigations. Many people have forgotten it but Sen. Hoey was chairman of the committee later chaired by Sen. (Joe) McCarthy of Arkansas. In Hoey's day, no witness complained about not getting a fair deal. He was considerate, kindly, yet never deviated from his determination to get the facts. He aroused President Truman's resentment when he investigated Truman's military General Henry Vaughan. All there were Democrats, Hoey the Democrat went through with the investigation of the intimate friend of a Democratic President.

Pearson called Hoey and Gardner "two great North Carolinians."

Lee B. Weathers

Bloody murder called Shelby's new journalist into action that December morning in 1911.

Behind the wheel of an early model automobile struggling along a pot-holed dirt road, 24-year-old Lee Weathers hurried toward the scene of a double ax slaying. Lee, who had bought the *Cleveland Star* on January 1 of that year, would be the first reporter to get a crack at the story. As owner of a small semi-weekly newspaper, Lee wore many hats: editor, publisher, bookkeeper, circulation manager and advertising director. On this morning, he was a reporter.

Decades later, when he wrote a history of Cleveland County and included personal memories, he recalled details of that December morning. Lee showed up early for work, as usual, and answered the phone. A Mr. Stamey in Fallston had an urgent message for Sheriff D.D. Wilkins but couldn't get through and called the *Star* with the news: a well-known farming couple, John and Clayton Dixon, had been beaten to death. Lee notified the sheriff and then hit the road.

What a newsy week it had been already. Just two days before the Fallston murders, the *Star* ran a story about Shelby Police Chief Harvey Jetton's 3-month-old daughter dying of bronchial pneumonia. Next came an account of how farmer William Wilson of the Earl community had died. While helping uncouple two box cars on the local railroad tracks, Wilson got his foot caught. "This threw him down and dragged him under the wheels," Lee wrote. "The car wheel caught his right leg and the knee and mashed it into jelly." Compelling stories. But they didn't come close to the Dixon killings. Readers everywhere would devour the smallest details of this shocking crime and Lee was about to nail the exclusive. After this initial scoop, he wrote many stories about every aspect of the case: arrests, trials, conviction, and one suspect acquitted.

The year 1911 would be a memorable one for Lee Beam Weathers. Newspapering had a lot to do with it, but not everything. Lee also made time for romance. As he courted a young lady, Arthur Clough's recording of "Down by the Old Mill Stream" charmed the nation:

> My darling I am dreaming of the days gone by
> When you and I were sweethearts beneath the summer sky
> Your hair has turned to silver, the gold has faded, too;
> But still I will remember, where I first met you.

Perhaps Lee hummed it to Miss Williewee Wiseman in the months before they married in November 1911 in her hometown of Danville, Virginia. The couple stayed together until her death in 1937 at the age of 51. Two years later, Lee married Breta Noell Clary of Roxboro.

From 1911 until his death in 1958 at age 71, Lee ran the paper, which changed its name in 1936 to the *Shelby Daily Star*. Under his watch, 47 years of news flowed through its pages—from the minutiae of daily life to the decline of local cotton culture and rise of a new industrial revolution.

News of every kind, large and small. But one story may have stood out in Lee's memory: The Dixon murders, his first big scoop after taking over the *Star* in 1911.

An early morning phone call at the office. Rushing to the crime scene over a bumpy country road. Witnessing what an ax can do to human flesh. Lee was there,

Individual stone for Lee Beam Weathers, local newspaperman, author, editor, and North Carolina senator. His family plot illustrates a common pattern of erecting a large stone in honor of the family as a whole but putting information about individual family members on smaller stones.

and he covered the subsequent trials and sentencings of those involved. It was a story that drew readers in and held their attention—for a while. Lee realized how quickly sensational stories of the moment became old news. Many forgot the 1911 murders, but not Lee, who mentioned the case in his book *The Living Past of Cleveland County: A History*.

News made up the fabric of Lee's life. When Sunset Cemetery claimed him, he slept surrounded by gravestone names from the columns of the *Star*. Sunset stamped "30" or "end of story" on a long journalistic career.

Gender Formation in the Cemetery

June: Gender—those attributes that make us male or female—has less to do with biology than with sociology. You can read academic treatises or popular novels to learn about gender, and people have devoted entire careers to studying it. But if you want a crash course in gender formation, just take a stroll through your local cemetery.

Nineteenth- and many twentieth-century tombstones in Sunset Cemetery typically define men by their accomplishments and women by their relationships. Children buried in Sunset are also defined by relationships, as the daughters or sons of their parents. It's almost as if women remain perpetually infantilized, lumped in with the children as in the standard practice of evacuating the "women and children first" from a sinking ship. Fay Webb Gardner and Bess Gardner Hoey, for example, were both first ladies of North Carolina and remarkably accomplished women. They were as much a part of the so-called "Shelby [Political] Dynasty"

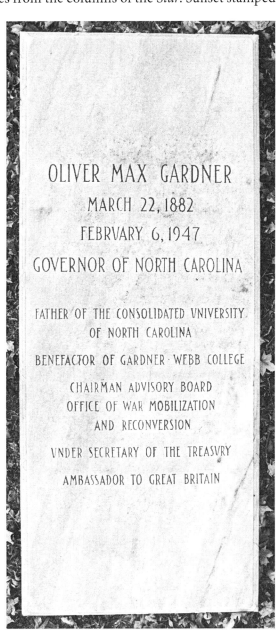

The marble ledger stone for Gov. O. Max Gardner listing his public accomplishments.

of the day as their famous husbands. But you would never know that from their tombstones.

Governor O. Max Gardner's political career is summarized handily right on the imposing marble slab that covers his grave:

OLIVER MAX GARDNER
MARCH 22, 1882
FEBRUARY 6, 1947
GOVERNOR OF NORTH CAROLINA
FATHER OF THE CONSOLIDATED UNIVERSITY OF NORTH CAROLINA
BENEFACTOR OF GARDNER-WEBB COLLEGE
CHAIRMAN OF ADVISORY BOARD
OFFICE OF WAR MOBILIZATION AND RECONVERSION
UNDER-SECRETARY OF THE TREASURY
AMBASSADOR TO GREAT BRITAIN

In contrast, the matching ledger stone for his wife, Fay Lamar Webb Gardner defines her entirely in terms of relationships:

FAY WEBB GARDNER
SEPTEMBER 7, 1885
JANUARY 16, 1969
WIFE OF
OLIVER MAX GARDNER
DAUGHTER OF
JUDGE AND MRS. JAMES L. WEBB
MOTHER OF
MARGARET LOVE GARDNER BURGESS
JAMES WEBB GARDNER
RALPH WEBB GARDNER
O. MAX GARDNER, JR.

I cannot imagine more clearly gendered gravestones. The gender distinctions extend even to Mrs. Gardner's parents. Her mother's given name was Kansas Love Andrews, but she is identified only as Mrs. James L. Webb. Her husband not only retains his given name but is identified by profession as well. He is JUDGE James L. Webb.

What makes all of this so interesting is that "Miss Fay," as she was affectionately known, could have had an impressive list of

The marble ledger stone for Fay Webb Gardner listing her relationships. Her stone is gendered female.

accomplishments on her tombstone. In addition to praising her civic contributions in traditionally female arenas such as garden, music, and literary societies, *The Dictionary of North Carolina Biography* lauds her "less conventional" executive skills as well: "She owned and managed business properties, was an executive of Cleveland Cloth Mills of Shelby and … director of Gardner Land Company." She and her husband infused the struggling Boiling Springs Junior College with so much money and energy that the trustees renamed the revitalized school Gardner-Webb College in honor **of them both**.

She was an astute politician and a tireless campaigner for the Democratic Party. The *Dictionary of North Carolina Biography* also points out that "she served on the state and national democratic committees and was twice elected a delegate to the Democratic National Convention. She helped to arrange several important Washington politico-social events including President Harry S. Truman's birthday dinner in 1954 and John Kennedy's inaugural ball in 1961." William C. Friday, the president of the University of North Carolina, said of the woman who organized JFK's inaugural ball: "It was often suggested, not entirely in jest, and freely admitted by Governor Gardner himself, that she was his equal if not his superior as a politician." In fact, Friday speculated, "In another time and place, 'Miss Fay' could have ascended to the highest levels of leadership in America and perhaps become our first woman President."

A short stroll away, a cemetery visitor finds the graves of Gov. Clyde Roark Hoey and his wife Bess Gardner Hoey, sister of O. Max. Gardner. The inscription for Gov. Hoey is predictable:

CLYDE ROARK HOEY
DEC. 11, 1877—MAY 12, 1954
GOVERNOR OF NORTH CAROLINA
1937–1941
UNITED STATES SENATOR
JAN. 3, 1945—MAY 12, 1954
ONE OF THE GREAT, YET THE PLAINEST AMONG US.
"WELL DONE, THOU GOOD AND FAITHFUL SERVANT."

Hoey's wife, however, is described very differently:

BESS GARDNER HOEY
WIFE OF
CLYDE ROARK HOEY
DIED FEBRUARY 13, 1942
RADIANT IN LIFE
TRIUMPHANT IN DEATH
SHE LOVED MUCH AND WAS MUCH LOVED

The pattern is quite clear: Mrs. Hoey takes her identity from relationships—both as a wife and as one who "loved much and was much loved." One more interesting, gendered detail is that the tombstone gives Bess Hoey's death date but not her birth date, perhaps as a nod to the stereotype of older women as undesirable. Her biographer, Grace Rutledge Hamrick, notes that she "never told her age."

Margaret Elizabeth "Bess" Gardner Hoey was much more than that, of course. By all accounts, she devoted her life to the welfare of children. After her mother's

death, she helped raise her younger brothers and then gave up some of her inher-
itance to send her brother, O. Max Gardner, to college. Biographers extol her as a
gracious hostess when she was First Lady of North Carolina, but an on-line encyclo-
pedia of famous North Carolinians includes this intriguing suggestion: "While Governor Hoey had a reputation as an excellent orator, his wife obviously had much the
same gift. She spoke often on the subjects of highway beautification, women's roles,
and the welfare of children." Perhaps like her husband, she could have been called
a "silver-tongued orator." Bess Hoey also had a long-term influence on Sunset Cemetery itself. According to Grace Hamrick, "as first president of Shelby Civic League in
1907, she lined the avenue into Sunset Cemetery with sugar maple trees." The colorful trees honor the many Civil War veterans buried in Sunset.

In their lifetimes, Fay Webb Gardner and Bess Gardner Hoey came to exemplify the attributes of the True Woman, a gender ideal for white, middle-class
women in the nineteenth century. In a classic description of this woman based on
her study of popular literature of the era, the scholar Barbara Welter describes her
as pure, pious, domestic, and submissive. Perhaps Mrs. Gardner and Mrs. Hoey
were exemplary in purity, piety, and domesticity, but I doubt anyone would call them
"submissive" even though their tombstones might suggest otherwise.

Still, we should not import our twenty-first notions of womanhood onto these
"radiant" examples of an older ideal of femininity. Nor would they want us to. On
January 17, 1932, First Lady Fay Webb Gardner confided to her diary that she had
spent the morning "abed" feeling "real lonesome" while her husband, Max, was
away on official business. Her musings show her content in a life defined by relationships rather than public accomplishments: "Thought of our married life and all it had
meant. It isn't always an easy job, but nothing that is worthwhile is, but by and large
it is the most soul-satisfying and best paying career that any woman can espouse."

John P. McKnight (1908–1987)

Joe: He traveled the world as a correspondent and foreign diplomat, covering
wars, revolutions, and hurricanes, but when the end came, Sunset Cemetery was his
final resting place.

John Proctor McKnight was the son of J.S. and Nerva Proctor McKnight and
grew up in Shelby. A lover of books, he was a 1928 Phi Beta Kappa graduate of Davidson College. His first newspaper job was with the *Wilmington Dispatch* soon after
graduation. He joined the Associated Press in 1930. In the summer of 1933, he was
stationed in Havana, Cuba, when his kid brother, C.A. "Pete" McKnight, came down
from Shelby to teach English in a Cuban school while learning Spanish.

"It turned out to be quite a summer," the *Raleigh News & Observer* wrote in a
1952 "Tar Heel of the Month" profile on Pete McKnight, by then editor of the *Charlotte News*:

> For one thing, Cuba had a terrific revolution. John was covering it for The Associated Press,
> and Peter managed to see quite a bit of it. Once, he remembers, they were in the National Hotel
> in Havana. The hotel was guarded by a large number of troops and some of them had large-size

guns. One of them fired a cannon, and there was considerable return fire. Pete remembers diving head first over the counter of the Western Union booth in the lobby, and sitting out the firing from that point of safety. He remembers, too, watching from a balcony as troops fired into a large crowd of people killing more than a score of them.

Then, as if a revolution wasn't enough, the McKnight brothers were there that summer when one of the worst hurricanes in Cuba's history struck the island. They were in the town of Cardenas near the beach when the storm swept ashore and began battering Cuba. "They were in a stone house and when the storm was over their house was the only one left standing for a radius of at least two blocks," the story reported. The experiences of that summer would inspire Pete McKnight to follow a career in newspapers like his big brother, John. Eventually, that career would lead him to the editorship of the *Charlotte Observer*.

Meanwhile, John went on serve as an AP correspondent in Mexico City, Spain, Portugal and Rome. As his 1967 obituary in the *Charlotte News* reported, McKnight also served in the Army from 1942 to 1943. In 1961, he joined the U.S. Information Service, working in Rome, South Korea, Brazil and Argentina. John was a Brookings Institute Information fellow in 1962 and a research associate at the National War College from 1967 to 1968. Davidson College awarded him an honorary doctorate in 1983.

John's book *The Papacy: A New Appraisal* won the North Carolina Mayflower Award for the best nonfiction book of 1952. While he was writing it, living in Chapel Hill, McKnight also wrote editorial pieces for the *Charlotte News* where he had once been state editor. He produced a three part series on Civil Rights in 1950, the first of which was about a 26-year-old Durham man who had been arrested for seeking signatures for a peace petition that had Communist backing. John asserted that everyone might not approve of the young man's actions, but

you cannot get away from the fact that he has posed a question to a democratic way of life. And behind that question are others yet larger; how shall we win the hearts of men to practical democracy if fear of Communism causes us to repudiate the very virtues that make ideal democracy dear to much of mankind and what profits us victory in the cold or hot war with totalitarian Communism if the price we pay for that victory is our grand birthright of freedom?

According to his obituary, John was fluent in Spanish, French, Italian and Portuguese and a storehouse of knowledge about many things. He had traveled far and wide and written with great clarity, insight and grace. His burial in Sunset Cemetery was private and his grave marker plain and simple, listing none of the many accomplishments in his 79 years on earth. The Shelby boy had done his best and if he had chosen an epitaph for his grave, maybe it would have been that of another well-traveled writer, Robert Louis Stevenson: "Here he lies where he longed to be. Home is the sailor, home from the sea and the hunter home from the hill."

VIII

Cultural Heroes

S/Sgt. Bonnie G. Wright (1918–1945)

Joe: The stories he could have told. Staff Sgt. Bonnie, a paratrooper, fought in the biggest battles in World War II. Sicily, Normandy, and Holland: the odds of surviving any of those awesome combat jumps—burdened with 100 pounds of gear and under fire from enemy soldiers on the ground—were stacked against him and his fellow sky soldiers.

Leading a platoon of the elite 82nd Airborne Division, Bonnie Wright of Shelby, North Carolina, might have seemed invincible. But he knew the longer he stayed in the thick of things the greater the chances of luck running out. On a bitterly cold day in late December 1944, Sgt. Wright and troopers went up against German panzer forces in the frozen country of Belgium. It was part of a desperate last-ditch effort by the Reich to end the war.

Known as the Battle of the Bulge, it would go down in history as the war's largest campaign and Sgt. Bonnie Wright of Shelby, North Carolina, did his part. The stories he could have told. If only the sergeant had lived. The wartime odyssey of Bonnie G. Wright, as for so many others, began with the Japanese surprise attack on Pearl Harbor, December 1, 1941. With patriotism aflame in the land, civilians rushed to take the oath in some branch of the military. Twenty-three-year-old Bonnie Wright was no exception, but first he had important business to take care of. In January 1942, he married Thelma Glover. Then, in February, he joined the U.S. Army. At some point early in basic training, Bonnie made a decision that would transform him from a regular soldier into something approaching a mythic warrior: He volunteered for the paratroopers. A new outfit had organized, and it appealed to men looking for adventure—along with $50 extra a month in pay.

The 505th Parachute Infantry Regiment, Second Battalion of the 82nd Airborne Division at Fort Bragg, North Carolina, would become Bonnie's heart and soul in the army. Not everyone made the cut. The handsome young commander of the 505th, James Gavin, was tough as nails and expected the same of his volunteers. He put them a training program so grueling that only the strongest made it to graduation. Like his commander, later known as "Jumping Jim Gavin" because he parachuted into battle with his men, Bonnie Wright was handsome and tough. A boxer in civilian life, Bonnie he could take anything "Jumping Jim" dished out. He made the grade and joined a regiment that would achieve legendary status in World War II.

In the 1943 invasion of Sicily, the 505th spearheaded the campaign and fought the infamous Hermann Goring Panzer Division, beating it to a standstill. Bonnie was wounded and missed the next combat jump in Italy. On leave while convalescing, he visited family in Shelby and someone took a photo of him holding his baby daughter, Patsy. It was the first and last time they saw each other. Bonnie returned to his regiment in time for the Normandy invasion. He jumped with the 505th three hours before the beach landings and helped liberate the village of Ste.-Mère-Église in France. Newspapers around the world ran stories about the liberation of the first town in Europe.

The *Charlotte Observer* ran a list of North Carolina soldiers who had participated in the capture of Ste.-Mère-Église—Bonnie's name among them. Years later, when Shelby moviegoers watched *The Longest Day*, based on Cornelius Ryan's best-selling book, they may have gasped when a character played by actor Red Buttons, parachuted into Ste.-Mère-Église and got caught on a church steeple, dangling there as German soldiers swarmed down below. Some may have known this scene was based on an actual incident, and that the stranded paratrooper was in the 505th Parachute Infantry Regiment with Shelby's own Bonnie Wright.

During "Market Garden," the massive Allied invasion of Holland chronicled in the Cornelius Ryan's book *A Bridge Too Far*, Bonnie and his regiment captured the great Nijmegen Bridge over the Waal River. In a post-war memoir *On to Berlin*, Gen Gavin wrote about the way the 2nd Battalion, of which the 505th was a part, performed in battle: "It was the battalion that destroyed the German Kampfgruppe that attempted to move from Cherbough to Ste.-Mère-Église in Normandy. It was the battalion that, attacking from rooftop to rooftop, destroyed the German bridgehead holding the southern end of the Nijmegen Bridge. It was an aggressive, tough, battle-seasoned battalion."

The 505th rested a while after the Netherlands campaign wound down. Still in Holland, Bonnie scribbled a post card message to his baby daughter, Patsy, back in Shelby. She couldn't read it then, but the post card would be a treasured keepsake when she grew older: "Hello daughter, Wonder what my little girl could be doing tonight? I got the picture that you sent and you are a beautiful little lady now. Take care of mother for me. Love always, Daddy." The war was obviously nearing the end, and Bonnie probably counted the days until he could be reunited with baby Pasty and his wife, Thelma. Then in that frozen December 1944, the supposedly beaten-down Germans did something totally unexpected. They mounted a huge, surprise breakthrough along 70 miles of the Allied line in the rugged Ardennes. It was one last, desperate push. Ill-equipped for winter fighting, the 505th went up against Germany's two best panzer divisions, ultimately pushing them back to their own border. Another major accomplishment that would go down in regimental history. But Bonnie would not be around to savor the glory.

In a history of the 505th regiment written after the war, a soldier in Wright's platoon remembered seeing the platoon sergeant on a roadside, wounded by artillery fire. Bonnie died later in a hospital, and was among 15 Co. F paratroopers killed or wounded in the battle. He was buried in the 57-acre American Cemetery and Memorial in Henri-Chapelle, Belgium. Bonnie Wright's name, along with other paratroopers in the 505th regiment, was included on postwar memorials erected in Belgium.

Two years later after his death, Bonnie's remains, along with 5,600 American war dead from military cemeteries in Europe, were shipped back to the U.S. Shelby's Co. M, 120th Infantry Regiment of the National Guard. The American Legion, and the VFW gave Bonnie a full military burial in Sunset Cemetery. A small portrait was embedded in the grave marker.

Bonnie's wife, Thelma, remarried. Her daughter, Patsy, grew up, married, and had three daughters. As little girls, they joined their grandmother on Saturday afternoons for a weekly ritual: tending family graves in Sunset Cemetery. Special

A ceramic portrait of S/Sgt. Bonnie G. Wright shows the face of a young man who was movie-star handsome. Many early-twentieth-century tombstones in Sunset bear these small ceramic plaques.

attention went to the graves of her two husbands, Bonnie Wright and Paul Ropp. Thelma supervised the granddaughters as they mowed grass, raked leaves, picked up sticks, and groomed the ground to perfection. Nothing less would do. If Grandmother didn't think they had done a good enough job, she made them start over. Still, the girls found time to run and play around the cemetery. As the granddaughter grew older, they encountered women who had known Bonnie Wright back in the day. Thinking back, the women would say things like "Oh my God, he was handsome." The granddaughters already knew that. They had seen photos of Granddaddy in the trunk.

The trunk: almost a sacred object in the family, overseen by their grandmother and later their mother. The girls weren't allowed to look inside without permission. But when they got the OK, they reached down into the contents and pulled out wonderful souvenirs Grandfather Bonnie Wright had had sent home from the war. Things like the remnants of his parachute Thelma used to make handkerchiefs for women in the family; medallions from battle victims; a swastika-engraved pin; a ring; St. Christopher medals; coins—German, French, British; a prayer book; small Bibles, one in German, another in Dutch. Photos of Bonnie and Thelma. A photo of Bonnie dressed as a boxer. Letters to Thelma, expressing his love. And a curious, handwritten

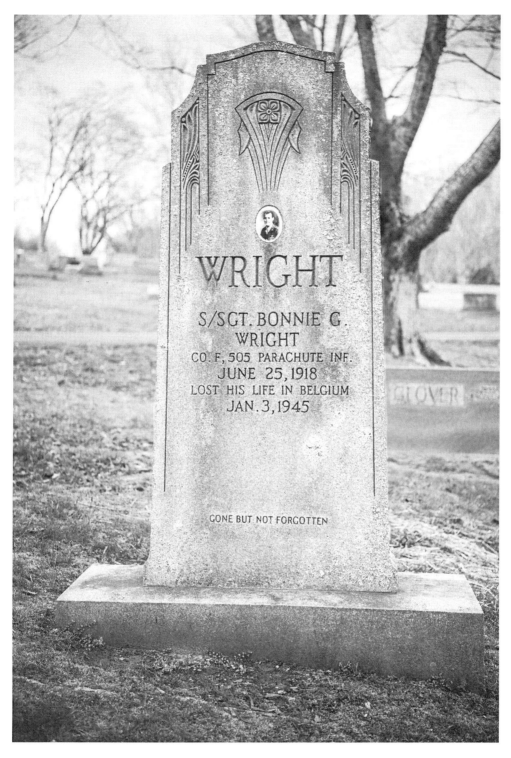

The tombstone for S/Sgt. Bonnie G. Wright, paratrooper and World War II hero. After dying in the Battle of the Bulge, Sgt. Wright was first buried in the American Cemetery and Memorial in Henri-Chapelle, Belgium, and later brought home to Shelby.

song entitled "I'm Sorry I Said Goodbye." Thelma may have saved the song because of the title. She and Bonnie were sorry he had to go away, and it made her cry. But they overlooked the part in the lyrics about a quarrel.

> Believe me dear, I'm sorry
> So sorry that I made you cry
> I didn't mean to hurt you
> I'm sorry that I said goodbye.
>
> Somehow we had a quarrel
> I don't remember why
> I love you so, my darling
> I'm sorry that I said goodbye.
>
> You will always be my darling
> And I will love you till I die
> I wish that I had believed you
> I'm sorry that I said goodbye.
>
> Believe me dear, I love you
> And only if you'll let me try.
> I'll promise to you my darling
> I'm sorry that I said goodbye.

For the granddaughters, everything in the trunk was a treasure. Each object had a story that Sgt. Bonnie Wright could have told them, but they'll never know. Yet the trunk offered them faint echoes of his experiences in World War II. And the simple inscription on his marker in Sunset Cemetery—he was in Co. F, 505th Parachute Infantry—made it clear: This young man from Shelby, North Carolina, was an American hero.

Hugh F. Hamrick (1914–1949)

No more bayonetings or beatings, back-breaking labor, endless jungle horrors. Brain fevers and other unspeakable torments are gone forever. Bataan Death March survivor Hugh F. Hamrick is at peace. Like Bonnie Wright and the many other World War II veterans buried in Sunset Cemetery, Hugh could tell stories that would make the blood run cold. The son of Mr. and Mrs. V.H. Hamrick of Boiling Springs, Hugh ran a Shelby service station and extensive farming operation before being inducted into the U.S. Army in May 1941. By October of that year, he had arrived in the Philippines, assigned to the 803rd Engineering Aviation Battalion.

Many years later, another Cleveland County soldier serving in the Philippines told a *Shelby Star* reporter how good the duty was in the Philippines during those pre-war days. Coy Langford, who was also a Bataan Death March survivor, recalled that young soldiers and sailors had a ball there in their off-duty hours. But Hugh, if he was so inclined, got only a small taste. On December 8, eight hours after the Japanese attacked Pearl Harbor, they struck the Philippines.

Hugh was captured by the Japanese in April 1942. As captives were rounded up and herded toward prison camps, he was an eyewitness as to how the 65-mile march got its name. Japanese guards bayoneted or shot prisoners who fell down. The heat was unbearable, and prisoners like Hugh who managed to stay on their feet got only a few swallows of water. Prison was also hell. Thousands died in the camps from dysentery, malnutrition, and other diseases. But Hugh was tough and held on—for 3½ years. Then in September 1945 his parents in Boiling Springs got a message that their son had been liberated. Formerly a prisoner in the Philippines, Hugh had been moved to Osaka, Japan, where he worked in a coal mine.

The odds had been stacked against him, but in late 1945, by some miracle of fate, Hugh came home to Shelby. (His fellow Bataan Death March survivor Coy Langford also made it back to Cleveland County.) Hugh's reunion with family and friends must have been a time of great joy. But probably lurking in the background of his mind were visions of fellow soldiers who weren't as fortunate; their pitiful remains lay in graves back in the Philippines or Japan.

Hugh started over, resuming his prewar work at the service station and farm. In 1947, Hugh's wife, Dovie, gave birth to a baby girl the couple named Melinda. The peaceful scenes of home were soothing to his battered soul. He had weathered the storm of war and felt the embrace of a welcoming community. He had a new wife and daughter. Happiness filled his cup. But the war wouldn't let go of Hugh. He suffered from reoccurring attacks brought on by a rare brain disease he had contracted as a POW.

When the attacks struck, Hugh fought back. He was, after all, a survivor. He had beaten the odds before. He had a wife and daughter, and he wanted to stay around for them. But the disease pounded away at a body that had already been through so much. And on May 21, 1949, Hugh died at Moore General Hospital in Swannanoa. He was 34. After funeral services at Shelby's First Baptist Church, Hugh was buried in Sunset Cemetery. Dovie would remarry and have another daughter, Jenny. Dovie died in 1997 and joined Hugh in Sunset.

Like Sgt. Bonnie Wright, Hugh had left behind a little daughter who would have few, if any, memories, of her father. Melinda Hamrick had a long career in social services, aiding families in need. She was director of the Moore County DSS office and later assistant director of the North Carolina Department of Social Service. She died of natural causes after a period of declining health on May 14, 2020, seven decades after her father. Melinda never married and her obituary listed no survivors. But it mentioned that her father, Hugh, had survived the Japanese POW camps. And that he had died when she was about two years old. She had been cheated out of growing up to adulthood in the aura of his love. But he was always her dad. A survivor. And she was proud of him.

Expatriation and Visualization

June: The story of how Bonnie Wright's body came to rest under a handsome granite stone in Sunset Cemetery includes a number of scenes of which average Americans are completely unaware. They may not know, for example that, as military historian Joe R. Bailey explains, the disposition of the American war dead was under the auspices of the U.S. Army's Quartermaster General. According to Bailey, if a soldier died in battle, his body was cared for by a member of the Quartermaster General's Graves Registration Corps. The work was often horrific, but the teams assigned to Graves Registration handled it with as much dignity as possible, usually covering the bodies of the dead to preserve the morale of the other soldiers as they were carrying bodies to collection stations via routes beyond the vision of those still alive.

Their work was dangerous because the enemy sometimes booby trapped the bodies, often by attaching a hand grenade to the deceased soldier's dog tag. When a member of the Graves Registration Corps pulled out the dog tag to ascertain the soldier's identity, the action also pulled the safety pin from the grenade. Graves Registration Corps members soon learned to take defensive actions such as tying a 200-foot rope to the dog tag and pulling it to ensure their own safety.

Since Sgt. Wright died in a hospital, his body would not have been collected from the field of battle in this way. However, his personal possessions, all of the memorabilia now preserved in the sacred trunk, would have been carefully collected, logged, and returned to his wife and daughter by the Graves Registration Corps. His granddaughters have carefully preserved registered letters from the War Department to his wife documenting this process. In the cemetery in Belgium where he was buried temporarily, the Corps would have made sure that one of his dog tags remained with his body and one was attached to his gravemarker.

The Quartermaster General's office of the War Department was also charged with returning the bodies of soldiers whose families wished to bury them stateside. In December of 1946, the office issued a pamphlet titled "Tell Me About My Boy" to explain to grieving families how the bodies of their war dead would be handled. As the pamphlet explained, "Tell me about my boy" was the "request most frequently sent to the Quartermaster General of the Army" seeking information.

The next of kin had a number of choices. The body could remain in the country in which the soldier fell and be buried in a permanent cemetery such as the one at Normandy Beach with a proper religious ceremony conducted by a "Catholic, Protestant, or Jewish" clergyman and marked by a "tombstone, cross, or Star of David." Alternatively, the body could be sent to a private cemetery in a foreign country or repatriated to the United States to be buried in a national cemetery such as Arlington or a private cemetery such as Sunset. Thelma obviously chose the last option for the final interment of her husband. According to the "Tell Me About My Boy" pamphlet, each body was accompanied by a military escort "from the ports of New York and San Francisco to the fifteen distribution centers. From these centers a military escort of equal or higher rank, grade or rating and same branch of service of the deceased [was] designated to travel with the remains to the point designated by next of kin."

This military escort probably stayed with Sgt. Wright's body until a local funeral home took over, and he almost certainly paid his respects to Thelma and Patsy before leaving. Perhaps he even stayed for the funeral or at least visited the home where the coffin lay in state, draped with an American flag and surrounded by elaborate floral arrangements. Later, the U.S. Army issued the official gravemarker that now serves as his footstone. The family, however, would have ordered the granite marker that stands at the head of his grave. It is taller than the other markers around it, perhaps as an indication of pride in their soldier and the hope that visitors will take note of his grave site and pause in gratitude for his service. The marker is nicely designed and decorated with graceful line drawings and stylized flowers. The flowers could be poppies, which became symbols of remembrance for the war dead after World War I. Nothing about the stone is particularly unusual, however, except for the ceramic miniature of Sgt. Wright in his uniform at eye level on the marker.

A good handful of these charming portraits appear on gravestones in Sunset, mostly on stones from the same era. They became popular on gravestones starting in the mid-nineteenth century, when modern photography made them possible. Occasionally it is even possible to find an older daguerreotype on a gravestone, especially if it has been preserved under a metal cover to prevent it from fading. The use of ceramic portraits on gravestones seems driven mostly by local custom. Bohemian National Cemetery in Chicago, for example, boasts a ceramic portrait on almost every gravestone. A picture of the deceased on a gravestone is a way to personalize it, but it is also a way to focus attention on the missing person. As the French philosopher Gaston Bachelard observes in his classic work *The Poetics of Space*, an effective way to emphasize something is to miniaturize it. The little lambs on gravestones of children are more poignant because they are miniaturized. They remain forever small, just as the little ones who never got to grow up. In the case of Bonnie Wright, who has remained a big presence in his family, we might remember that he was only twenty-six when he died. His place in the world is now reduced to a gravesite and to the picture that sparks the imagination of the viewer. What would this movie-star-handsome man have become if he had lived?

Occasionally, the pictures that appear on ceramic plaques on gravestones were taken postmortem. Postmortem photography were common in the nineteenth century before most families had access to cameras and when professional photography was expensive. A quick Google search turns up hundreds of examples, sometimes of bodies laid out in coffins but just as often of bodies elaborately posed. Dead children propped up beside their living siblings or in the arms of their mothers are not uncommon.

What would prompt our ancestors to engage in what seems to the twenty-first-century eye to be a profoundly morbid custom? One answer is simple practicality. If a person, particularly a child, had never been photographed, the postmortem picture was the only chance to preserve the likeness of the deceased. The famous author Harriet Beecher Stowe kept a postmortem picture of her son Charlie, who died in 1849 of cholera at eighteen months, on open display in her home. Many families displayed such portraits in a time when infant mortality was high. Sunset Cemetery is also the final resting place of a baby whose tombstone includes a postmortem picture of a child who was "born sleeping." It is the only modern postmortem picture I have ever seen on a tombstone. Little Karsyn Max Franklin was stillborn on January 2, 2018. His obituary names his parents, Cory and Brittany; his brother, Kadyn; grandparents and great-grandparents.

He was obviously a treasured child, and his family obviously wanted to

BABY

KARSYN MAX
BORN SLEEPING
JAN. 2, 2018

"BECAUSE OF YOU,
WE BELIEVE IN ANGELS"

FRANKLIN

Tombstone for Karsyn Max Franklin, who was "born sleeping."

preserve his likeness. In fact, a different postmortem picture appears with his obituary in the *Shelby Star*. We know that someone had prepared a little shirt for him with his name embroidered on the front, and that he had a full head of dark hair. We know from his epitaph that his family believes he lives on. It says, "Because of you, we believe in angels."

In Sunset Cemetery, both Bonnie Wright and Karsyn Franklin live on in memory but

Postmortem photograph of Karsyn Max Franklin, a stillborn baby. Postmortem photographs were popular in the nineteenth century but are rare today.

also in imagination prompted by miniature portraits that remind us even lives cut short still matter.

Ann Eliza Stough (1826–1888)

Joe: A twenty-first-century vandal pushed Ann Eliza Stough's gravestone off its foundation—an insult to the memory of a distinguished preacher's wife, "a good woman" as a contemporary newspaper called her. Time has done its work on the stone flat on the ground. But when it caught the eye of passersby who stopped and looked closely at the inscription, they saw this 62-year-old person Ann Eliza was the wife of the Rev. A.L. Stowe. Arched over the top of the moment were the words: "In Loving Remembrance."

Then, if the light were just right, passersby would see a verse from a poem, and if they were well-read in American literature, might have recognized the source: "Resignation" by Henry Wadsworth Longfellow:

There is no Death! What seems so
   is transition;
This life of mortal breath
Is but a suburb of the life elysian,
Whose portal we call death.

Longfellow, one of America's most popular poets, had been dead six years when Ann Eliza passed away, but

The Ann Eliza Stough stone, which includes a verse from Henry Wadsworth Longfellow's "Resignation," written in 1848 after the death of Longfellow's 17-month-old daughter, Fanny. The verse describes death as "a portal" to the "life Elysian." The verse is popular on nineteenth-century tombstones across the nation.

his works hadn't been forgotten. In the biography *Longfellow: A Rediscovered Life*, author Charles Calhoun wrote that Longfellow composed "Resignation" after the 1848 death of his daughter Fanny, age seventeen months, as a way to deal with his grief. It became one of his most popular short works among Victorian readers.

Brief death notices for Ann Eliza noted that she had been an invalid for many years. They described her as "a useful woman" and a "worthy woman." The *New Era* in Shelby noted she was the former Miss Horton, born February 28, 1826, in Chatham County in central North Carolina. "Her early life was spent in the central portion of the state, where she has many friends and relatives," the paper reported. "Mrs. Stough has been a resident of Shelby for the past 12 years and leaves many friends who mourn their loss. Her funeral took place Tuesday afternoon from the Baptist Church, Rev. J.M. McManaway conducting the service."

Shelby First Baptist Church was where Ann Eliza's husband, A.L. Stowe, had been pastor. Born in Hamburg, Germany in 1825, he had been educated for the Catholic priesthood but became a Baptist after coming to Norfolk, Virginia, in 1847. According to the *History of First Baptist Church of Shelby*, Stough became a Baptist preacher in the Sandy Creek Association of Virginia and was a chaplain in the Confederate Army during the Civil War. He pastored Shelby First Baptist Church from 1875 to 1879, when he left Shelby to preach in Mecklenburg County and churches in South Carolina. A year after Ann Eliza's death. The Reverend Stough married Mary C. Walker of Fort Lawn, South Carolina. He died in 1909, and she passed away in 1928. They are buried at Flint Hill Baptist Church Cemetery near Fort Mill, South Carolina.

Back in Sunset Cemetery, Ann Eliza's gravestone stood for decades until uncaring hands knocked it to the ground. But time has not erased her name yet or wasted the inspiring words of a great American poet.

Henry Wadsworth Longfellow, Cultural Hero

June: Henry Wadsworth Longfellow was a rock star in his own time, and his influence on the nineteenth century could hardly be overemphasized. Queen Victoria's star-struck servants, to her amusement and delight, hid themselves around Windsor Castle hoping to catch a glimpse of the great man when he came to visit in 1868, according to Longfellow's biographer Nicholas Basbanes. Longfellow also visited Charles Dickens, whom he considered a friend, and learned that he was more popular than Robert Browning and Alfred, Lord Tennyson, in their own country. Professor of Modern Languages at Harvard College, Longfellow was a gifted linguist who taught French, Italian, Spanish, and German. According to Basbanes, he also quickly picked up Swedish, Danish, Finnish, Icelandic, and Dutch on a trip to Europe. He was known for one of the finest translations of Dante's *Divine Comedy* and for over 400 poems in addition to novels, travelogues, and textbooks.

But most of all, he was one of the Fireside Poets whose work families read aloud or recited for pleasure as they relaxed in front of an open hearth in the evenings. There was a time when reciting "Listen, my children, and you shall hear" would be sure to inspire someone else to continue, "of the midnight ride of Paul Revere."

Everyone knew *Evangeline*. The *dramatis personae* of *The Song of Hiawatha* were household names. Schoolchildren across the nation memorized "The Village Blacksmith." And the verse from Ann Eliza Stough's tombstone from Longfellow's "Resignation" was a comforting standard for tombstones across the nation. Longfellow eloquently voiced ideas that helped people put the history of their young nation to good use, create a genuinely American literature, and cope with loss and grief.

Today, English departments in American colleges and universities rarely teach Longfellow except as a curiosity. His work no longer appears in anthologies. In fact, almost the only way people notice Longfellow at all is at Christmas when they sing the words of his Christmas carol "I Heard the Bells on Christmas Day," and even then it is common to sing the words without knowing the author. Some might say Longfellow is simply outdated, but there is more to it than that. Longfellow exemplifies ideas about poets very different from those of contemporary people, who often view them either as composers of verse suitable for Hallmark greeting cards or as the weird obsession of English professors who smugly analyze their impenetrable writing. Longfellow would not have recognized himself in either of those descriptions. Instead, his poetry reflects the emphasis on community that characterizes icons and epitaphs in the older part of Sunset Cemetery. Longfellow took his role as a public voice very seriously. The horrors of the Civil War inspired "I Heard the Bells on Christmas Day," for example, and its comforting message had much to say to the nation as a whole.

Like many fathers, Longfellow was wracked by worry for his nineteen-year-old son, Charley, who ran away to join the Union army less than two years after the loss of his mother. Fanny Appleton Longfellow died from wounds suffered at home when her gown tragically caught fire while she was sealing envelopes with hot wax. Basbanes quotes a letter from Henry Longfellow in which he tells his younger son, Erny, on June 22, 1863, about the unsettling experience of hearing cannon fire mixed with peals of church bells as he sat at Charley's bedside hoping he would recover from the "camp fever" (probably typhoid fever, according to Basbanes) that had left him dangerously ill. Longfellow eventually used the memory in the poem "Christmas Bells."

When "Christmas Bells" became "I Heard the Bells on Christmas Day," however, it lost the verses that linked it undeniably to the Civil War.

> Then from each black, accursed mouth
> The cannon thundered in the South
> And with the sound
> The carols drowned
> Of peace on earth, good will to men.
>
> It was as if an earthquake rent
> The hearth-stones of a continent,
> And make forlorn
> The households born
> Of peace on earth and good-will to men.

Without those verses, the poem is an initially sad story, disconnected from historical context, of a man who hears church bells on Christmas Day but realizes that "there is no peace on earth." But the bells speak to him in the end, reminding him that "God is not dead; nor doth he sleep!" and "The Wrong shall fail,/The Right prevail." The carol delivers a comforting message for all time, but to Americans in 1863, it must have addressed the question: "How could God let this happen?"

Longfellow also saw himself as a poet for all Americans at the beginning of the Civil War. "Paul Revere's Ride" was written in 1860 although the setting for the poem is April 18, 1775, just before the opening battle of the Revolutionary War. It was published in the January 1861 issue of *The Atlantic Monthly*. In fact, the issue came out on the very day that South Carolina seceded from the Union. Longfellow changed several historical details of the story. For example, Paul Revere was the person who hung two lanterns in the steeple of Old North Church, not the one and only recipient of the message. Also, he was not the only man who rode that night to warn the citizens of "every Middlesex village and farm" that "the British are coming" (a phrase that is not even in the poem). Finally, Longfellow left out the fact that Paul Revere was, in fact, captured by the British on his ride and detained for a few hours while others finished warning the Patriots.

Henry Wadsworth Longfellow took some poetic license with the story to rally Americans for the coming War Between the States that he obviously saw as a crisis in which the future of the American experiment itself was at stake. Paul Revere was not the only Patriot riding the night before "the shot heard round the world"— but focusing on what one man alone could do to save the nation spoke to every eligible soldier who doubted his value in the fight and every parent who hesitated to send that young man to battle. And the poem evoked the sacred founding myth for the nation. The last few lines are a call to arms: "In the hour of darkness and peril and need,/ The people will waken and listen to hear/ The hurrying hoof-beats of that steed,/ And the midnight message of Paul Revere."

Basbanes points out that "Paul Revere's Ride" is "the most memorized poem in American history, its cadences mimicking the sound of a horse galloping through the countryside, the rider alerting the citizenry to redcoats on the march." The galloping rhythm of "Paul Revere's Ride" makes it easy to memorize, but it also speaks to the fact that nineteenth-century people took pleasure in reading poetry aloud. It is fun to analyze these poems in a classroom, but they are accessible to almost everyone who can read. Today we value complexity, irony, and difficulty in poetry. These are marks of craftsmanship that requires hours of analysis with a good dictionary and, perhaps, the guidance of a patient English professor for full understanding. Longfellow's more-subtle craftsmanship, aimed at entertaining as well as guiding the public, was of a different kind. His accessibility seems suspect to a modern audience.

Longfellow's take on death in "Resignation," is another example of his role as a public poet, this time speaking to a nation in which the loss of children was common. It begins by invoking the common image of "the vacant chair" at the hearthside and the grief that was an unwelcome guest in many homes. "Resignation" is a meditation on the death of a child. Its language employs the *lingua franca* of grief management in the mid-nineteenth century. For example, it expresses elegantly the common ideas that dead children are safe children who can never sin and that they will grow up in heaven, ready to greet their parents some day:

> She is not dead,—the child of our affection,—
> But gone unto that school
> Where she no longer needs our poor protection,
> And Christ himself doth rule.
>
> In that great cloister's stillness and seclusion,
> By guardian angels led,
> Safe from temptation, safe from sin's pollution,
> She lives, whom we call dead.

Notice especially Longfellow's use of the word "safe" at the end of the passage. It is the same idea his contemporary, Fanny J. Crosby, used in her much-loved hymn "Safe in the Arms of Jesus."

Such poetry is not original in the modern sense, nor does it purport to be. Its focus is not on the brilliance of the poet or on the marketability of the verse. It is on a common trove of beliefs that kept people of another age from giving up in the face of unbearable loss. In the twenty-first century, people have trouble even saying the word "death," and the death of a child is—as it always has been—the most unnatural of losses. Yet today, we condemn ourselves to grieve alone. Prolonged grief itself, modern people believe, is a sign of mental disturbance that needs therapeutic intervention. Longfellow's declaration at the beginning of Mrs. Stough's epitaph—"There is no Death! What seems so is transition"—is a cliché, something so common we imagine no one could take it seriously.

But what if we looked at it as a nineteenth-century cemetery visitor might have, as a triumphant assertion of something we need to remember? Perhaps it seems common, not because it is trivial, but because it is a truth widely held. And the last stanza of the poem could have come right out of a chapter in a contemporary death counselor's handbook about the necessity of acknowledging grief:

> We will be patient, and assuage the feeling
> We may not wholly stay;
> By silence sanctifying, not concealing,
> The grief that must have way.

Perhaps we should take a leaf out of Longfellow's playbook. Patient acceptance of grief that "must have its way" is likely healthier than denial of death.

Margaret Stroebe, Mary M. Gergen, Kenneth J. Gergen, and Wolfgang Stroebe describe the modern prescription for grief as a mandate to break our bonds with the deceased so the mourner can quickly "move on" and get back to "real life." In contrast to the "Breaking Bonds" model for grief, our nineteenth-century ancestors might have encouraged us to acknowledge our broken hearts. During the mid-nineteenth century, according to these sociologists, Americans "placed love at the forefront of human endeavors" and valued bonds with other people to the point that "the death of an intimate other constituted a critical point of life definition." In the "Broken Hearts" model of grief, breaking one's bond with the deceased by putting grief aside too quickly would have diminished both the importance of the relationship and one's own value as a human being.

Ann Eliza Stough's tombstone, properly considered, should give us pause. Longfellow's poetry is due a second look. And modern people have much to learn about death, grief, and mourning from those who managed them better than we do.

Don Gibson (1928–2003)

Joe: The little boy with a stutter hated school and quit in second grade. Teachers and classmates didn't seem to care. Shy and sensitive, Don Gibson wandered the streets, a poor kid from a South Shelby mill village, not particularly interested in anything. Except music. Any kind of music—hillbilly, classical, jazz, Stephen Foster compositions like "Beautiful Dreamer"—it didn't matter. The power of music could penetrate Don's shyness and touch his soul.

The melodies swirling in his imagination came from records, radio, back porch pickers, local bands and totally unexpected sources like a GI buddy returned from Paris shortly after World War II. Don told a *Charlotte Observer* reporter the soldier had with him 78 rpm recordings by a gypsy guitarist named Django Reinhardt. This musical magician stirred Don's romantic spirit. The unique guitar style of Django from Paris, France, would echo one day in the Shelby boy's picking.

Don may have dreamed of a career in music. But could he have ever imagined a future in which he would be considered a songwriting genius and a pioneer of something called "The Nashville Sound"? Rock 'n' roll hadn't arrived in force yet, but when it did, a sharp decline in the sales of country music records would follow. In an effort to reverse that trend, "The Nashville Sound" replaced the twang of the honky tonk of old country with strings and choruses and smooth arrangements. It was a more pop sound. Don and RCA record producer Chet Atkins led the way for this new wave in country music, starting with Don's original composition "Oh, Lonesome Me." But that was still far in the future.

Still working odd jobs around Shelby, Don played in bands like The Sons of the Soil, broadcasting over Shelby radio station WOHS. The group patterned its smooth harmonies after the popular western group Sons of the Pioneers. Don's heart and soul overflowed with music. "The only thing I was ever good at was music," he told a reporter many years later. Young Don Gibson must have known that in the long run music might not get him very far in life. But that didn't stop him from trying—and hoping for a break. And finally, it came. A friend helped him land a performing job with radio station WNOX in Knoxville, Tennessee. The position didn't pay much, but Don couldn't afford to ignore it. WNOX was steppingstone to the Grand Ole Opry, so he packed up and left Shelby on a great adventure. For the rest of his life, he only returned to his hometown as a visitor.

The Knoxville radio gig was a struggle. To make ends meet, Don played beer joints and lounges. Fans of pure country music noticed he didn't sound like twangy singers of the day. Don had a smoother, more soulful voice that maybe didn't sit too well with purists. At any rate, Don's dreams of a successful musical career still seemed far away and probably on shaky ground at times. He started drinking more.

Despite the uncertainty, he kept writing songs, following the method that he always used: simplicity. First, he hummed a melody. Next, he played around with words, not writing anything down, just seeing where the tune would lead. Often, it led nowhere. One day in 1955, Don hummed a plaintive melody, and words started flowing. From the depths of his imagination, a ballad of lost love took shape: It was called "Sweet Dreams of You." Don would record the song and see it hit the top ten list on Billboard's country charts. That was just what he needed: he quit the beer joints and took up songwriting full time. The sudden flame of success eventually cooled, but Don continued to hum melodies and write lyrics.

What happened next became part of the Don Gibson legend. On June 7, 1957, living alone in a trailer outside Knoxville, watching a repo man pick up his vacuum cleaner and TV, Don strummed his guitar as words and melodies tumbled in his mind. When he wrote it all down, he had made history. In that one afternoon, Don turned out two of country music's greatest songs: "I Can't Stop Loving You" and "Oh, Lonesome Me." Two songs that made him a superstar. (More than 700 artists would record "I Can't Stop Loving You," including Ray Charles.) In a burst of creativity, he sang of heartache and loneliness in works like "Blue Blue Day," "Too Soon to Know," "Who Cares," "I'm Hurting," "Give Myself a Party," "A Stranger to Me," and "Oh, Such a Stranger." Using simple language and riveting melodies to communicate strong emotions, Don delivered a message in his own distinctive style.

Now, instead of beer joints and bars, Don played the Grand Ole Opry, American Bandstand, huge coliseums and the Hollywood Bowl. On one tour he met newcomer Patsy Cline and they became friends. Patsy said she wanted to sing like a female Don Gibson. Her version of Don's "Sweet Dreams" was Patsy's biggest hit, released a week after her death in a 1963 plane crash. "Sweet Dreams" became a country music standard.

For all his success, the shy and sensitive Don hated performing in front of live audiences. He drank more and got into drugs. His personal life suffered: Two divorces, an accidental overdose, missed concerts. "A crazy time," Don told a reporter later. "I was running from fame. I didn't know how to adjust to it. Fame turned me every which way but loose. It was a wonder I didn't die."

In 1967, Don returned home to Shelby to spend time in care of a family circle. And it was during this stopover that he met Barbara "Bobbi" Patterson, a family friend he had known since she was a little girl. Like him, she was shy and sensitive, but she also had a stability missing from his personality. They married that year and Bobbi was determined to help her husband rebuild his life. And although it wasn't easy, she helped him.

In 1984, Don quit the road and returned to Nashville. He was inducted into the Nashville Song Writers Hall of Fame and in 2001 into the Country Music Hall of Fame. Don died in 2003 at the age of 75 and was buried in Sunset Cemetery. He rests under a large monument that Bobbi selected. Listed on the stone are Don's biggest hits and artists who recorded them—from Elvis and Sinatra to Ray Charles and Roy Orbison.

The life of the homegrown artist buried there is distilled in one of those song titles. Did a shy boy wandering the streets of Shelby ever dream that "(I'd Be) A Legend in My Time"?

The back of the Don Gibson memorial celebrating his songwriting history. Songs such as "Oh, Lonesome Me," "I Can't Stop Loving You," and "Sweet Dreams" made Gibson a household name and earned him a place in the Country Music Hall of Fame.

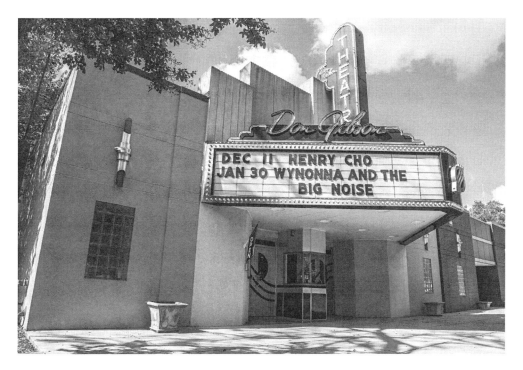

The Don Gibson Theatre in downtown Shelby, named in honor of country music great Don Gibson. The Art Deco building was built in 1939 as a cinema but eventually fell into disrepair. A capital campaign raised money to renovate it, and it reopened in 2009 as a 400-seat concert venue named for Shelby's legendary singer-songwriter.

The Don Gibson mural on the side of Miss Molly's Boutique in downtown Shelby. Painted by Scott Nurkin, it was completed in July 2020 and includes the lyrics to "I Can't Stop Loving You" next to a portrait of a young Don Gibson. The Uptown Shelby Association received a grant from the City of Shelby to initiate the project, and the Earl Scruggs Center was instrumental in planning the project and bringing it to fruition.

Art in the Cemetery

June: Sunset, like many large municipal cemeteries, is an open-air art museum. Even though most Shelby residents have not been rich enough to erect elaborate mausoleums or bespoke sculptural installations, the cemetery does include hand-carved marble tombstones, clever etched designs, and one impressive piece commissioned to honor Don Gibson, a man who, in the words of one of his songs, became "a legend in [his] time." The phrase itself is part of an ironic, self-deprecating lament for a man who, the lyrics suggest, should be famous for surpassing everyone else in heartbreak and loneliness. But Gibson's wife, Bobbi, has given it new meaning by honoring her hero with a classical-style monument celebrating his public legacy and, more subtly, the love of her life.

Ron Ledbetter of Shelby's Riverhill Monuments, which advertises its work as "Artistry in Stone," designed the Gibson monument. The massive memorial required 26 ½ tons of polished green granite imported from India. It is so heavy that the first step in erecting it was sinking a base of concrete and steel six feet into the ground. The obvious intention is to preserve Mr. Gibson's memory for eternity.

Gibson's widow, Bobbi, explains that the inspiration for her husband's memorial was the marker on the grave of Civil War General William Brimage Bate (1826–1905) in Mount Olivet Cemetery of Nashville, Tennessee, the home of country music where the Gibsons maintained a residence. Bate, who eventually became Governor of Tennessee and a U.S. Senator, is buried there in Confederate Circle.

A quick comparison of the two monuments shows that they are remarkably similar. Both feature a handsome bronze plaque of the deceased on a tablet between Doric columns. Both feature the last name of the man memorialized in capital letters just under the cornice. Both are solid and imposing, suitable for inspiring reverence and awe.

In fact, both memorials exemplify the three cornerstone principles of the Roman architect known as Vitruvius: strength, utility, and beauty. The treatise on architecture by Marcus Vitruvius Pollio, who lived in the first century BCE, was rediscovered during the Italian Renaissance. It is a primer on classical style that influences our sense of what a noble monument should look like even today. Strength, utility, and beauty require balance, symmetry, flawless materials, consistently crafted elements. These remind the viewer of the importance of those memorialized and, perhaps more importantly, of their values and enduring legacy.

An obsession with classical architecture and funerary symbols was important during the establishment of the United States as a nation. After patriots won the Revolutionary War and the Constitution was ratified, the nation was faced with the stark fact that, in contrast to the Old Country that European settlers left behind, the new nation had no usable past. One solution was to borrow history. The beloved Fireside Poet William Cullen Bryant, for example, borrowed history from the land itself and from native Americans in "The Prairies." In this poem, the speaker riding his horse over the American prairies realizes the land under him is

Bobbi Gibson in front of the memorial to her husband, country music legend Don Gibson. The monument, designed by Ron Ledbetter of Riverhill Monuments and made of 26½ tons of polished green granite from India, is modeled on the grave marker for Confederate General William Brimmage Bate in Mount Olivet Cemetery of Nashville.

made of the dust of former civilizations. His nation might be new, but the land itself is not. And he can imagine himself as an extension of the ancient inhabitants of the prairies.

In art and architecture, the classical ages of Greece and Rome offered another history to appropriate as a way to emphasize the civilized taste of the new Americans and the promise of the new country. If the American democracy could be seen as an extension of Greek democracy, why not borrow the symbols associated with that civilization? We might lack our own golden age, but neoclassical symbols could fill in the gap with those revered in ancient Greece and Rome. Blanche M.G. Linden cites Thomas Jefferson as someone who articulated many of these ideas. To him, neoclassical style "suggested a negation of luxury destructive to the republic. Its simplicity, visual purity, and restrained ornament were metaphoric of civic virtue, orderly and logical like the Constitution, an emblematic denial of the baroque tastes of monarchies and aristocracies." These values influenced sculptor Horatio Greenough to portray President George Washington in a Roman toga for the marble statue that is now housed in the National Museum of American History in Washington, D.C.

As another manifestation of neoclassical style, the older part of Sunset Cemetery and of most American cemeteries during the first century of the American Republic is filled with urns, weeping willows, obelisks and other classical symbols. The graves of O. Max and Fay Webb Gardner are covered by classical marble ledger stones, but behind them are three Doric columns, an appropriate memorial to these important citizens who contributed much to the culture of the area.

Most viewers appreciate the spirit of these monuments without having to identify their architectural features. Bobbi Gibson does not speak of Doric columns on her husband's gravemarker, but she is proud that the design echoes that of a hero. And she shyly admits that it is larger and more elaborate than other markers in the cemetery to symbolize her "big love" for Don Gibson.

The Gibson memorial is a blend of nineteenth-century sensibilities and the tastes of twentieth and twenty-first-century people. Tombstones in the nineteenth-century sections of American cemeteries emphasize shared values such as Christian faith and honorable military service. They include many repeated community symbols such as hands with fingers pointing up and the opening gates of heaven.

Some include personalized inscriptions, but often the epitaphs are familiar scriptures or hymns adapted to make them particularly appropriate for the person memorialized, stock expressions of community values, and narratives that inspire reverence for valor, love of country, reverence for one's mother. William Bate's monument is a good example of a memorial that emphasizes shared community values. Below his bronze profile is a quotation from Psalm 46: "God is my refuge and strength."

In the newer parts of Sunset, the attention shifts to maintaining a memory of what made an individual unique rather than of what the person shared with others. The green granite of the Don Gibson memorial is "the exact color of his eyes." The

Doric columns behind the graves for O. Max Gardner and Fay Webb Gardner reflect the taste for neoclassical architecture that linked the nation to the ancient civilizations of Greece and Rome. Thomas Jefferson recommended elegant, simple neoclassical style as a symbol of the nation's rejection of "the baroque tastes of monarchies and aristocracies."

words underneath his bronze likeness quote Joe DePriest's obituary for Don Gibson. It ends with the words "An American original. A true legend in his time." On the base of the memorial are personal symbols of Don Gibson's life: a picture of him and Bobbi from a 1972 publicity photo, their wedding date, and a Masonic symbol. The Masonic symbol is a personal reference to Don Gibson's father who died when he was seventeen. Though Don never knew him, he was proud of sharing a connection through being a Mason.

The back of the Don Gibson memorial lists the names of his most famous songs and the artists who performed them. It includes lyrics from "I Can't Stop Loving You." The song Bobbi treasures most, though, is a "simple" song written just for her in 1969: "Loving You I Will Always." She remembers Don as the man who bought fast-food burgers for dogs because he loved animals. As the man whose cremains are interred in an urn with pillars like a bookcase because he loved books. "He never gossiped," she says. "He was a good man."

An old adage says that people die twice: when physical life ceases, and when no living person remembers them any more. The Don Gibson memorial includes prompts to memory for those who loved him best. But it is also a very public memorial to ensure that his legacy lives on even when they are gone too.

Bobby "Pepperhead" London (1945–2010)

Joe: They came from far and wide to bid Pepperhead goodbye. Sitting with other family members in the nearly 1,500 seat Malcolm Brown Auditorium at Shelby High School, Claude London was amazed at all the people who had turned out for his older brother Bobby London's funeral service in July 2010. Local churches couldn't accommodate the anticipated crowds so the service was moved to the big auditorium which quickly filled. Another 500 waited outside.

Bobby, nicknamed Pepperhead, had died suddenly at the age of 64. But his fame and personality lived on, as did his favorite saying: "I wanna thank you." Bobby had been the lead singer for a local soul music band called The Ambassadors that had flourished in the 1960s. The group had played gigs up and down the East Coast and had not only opened shows for big name artists, but in some cases performed with them. The Ambassadors had a hit record, "Apple of My Eye," and the band's connections read like a roster of soul greats: James Brown, Johnny Taylor, the Four Tops, the Isley Brothers, the Commodores, Wilson Pickett, Otis Redding, George Clinton, Parliament, and the Funkadelics. Claude had seen the Ambassadors perform at Shelby's Holly Oak Park and remembered the pride he had felt in having two brothers up on the stage—Bobby singing lead and Billy doing backup vocals.

Waiting for the service to begin that July day in 2010, Claude London recalled the power of Bobby's voice and his charismatic personality, both of which remained strong long after the Ambassadors faded from the scene. Bobby continued singing in church choirs, weddings and other special functions. Bobby's voice also expressed itself in other ways—ringing out loud and clear. At Shelby High School football games, it boomed. Bobby was the ultimate fan of the school where the mascot was a

Golden Lion. Fans on the opposite sides of the stadium from where Bobby sat would hear his thunder-like encouragement to the home team. "That's the Pepper," they said, knowingly.

In Brown auditorium, Claude kept thinking: Bobby had left this life so quickly. His mind drifted back to childhood days when Bobby and his ten siblings grew up under the tender care of their mother, Elease. Claude loved his father, but for reasons that were never quite clear, he never came around much. The burden of raising the children fell mostly to Elease. They lived in an east Shelby neighborhood known as "Dog Alley." Times were hard but all the family members chipped in. "Mother was our strength," Claude recalled. "She taught us responsibility and love. We had to go to church and we had to go to school. Whatever gifts we have we owe to her and are grateful." Music was also a tie that bound the family together. Music seeped into their blood. Bobby embraced it with a passion that ran especially deep. Claude remembered his brothers and sisters gathering in the neighborhood to sing while little Bobby pounded away on a trash can lid like it was a drum. As Bobby got older he sang in local groups and became part of a band managed by Edgar Campbell that performed regularly at Lake Lure.

Growing up in a time of segregation Bobby attended the all-black Cleveland School where the dominant figure was legendary principal James Hoskins. For students he was a guiding light.

"He was more than a principal," Claude said. "He was like a father. Mr. Hoskins had an influence on all of us." Because of family hardships, Bobby had to leave Cleveland School for a while to help his mother. But he would eventually graduate from high school. And he would become a key member of a new local band, The Ambassadors. Bonny Clyde, the group's saxophone player, dubbed Bobby "Pepperhead" because of his spicy personality. "My brother was a bubbly person," said Claude. "He was an intense person. Something about him would draw you to him."

The Ambassadors arrived on the scene when soul music, which originated in the African American community, was gaining wide popularity through the efforts of national artists like Ben E. King, Marvin Gaye, the Temptations, and Aretha Franklin, along with the artists the Ambassadors would meet. The soul group from Shelby, North Carolina, would make their mark. They had their moment in the sun and then moved on. Following his years with the band, Bobby worked as a shipping clerk for J & C Dyeing Company for 20 years and then joined Combustion Engineering before joining Reliance Electric, later known as Balder Electric. He had planned to retire from this company. Meanwhile, he looked forward to Friday night high school football. Bobby's impassioned cheers for Shelby High not only told players how to play, but umpires how to call the game. Later, he became an official, refereeing with the North Carolina High School Athletic Association.

Church was always an important part of his life. Bobby was a devoted member of Mount Calvary Church where he sang in the all-male, adult and senior choirs. For several years, he sang with the Spartanburg Gospel Music Workshop of America Choir. And then, on July 27, 2010, it all came to an end. During Bobby's funeral, the gospel music touched Claude's heart as it stirred memories of his brother that came back in vivid flashes. And then the service was over and they took Bobby to Sunset

The tombstone for soul musician Bobby "Pepperhead" London individualized with the mascot of his favorite team, the Shelby Golden Lions. The Rev. Claude London stands in front of his brother's grave.

Cemetery. He rests under a monument with images of him as a young man and older gentleman, along with a Shelby High Golden Lion.

Also engraved on the stone are the words he wished for so many—words that so many now wished for him: "I Wanna Thank You." Fans of the Ambassadors might stop by his grave and remember his powerful voice singing lead vocal on the group's hit record: "Apple of My Eye."

Sports: The New American Religion

June: We know that Bobby "Pepperhead" London was a man of faith and an active church goer. But the words and pictures on his tombstone are a testimony to his sparkling personality, and his devotion, not to Christianity, but to the Golden Lions football team. Demonstrating allegiance to a team, athlete, or specific sport is a pattern in the newer section of Sunset Cemetery and among some of the newer graves in the older section. Sports has supplanted Christianity as the religion of Cleveland County—at least in the cemetery.

Churches in the area are still the center of social life for many people, but things have been changing over the last two or three decades. When I moved to Cleveland County in 1994, the two bits of wisdom I heard from many people were variations on one of the following:

> You can't throw a rock in Cleveland County without hitting a church.
> There are three religions in Cleveland County: the Baptist church, NASCAR, and ACC bas-ketball. And not necessarily in that order.

If religion is still important to Cleveland County, why then are religious refer-ences so much more pronounced in the older sections of Sunset than the newer?

Partly it is because nineteenth- and early twentieth-century technology made commissioning a unique tombstone too expensive for people of moderate means. As a result, memorialization in the older section of Sunset uses stock symbols that show that Christianity, specifically Protestant Christianity, was the bedrock of life for most locals. References to the departed as "asleep in Jesus" and the open gates of heaven, for example, describe beliefs held in common by the community. Tomb-stones repeat them over and over. As the historian Albert N. Hamscher points out, "cemeteries are inherently conservative places." Once a certain style becomes the norm, it tends to be replicated for decades.

An intermediate era of tombstone design that makes fewer references to reli-gion became popular in the half century between approximately 1920 and 1970. Many of these tombstones are solid blocks of granite adorned primarily with what people in the monument business call "bandaids and cabbages," a rectangular banner for the names and dates of those interred, and some rosettes (often cab-bage roses) in the corners. These stones also sometimes have standard Christian symbols such as praying hands, but they offer little information about the personal beliefs of the deceased. Like the oldest stones in the cemetery, they focus on the community rather than the individual. All that began to change in the early 1970s when advancing technology made inscribing tombstones with everything from Scrabble boards to fishing lures possible. Sandblasting secular designs on granite was certainly possible before this, but it could not achieve the detail of laser etching that allows the reproduction of photographs such as Bobby London's. And even when the technology allowed more personalized depictions of personal beliefs, organized religion did not become the usual focus.

Hamscher points out in "Pictorial Headstones: Business, Culture, and the Expression of Individuality in the Contemporary Cemetery" that the rise of very personalized tombstones with portraits of the deceased and representations of hobbies and individual interests resulted from a convergence of several historical events in the early 1970s. First, the monument industry was in a slump. In addition to the uninspiring nature of the stones from the middle decades of the twentieth century, monument companies found that new memorial parks such as Cleveland Memorial Park in Boiling Springs, a few miles from Shelby, and the increasing popularity of cremation were threatening their businesses. These memorial parks are commercially owned by companies such as Service Corporation International (SCI), and, unlike church or municipal cemeteries, they are driven by profit.

As a result, in an effort to squeeze in as many bodies as possible, the graves are not necessarily arranged with the traditional east/west orientation. Memorial parks also allow only small, inconspicuous markers that simplify mowing the grass but generate little income for monument companies. And at the same time memorial parks were becoming popular, an increased acceptance of cremation reduced the demand for grave plots and tombstones altogether as many families opted for spreading ashes at places of emotional significance or placing them in columbariums, which memorial parks conveniently provided.

The technology for producing truly personalized tombstones could not have come at a better time from the standpoint of monument dealers, whose conventions and trade magazines such as *Monument Builders News* and *Stone in America* promoted revitalizing the industry by selling individualization to their customers. These choices became increasingly popular among Baby Boomers, who tended to reject the boring, stodgy tombstones of their parents' generation just as they rejected their military-style hairstyles and Bing-Crosby-era music. Hamscher quotes John Diannis, executive vice president of the Monument Builders of North America, who wrote in 1976 that the technology of his time "tends to reduce everyone to a set of numbers: social security numbers, bank account numbers, charge card numbers, zip codes, the numbers go on and on. There is a de-personalizing effect in all of this." One way to combat being turned into a number is to emphasize one's individuality.

Hamscher also sees the early twentieth century as a time when leisure activities became more important than work. He speculates that, as a result, sports symbols displaced religious symbols in the cemetery. But I think it's more than that. From what I have seen in Sunset and other cemeteries from coast to coast in the United States of America, it's not just a matter of one symbol displacing the other. It's looking more and more as if one religion is replacing another.

Church attendance in Cleveland County is declining in many of the long-established churches, mirroring a nationwide trend. According to the Pew Research Center, in "telephone surveys conducted in 2018 and 2019, 65% of American adults describe themselves as Christians when asked about their religion, down 12 percentage points over the past decade. Meanwhile, the religiously unaffiliated share of the population, consisting of people who describe their religious identity as atheist, agnostic or 'nothing in particular,' now stands at 26%, up from 17% in 2009." Attendance at live or virtual sporting events, meanwhile, is booming. It's not hard to figure out why. Religion in America has increasingly been a divisive factor in American culture, particularly since evangelical support helped send Donald Trump to the White House in 2016. At the same time, doctrinal religion can seem out of touch, too obsessed with the hereafter to be of use in the here and now.

"Real" life, meanwhile, is increasingly digital, especially for Generation Z, the young people born in 1995 and later. According to sources such as Corey Seemiller and Meghan Grace's *Generation Z Goes to College*, they now comprise about 25 percent of the population, our largest cohort, and they live in a phigital world, one in which the boundary between physical and digital spaces is blurred. They are likely to describe themselves as "spiritual" but not "religious." Studies show that their attention span is about eight seconds, the length of time it takes to watch an Instagram video. They are continually sleep deprived because they stay up late, even wake up in the night to check their phones. Their parents are little better.

In a world of harried and sleep-deprived people, sports is pure pleasure. It doesn't require dressing up and getting up early on Sunday. Games can be enjoyed entirely online while scrolling through social media, texting, and pursuing the intoxication of click bait. It is available in bite-sized chunks, and its demands

A tombstone celebrating a "Home Run to Heaven" reflects the conflation of sports and religion in Cleveland County and across the nation.

The Carl Love stone shows the young man dressed in Crest High School colors scoring a touchdown, an apt metaphor for earning a heavenly reward.

for time and money can be ignored guilt free. More than that, sports offer everything that makes religion appealing without the downsides: a sense of belonging to a group of like-minded people, history and traditions to treasure, creeds that promote ethics such as fair play and hard work, thrilling rituals, moments of transcendent bliss, even approved ritual garments and music. Is it any wonder that the new parts of Sunset have tombstones with epitaphs such as "Home Run to Heaven" and scenes that show a Crest High School football player scoring a touchdown?

Sports even provide saints to emulate and worship. One unfortunate loss as a result of the Protestant Reformation was the demotion of saints back to the realm of the ordinary. In the Catholic tradition, only those capable of superhuman endurance and the ability to work miracles become saints. Protestants decided all Christians could be called "saints," which stripped the word of its glory. We still need our heroes. In Cleveland County, North Carolina, those heroes could be NASCAR stars. One footstone in the newer section of Sunset boasts a car labeled with the number 3 for the late Dale Earnhardt and the words "Victory Lap to Heaven." Several years ago, the novelist Sharyn McCrumb visited Sunset Cemetery and was delighted to find this small stone. At that time her latest novel was nearly finished. It was a modernized version of Geoffrey Chaucer's *The Canterbury Tales*. Chaucer's work is a collection of tales told by pilgrims traveling from London to Canterbury to visit the grave of St. Thomas Becket. McCrumb borrows Chaucer's frame story but changes the pilgrimage so that the travelers are visiting racetracks and other locations significant to the life of the Dale Earnhardt via a chartered bus driven by

James Price, shown here with his "muscle car." The stone reflects both the personality of the man memorialized and the importance of sports in Cleveland County culture.

The front of the James Price stone includes a ceramic portrait of Mr. Price and an evocation of family solidarity. Many stones in the newer section of Sunset Cemetery incorporate laser-etched portraits on the memorials in keeping with the focus on individuality celebrated in modern cemeteries.

a former NASCAR driver. Along the way, each pilgrim experiences a life-changing miracle. Is it any wonder that Sharyn McCrumb titled her novel *St. Dale*?

From a singer who was the Golden Lions most enthusiastic fan to the man who loved muscle cars, sports has become the way to both personalize the individual and create communities of memory. Tombstones with sports icons suggest that sports has taken on the purest functions of religion.

IX

Ministers to Body, Mind, and Soul

Henry Beckham "Beck" Quinn (1854–1924)

Joe: Beck Quinn—a Shelby landmark and legendary keeper of the lithia water Fountain of Youth—almost became a permanent resident of Sunset Cemetery one June morning in 1922. His Ford automobile came in close contact with a Southern Railway train and he narrowly escaped with his life.

The *Cleveland Star* reported that Beck thought he had cleared the railroad track, "but there was a man standing just in his way and thus trying to avoid the man he did not succeed in getting quite far enough from the track. The train stuck the rear end of the car, tore one of the fenders off, demolished a tire and a number of other minor injuries to the Ford, but he himself miraculously escaped unhurt."

Beck, a true town character well known all over North Carolina, was lucky that day. But the tide shifted, and on April 12, 1924, it bore him to Shelby's Silent City. The *Raleigh News & Observer* wrote that the 69-year-old Beck had died at his home on East Graham Street following "a protracted illness of asthma. The funeral services were conducted today by Rev. W.A. Murray, pastor of the Presbyterian Church, and interment was in Sunset Cemetery." "Uncle Beck Quinn Passes to His Reward" read a headline in the *Charlotte Observer*, adding the deceased "Was One of a Quintet of Unusual Characters Who Have Resided in Shelby." The *Observer*'s story noted that "Few people every visited Shelby without being drawn to the famed court square with its inviting lawns and stately trees and the majority of those have seen 'Uncle Beck' for he and his fountain house of lithia water and personal wit were part of the court square."

Beck owned Lithia Spring three miles north of town and piped the all-healing elixir to the court square, where he sold it for a penny a shot. "The source of the 'lift,'" the *Charlotte Observer* wrote,

> being a self-operating chain and bucket pump, the only one of its kind in operation in America. It was invented by a South Carolinian before the war and has been in faithful operation ever since. It works on the counterbalance principle. One bucket that was being filled at the spring below, which emptied the mineral water into a reservoir, was in turn filled with branch water to bring another bucket up from the spring.

Customers also got generous doses of his quaint wit. Shelby in the 1920s was still known as the City of Springs for its profusion of so-called healing mineral waters.

177

Most notable was Cleveland Springs, two miles east of the square. It had been a popular watering hole since at least the 1850s, and by the time of Beck's death, a third resort hotel was operating at the site.

The sulfurous tasting lithia water had been commercially bottled in America since 1888. But natural lithia springs were rare—and Lithia Springs of Shelby, North Carolina, was one of them. The alleged medicinal benefits were many—some people swore by the water; others ignored it. An advertisement in a February 1920 issue of the *Cleveland Star* stated: "STOP YOUR KIDNEYS AND BACK from giving you so much pain. You are gradually drifting into Bright's disease. Shelby Lithia Water will do the work. Nature's remedy only $1.00 for 5 gallons delivered to your home."

Beck's friend, *Charlotte Observer* editor Wade Harris, had written a series of sketches about some of Shelby's unusual characters. There was the Mill Man (J.C. Smith); the Drummer (Joe Baber); the Norwegian (T.W. Ebeltoft); the Major (S.J. Green); and The Water Man, Uncle Beck Quinn.

"Mr. Quinn was one man who stood in the love and affection of all the people of the town, with men and women and children alike, of all colors," Harris wrote in the *Charlotte Observer*. "He was a landmark whose removal will be of remark by the pilgrims to the city of mineral waters."

Beck was the son of Mr. and Mrs. Anonymous Quinn. According to family history, Beck's father didn't like his birth name, Aaron, and had changed it to Anonymous.

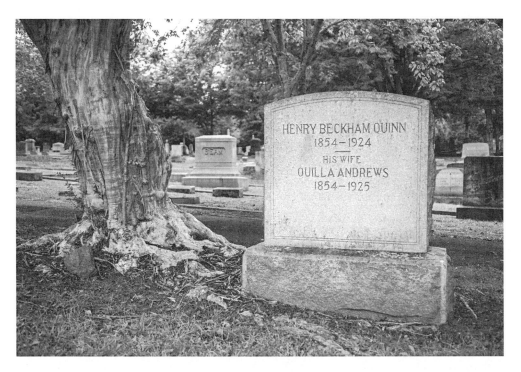

The plain granite stone for George Beckham "Uncle Beck" Quinn tells only his name and dates and those of his wife. The stone does nothing to reveal the personality of one of the most colorful characters in Shelby history. Mr. Quinn sold lithia water, a heralded elixir, from his spring for a penny a shot and dispensed homespun advice and tales along with the medicinal water.

A Civil War veteran, Anonymous Quinn was a tailor by trade and so was a brother, Stanford Montgomery Quinn, who left Shelby for the California Gold Rush in 1849, stayed two years, then came home. He died in 1854, and rests in Sunset Cemetery.

The *Charlotte Observer* called Beck Quinn's fountain on the court square "a gathering place for the retired and leisure class—the old fellows who start interesting stories with 'When I was a boy.'" The paper called Beck "the chief entertainer." By April 1924, Beck had told his last story on the court square and joined his kinfolk in Sunset Cemetery, where no doubt the storytelling, continued.

George Smyrnois (1888–1929)

February 19, 1929: Newspapers carried stories about president-elect Herbert Hoover's arrival in Washington by train from his Miami vacation home two weeks prior to his inauguration. The Associated Press also reported the soon-to-be Commander-in-Chief had a fondness for pies and that it made no difference what kind—cherry, custard or apple—just so long as it was pie. Some movie theaters were rerunning the silent epic *Wings* with Charles "Buddy" Rogers, Gary Cooper, and Clara Bow, which would win the first Academy Award that year. In the Shelby Hospital, Greek immigrant George Smyrnois was probably in no mood to follow current news events. As the *Cleveland Star* later reported, he was likely having a disturbing premonition. Smyrnois, 38, had told friends before he checked into the hospital for a routine procedure that in case anything went wrong and he didn't make it, he wanted them to make sure one thing happened after his demise. He was the owner and operator of The Chocolate Shop on South Lafayette Street in Shelby, a popular teenage hangout. Smyrnois wanted the Sunset-Cemetery-bound hearse to pause in front of The Chocolate Shop so customers could wave goodbye. The request might have struck friends as a little farfetched but as things turned out, George was right. He died on February 20, 1929, following an operation for what may have been a ruptured appendix. Two days later, a Palmer Mortuary hearse stopped in front of The Chocolate Shop, where bystanders bid a brief farewell to the proprietor.

George, who was single, got a substantial grave marker with a Masonic symbol embedded in the stone. Thus ended the Chocolate Shop era. Teenagers grew up, the Great Depression settled in, newspapers chronicled the rise of fascism in Europe. Shelby residents had many things on their minds other than the native of Greece who had come their way back in the 1920s. But a few around town probably heard about the will George Smyrnois had made out in February 1928, a year to the month before he died. He wanted a decent burial suitable to the wishes of his friends and relatives. George then bequeathed to his friend, local businessman Enos Beam, all of George's equipment in the store and all personal belongings located in the Beam Building on Lafayette Street. That included furniture and household items in the room George occupied in the nearby Fanning Building. He asked that after items were sold to cover any debts, the remaining funds be sent to George's parents, Mr. and Mrs. Eloolans Smyrnois in Georgitsi, State of Sparta, Greece. The *Cleveland Star* reported that Beam was proud of the fact that generations of his family members had been Masons. So it's

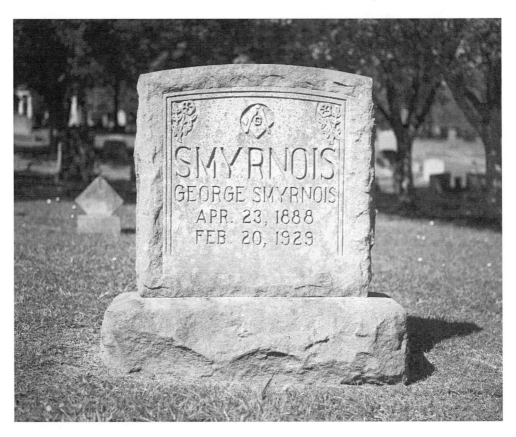

The beautifully carved George Smyrnois stone includes a Masonic symbol but does not reveal
that he owned The Chocolate Shop, a teen hangout. Having a premonition of his impending
death, Smyrnois, a Greek immigrant, asked that his hearse pass the shop on the way to Sunset
so that his customers could wave good-bye.

likely he welcomed George into the local lodge and saw to it the Masonic symbol got
on the gravestone.

So George, a native of Greece, rested in Sunset Cemetery, far from his own kin
but probably close to at least a few of the friends he had furnished a little joy in the
days of their youth at The Chocolate Shop.

The Rev. Hilary Thomas Hudson (1823–1892)
Dr. Joseph "Joe" MacDonald Reeves (1929–2015)

Rev. Hudson

They were both farm boys—one in the nineteenth century, the other in the twentieth, and they shared a love of books and learning. Both would become Methodist
ministers whose career paths would eventually lead them to pastor the same church
in Shelby. And, at the end of their lives, they both went to Sunset Cemetery.

A native of Davie County, Hilary Hudson was only five years old when his father died. The boy worked on the farm until he was 19 and then was apprenticed to a carriage builder. When Hudson died in 1892, his obituary in the *Raleigh Christian Advocate* described how hard he had studied on the side while working in the carriage trade. His diligent habits opened doors for him to attend an academy run by the Rev. Baxter Clegg in the county seat of Mocksville. This hard-working student who made excellent grades gained the attention of the right people. After Hudson finished the academy, friends helped him get into Randolph-Macon College in Ashland, Virginia. According to the *Christian Advocate*, he didn't have the means to finish the college courses and was forced to leave.

Next began his stint as a teacher, holding classes in a little school at Snow Creek in Iredell County. While there, he was licensed to preach. In 1851, Hudson joined the North Carolina Methodist Conference in Salisbury and was ordained as a deacon in 1853. Four years later, the brilliant young man was ordained an Elder. His assignments as a pastor took him all over North Carolina, from Washington, Salisbury, Hillsboro, Chapel Hill and Greensboro, to Fayetteville, Raleigh, Warrenton, Wilson, and, in 1874, to the Shelby Methodist Church.

Early on, Hudson had made a name for himself with his writing talent. At the *Raleigh Christian Advocate* he served as editor, associate editor, and corresponding editor. Right after the Civil War, when the paper's mounting debts spelled certain ruin, Hudson stepped up and bid on it from his private funds, saving the *Advocate* at the last minute. The owners never forgot that generous act. That same year, in 1868, Hudson's first wife Hattie Cole died in Raleigh. Their son, H.T. Jr., would grow up and become a practicing attorney in Shelby.

In 1872, H.T. Sr., married Mary Taylor Lee of Mecklenburg County. Their daughter, Vernia Lee Hudson, was born in 1877. A prolific writer, Hudson turned out books with titles like *The Methodist Armor*, *The Shield of the Young Methodist*, *The Prohibition Trumpet*, *Children's Lamp*, *The Red Dragon*, and *The Sun Clad Woman*. In 1883, the *Christian Advocate* gave its blessing to *The Methodist Armor* when it appeared that year. The book had received high praise "from our religious periodicals and is, we think, calculated to accomplish much good. It is published at our Publishing House in Nashville and is a credit to the House, as well. We predict for it a large sale and shall rejoice to see it in every Methodist family, believing it to be full of such information as is greatly needed." The *Advocate* urged its readers to buy and read the book.

Tragedy struck the Hudson family in 1877 while they were in Shelby, living in a residence on North Lafayette Street. Hudson and his wife, Mary, grieved over the loss of their eight-year-old daughter, Vernia. But the preacher continued his demanding schedule—more sermons, more books—always busy doing more of the Lord's work. By the summer of 1892, things were catching up with him. The *Advocate*, which regularly informed readers on the latest about the Reverend Hudson, reported on June 8 that he had been "suffering from la grippe, nervousness, insomnia and melancholy, together with over work in preparing another book for the press." He had improved, the paper went on, "and there is now hope that he will soon recover his usual health. He is one of the best men and has one of the finest minds, in some respects, in the state. We are rejoicing to learn that he is improving and hope he will soon be himself again."

But the rejoicing was short lived. On June 20, Hudson died unexpectedly in Morganton. "We cannot find words to express our high esteem for the character of Dr. Hudson," the *Advocate* wrote. "He was one of the loveliest characters and beautiful lives we've ever beheld." The preacher joined his daughter, Vernia in Sunset Cemetery. Mary came in 1915 and H.T. Jr., in 1925. All resting in a Victorian family plot surrounded by a substantial iron fence. A family together again.

Dr. Reeves

From the pulpit of Central United Methodist Church in Shelby, Senior Pastor Joe Reeves eulogized the recently deceased and framed their passage with appropriate spiritual context. Many were bound for burial in Sunset Cemetery, a spot where Joe himself would eventually rest.

When he died in 2015, a family member wrote an eloquent obituary that encapsulated the life of this dedicated man of God. He hailed from the North Carolina Mountains, one of eleven children farming the hillsides of the Walnut community in Madison County. "Joe Reeves

The stone for the Rev. H.T. Hudson, pastor of Central United Methodist Church, is a handsome marble monument with a neoclassical urn on top. It also memorializes his wife, Mary Taylor Lee Hudson, and his daughter, Vernia. All three lie in a fenced family plot. The Rev. Hudson's epitaph is an allusion to Gen. 5:24, which describes Enoch, who "walked with God."

divided his boyhood between the potato patch and the baseball diamond," the obituary stated, "stealing minutes from both to read as much as he could, especially when mountain rains left fields too wet to farm and second base too wet to field."

After serving in the U.S. Air Force with a tour in Korea, young Joe returned to the family farm in Madison County, plowing hillsides with two mules. One August afternoon as the sun beat down, Joe answered the call to preach and "traded the plow for the pulpit," his obituary noted. That call would lead him to nearby Mars Hill College and later the University of Tennessee and Duke Divinity School. He then launched a 40-year career as a minister with the United Methodist Church Western North Carolina Conference. He later earned a Doctor of Divinity from Drew University.

While at Duke, Joe met his wife, Betty Proctor of Olanta, South Carolina. They were married 54 years and had two sons, Stack and Shawn. Joe served pastorates in Charlotte, Elkin and Monroe. He was senior pastor at Central United Methodist Church in Shelby for seven years in the 1980s. Mariel Camp who, along with her late husband Tom Camp, has been a member of Central United Methodist Church for 50 years, said it was hard to describe Joe Reeves. "Joe was a wonderful preacher, whose deep, mellow voice had a certain cadence that pulled you into the narrative," she said, continuing,

> He was always there when a family needed him, even at 5 a.m. at the hospital with a child facing surgery. When he read a book, he understood the message and could explain in two sentences what the author took 300 pages to say. Somehow he had absorbed the deep peace of his beloved mountain farm where he grew up. He loved the people of his church, and they loved him back, and they would have kept him forever if the Methodist Church allowed it. To him,

The marker for the Rev. Joseph MacDonald "Joe" Reeves memorializes the beloved pastor of Central United Methodist Church of Shelby. The grave is recent enough to be marked as well by the small portable marker with a picture of the Rev. Reeves left by the funeral home. Many modern gravesites in Sunset retain these funeral home markers as long as possible.

The Methodist clergy emblem on the Rev. Joe Reeves' grave is a small bronze plaque with an image of the iconic Methodist circuit rider. The circuit rider served several different congregations, riding from one to another on a horse, especially during frontier days. Circuit riders are credited with spreading Methodism throughout the United States.

the church was all about people, and he would have willingly skipped all the meetings and conferences (and sometimes did). It wasn't that he talked a lot; in fact, his main strength was listening, really listening. The words "dignity," "gravitas," and "humility" don't do him justice, but they come close.

In 2004, women of the church put up money to print a soft-cover book of their pastor's prayers, which Camp edited. In the introduction to *Joe's Prayers*, the pastor wrote that

Conversations with God was an agreeable way to characterize what I attempt to do in prayer. For we do not pray, do we, with any expectation of changing God's mind about anything? We might want to do that sometimes, when we are aware that God knows us and loves us and understands our yearnings of the moment. Not to change God's mind but to adapt our own desires to God's will is our desire, in a trust that we are indeed loved by the One who will use our willingness to accomplish his own purpose.

A United Methodist Church clergy emblem went on Joe's stone in Sunset Cemetery. The image of an itinerant preacher on horseback was appropriate for a mountain boy who had traded the plow for the pulpit and shared with these early traveling ministers qualities of self-sacrifice, dedication, and hard work.

Theodore William Ebeltoft (1849–1932)

A fire alarm sounded in downtown Shelby at 5:00 that morning in January 1901, and T.W. Ebeltoft had set it off. A crowd quickly gathered on the square to watch as an entire block flamed up. Firefighting efforts were futile. Afterwards, when officials assessed the extensive damages, T.W.'s grocery/book store was considered a total loss. The *Charlotte Observer*'s account of the devastating fire listed property owners' names and the amount of their insurance. None of them except T.W had full coverage. He started over from the ashes and soon returned to his role as Shelby's revered sage.

Shelby and T.W. hadn't taken long to bond when he had arrived there as a new-comer about ten years before the fire. Word spread about this curious but enormously likeable man suddenly in their midst, running a combination grocery, confectionary and book store, the only one in town. "Food for the body, food for the soul" might have been T.W.'s mantra. The more folks knew about him, the more they may have thought of T.W. as a character from some Dickensian novel full of interesting characters. Born in Mobile, Alabama, to a father from Norway and mother from Georgia, T.W. grew up to become a Baptist minister. Sometime in the 1880s, he married Lila Springs, a member of the prominent Springs family of Charlotte. (Her father, Capt. John M. Springs, had manufactured Confederate uniforms during the Civil War.)

The Ebeltofts were living in Fayetteville when T.W. decided to retire from the pulpit and start a new chapter in his life "on the score of health preservation," the *Charlotte Observer* reported in 1932 when T.W. died. His death certificate listed kidney disease as the cause, and T.W. may have selected Shelby as his new home because of the town's famous lithia water, which many considered beneficial for kidney problems. At any rate, T.W. and Lila came to Shelby and moved into the former Eli Fulenwider residence on South Washington Street. Built in the 1850s, the two-story, white frame house had been home to Swiss pioneer Eli Fulenwider, a member of a family in the iron works business. T.W. opened his business on the court square and became known around town by some as "the Norwegian" because of his ancestry. When customers lingered to talk with the former preacher, they noticed that he listened like he really cared about what they had to say. And as he spoke to them about any subject, people were likely amazed at the depth of his knowledge.

The newcomer wasn't passive about Shelby, and T.W. became involved in the community, serving as treasurer for the school system and even becoming part owner of the local newspaper, the *Cleveland Star*. During World War I, he helped sell war bonds. "The Norwegian" was not only popular locally but somewhat of a celebrity statewide through sketches written by *Charlotte Observer* editor Wade Harris, who was married to T.W.'s sister. (Liza Ebelfoft's comings and goings were regularly reported in the *Star* and *Observer*.)

The *Observer*'s obituary for T.W. called him "a community personality that had been identified with the daily affairs of the town for many years and one who had made for himself a warm place in the neighborly hearts." When he had arrived from Fayetteville "to take up commercial occupation at Shelby.... He was quickly recognized by the people of that community as a man of fine intellectual attainments, a finished scholar and a man of brilliant man." According to the *Observer*, T.W. was nothing less than the Town Authority: "People would go to him for information on any subject as they would go to a Carnegie Library. When any matter of public concern disturbed, it was the custom of 'go to Ebeltoft—he knows.'" Down at the court square grocery/book shop, T.W. may have met youngsters like O. Max Gardner and Clyde Roark Hoey, future governors of North Carolina.

T.W. probably sold controversial bestsellers written by Shelby's own Thomas Dixon, Jr. Dixon may have even shopped there on visits to his hometown. By then he lived in New York City and in 1915 had a home in Los Angeles, where he worked with the director who was making the silent film epic *Birth of a Nation*, based on Dixon's novels *The Leopard's Spots* and *The Clansmen*. And surely T.W.'s book shop would have stocked the 1923 memoir *Thirty-one Years of Genteel Vagabonding by an Old Shelby Boy, an Erratic Romancer*, written by Henry Fullenwider. According to the *Cleveland Star*, which ran an installment, the book would appear under the name of John Robyn, "the stage name of Mr. Fullenwider … a great showman who delighted thousands in his travels over the United States playing in school houses as well as the big theaters of the country."

The *Star* called the current installment one "especially interesting to Shelby and Cleveland County people since it contains twits on people he [Fullenwider] recalls to mind so clearly." Here was a roll call of outstanding local folks, alive and deceased, T.W. could have known from firsthand experience or may have just heard about. They may have marched through the Norwegian's imagination as he read Fullenwider's "twits about this cast of Shelby characters":

> Departed, Robert M. Miller. The noblest Roman of them all.
> William P. Love. Southern gentleman of the old school.
> Jake W. Rudasill, now of Texas. Self-trained, his riches self-gained. A jovial,
>   most excellent man. Howdy, Jake.
> The late Chevis Froneberger. Who had tons of ringing good metal in him that
>   some failed to grasp.
> My erstwhile friend and playfellow Lee Rudasill. I know not where he is, but I
>   hear he still eats and lives at Easy Town.
> Harve Cabaniss. A clever lawyer, gentleman. Boys, get the rabbits.
> The late old Dr. Williams. Jocular and old-time baby catcher.
> C.R. Hoey, Attorney, orator and man of affairs.
> Editor Lee B. Weathers. Who has worked head and pen for transmuting failure
>   to success and sorry things to glad ones.

A Shelby book written by a Shelby native with a sense of humor and a sense of the past would probably have appealed to The Norwegian. As the years had passed, the rhythm of his life was fine-tuned there at the grocery/book store and his South Washington Street home. He and Lila welcomed their daughter, Elizabeth, who was born March 9, 1890. T.W.'s health issue wasn't mentioned in a July 16, 1902, item in the *Cleveland Star* but most Shelby readers probably knew it was there: "T.W. Ebeltoft is spending this week at Blowing Rock with his friend, Prof. S.G. Hardin. He is greatly missed in Shelby for it is so seldom that he leaves. All his friends will wish him a pleasant stay in the mountains."

Eight years after the Blowing Rock trip, T.W., and his wife welcomed guests to their home in Shelby. The *Star* duly noted the visit with this item: "Editor Wade Harris of The Charlotte Observer, Mrs. Harris and charming daughter, Miss Antoinette and Mrs. Springs of Charlotte motored to Shelby Sunday and were distinguished guests at their kinswoman's, Mrs. T.W. Ebeltoft. They were accompanied home by Miss Elizabeth Ebeltoft who will remain in Charlotte until this afternoon. Col. Harris is a great admirer of Shelby and the Shelby people and he spent a most enjoyable day here chatting with his numerous friends."

The numerous friends of T.W. continued to enjoy his company for slightly more than a decade. Then, on April 1, 1932, he passed on, going to Sunset Cemetery where his wife would join him in 1954 and their daughter join their parents in 1980. T.W.'s obituary in the *Charlotte Observer* noted that he had died "with the love and admiration of the entire town." The Town Authority had started yet another new chapter: holding court with old friends surrounding him in Sunset.

Cemeteries as Museums

June: Cemeteries and graveyards are open-air museums. They are more than collections of historical artifacts, and more than collections of art, though. They are, as the word "museum" suggests, places to muse—to ponder the mysteries of life and death and the way human beings create memories. They prompt questions and spur investigation. They can both comfort and trouble visitors. When people who love cemeteries choose them for strolls and recreation, they usually seek more than a pleasant place for a walk. They choose to spend time in places other folks avoid because cemetery lovers understand that the history of the culture is embedded in the most literal way in its graveyards and that contemplating mortality is the surest path to appreciating how precious life is. As with any museum visit, it can be a solo experience or one enjoyed with like-minded friends.

We have been asked how we chose the tales and tombstones discussed in this book. Some of the choices were easy. Joe DePriest had been wandering in Sunset and soaking up the stories of local characters like Uncle Beck Quinn and George Smyrnois all his life. His many decades as a journalist led to deep research into the lives of everyone from notorious outlaws to governors of North Carolina. And since he never meets a stranger, every phone call or interview or email exchange in the process turned into a friendship that led to new information. I, on the other hand, followed a more academic pathway in choosing the tombstones and details of cemetery design and American deathways I wanted to write about.

I was finishing a book on American women's hymns when I came to Cleveland County in 1994. Soon after, I spent a beautiful autumn afternoon touring Sunset Cemetery with a guide from the Historic Shelby Foundation. However, I stopped listening to the guide's words when we came to the Hudson family plot and I saw a stanza of Fanny Crosby's 1869 hymn "Safe in the Arms of Jesus" on a tombstone. I had been writing about that very hymn, and seeing it on a tombstone led to an epiphany: the culture that produced the hymn also produced that tombstone. The insight changed my life. I began haunting Sunset looking for hymns and icons such as "the gates ajar" and hands with fingers pointing to heaven that clearly related to the nineteenth-century American women's culture with which I was obsessed.

And then Joe and I met in June of 2019, when the Association for Gravestone Studies held its annual conference at nearby Gardner-Webb University. I was there for the lectures and as co-chair of the conference. Joe came for the conservation workshop at Sunset. Once we became acquainted, we began strolling Sunset together. Many of the tales and tombstones come from those walks when we spotted something of interest that led to research. The Bonnie Wright story is a good example. Sunset Cemetery is like a museum with hidden rooms and works of genius by artists whose work is just waiting to be discovered. We turned right one chilly November day when we would ordinarily have turned left and found Sgt. Wright's tombstone. A U.S. Army veteran himself, Joe immediately connected with another military man. He noticed that Sgt. Wright was a paratrooper who died in service to his country during World War II and began to muse about the stories he could have told.

I, on the other hand, was intrigued by the ceramic miniature of Bonnie Wright. What a handsome man! I had seen similar ceramic plaques on a few other tombstones in that section of Sunset. Affixing a ceramic portrait of the deceased to a tombstone was clearly a strategy used in the transitional time between the era when only the rich could afford to commission statues or bas-relief carvings on tombstones and the era of the late-twentieth and early twenty-first centuries when laser etching made portraits available to everyone. The plaque invited me to muse on the life of the man pictured there and to ponder how miniaturization affects the creation of memory. I also began wondering how that stone came to be in Sunset Cemetery. What path did Bonnie Wright's body follow before reaching this final resting place?

All of this musing led to investigation. Joe found an obituary for Sgt. Wright and the names of some of his descendants. I thought they sounded familiar and mentioned them one evening at a handbell choir rehearsal at my church in Boiling Springs. Another member of the group was a distant cousin—and he gave me the phone number for one of Wright's granddaughters. Joe contacted her, and the next thing we knew, we were interviewing people who could tell us all about Bonnie Wright and show us memorabilia carefully preserved by his family. I followed up by connecting the portrait on the stone to one on a more recent memorial in the newer part of Sunset. I also researched the process of repatriation for an American soldier who died overseas. Musing led to investigation and to more musing and, eventually, to two pieces of writing about Sgt. Bonnie Wright. The process was never systematic, which was part of its charm.

Anyone who loves cemeteries and tombstones and the rich history of humankind they preserve knows what it is like to find someone with the same interest. New England, with its rich trove of colonial gravestones was the site of the first effort to bring gravestone scholars together. According to Allan I. Ludwig in *Graven*

Images: New England Stonecarving and Its Symbols, 1650–1815, Peter Benes organized "a conference on gravestone carving called The Dublin [New Hampshire] Seminar, which took place in 1976." This group of scholars shared papers on their common interest in tombstones that year, and then the conference morphed into two groups with similar interests. The Dublin Seminar for New England Folklife continues, according to its website, to promote the study of all kinds of material and non-material cultural, including topics such as meeting houses, toys and games, and disability in the early centuries of New England life. Boston University published the papers from the first Dublin Seminar in 1977, and the Association for Gravestone Studies was formed that year as a separate organization for what Ludwig calls "all those people who had fallen hopelessly in love with old gravestones."

Today, the Association for Gravestone Studies (AGS) is an international organization with conferences each year in venues that range all over the United States and Canada. Participants come from Australia, New Zealand, the UK, Japan, and other countries in addition to every state in the union to share their research and "muse" with others in the open-air museums we call graveyards and cemeteries. One of the most notable features of those who study gravestones is their sheer diversity. It's been that way from the beginning. William E. Harding, for example, was a fourth-year medical student in 1976, when he gave his paper at the Dublin Seminar on a New England carver's shop: "Zerubbabel Collins' Successor and His Work in Bennington County, Vermont." Laurel K. Gabel, a research nurse and another important gravestone scholar, claims she was just "a housewife" when she attended her first AGS meeting in 1980.

In addition to academics in fields across the spectrum from art history to sociology to American studies to education, the organization today includes public historians, businessmen and women, a mathematician, an art librarian, museum directors, and a rabbi who is also a scientist and an Alpine ski instructor. Members associated with the National Park Service and with private restoration businesses conduct a conservation workshop each year in addition to the formal lectures, workshops, and tours that occur during the conference. In short, the Association for Gravestone Studies is like a well-functioning church whose members are very different and sometimes disagree but who are united by a common commitment. Laurel Gabel says that today she remembers only one paper from her first conference, "but it was the people!, the vibrating current of inspiration!, the subject itself! that sparked [her] obsession."

Spending time in cemeteries with like-minded people has sparked that obsession for many of us. I will never forget my first AGS conference at George Mason University in 1999. I had fallen in love with Sunset Cemetery and with the cultural markers I found in it, and I submitted a paper proposal shortly after finding AGS online. My acceptance was handwritten by Barbara Rotundo, another great gravestone scholar who served that year as the lecture chair. Her note chided me for addressing her as "Dr. Rotundo" because "we do not stand on formalities in AGS." She also warned me not to go over my twenty-minute time limit lest I court swift embarrassment at her hands. I traveled to Fairfax, Virginia, alone, knowing absolutely no one who would be there. I have never been so excited! Up until that point, I thought I might be the only one on earth with this particular passion.

When I checked in at the conference, I was directed to a room where people were gathering for snacks and fellowship. I immediately spotted two women sharing stacks of photographs, laughing and exclaiming over each one. They looked safe and approachable, and I thought they might be comparing pictures of their children or grandchildren. They were, I learned later, Laurel Gable, the woman I now think of as the greatest living gravestone scholar, and Jessie Lie Farber, the first editor of the AGS journal *Markers*. And they weren't trading photos of their grandchildren. The pictures were of tombstones. I knew I had come home. I had found my tribe.

X

Garden of the Enslaved

The "Colored Cemetery"

Joe: This is the barren ground. Enslaved persons rest here, their graves marked only by faint imprints in the ground. Anonymous souls lying forgotten on a slope beside white folks' markers. Little documentation about this section of Sunset Cemetery has come to light; oral tradition identifies it as a place for slaves and paupers.

Enslaved African-Americans were chattel, bought and sold on the Cleveland County court square like cattle or pigs. Their life stories are buried with them at Sunset Cemetery. Yet sometimes they seem to sing out across time: Anthems lifted up in the fetid holds of slave ships on the Middle Passage; chants shouted in scorching plantation fields; or fervent gospel pleadings to the Almighty.

Slave records in Sunset Cemetery are meager. But there are fleeting glimpses of what their lives were like in early Cleveland County court minutes and other official documents, along with newspaper notices. This item from December 1847 is typical: "NOTICE: There will be sold at the Court House in SHELBY on Saturday, the 1st day of January, next, on a credit of 12 months, TWELVE LIVELY NEGROES, belonging to the estate of Thomas Roberts, deceased. This December. J.M. Roberts Administrator." In the slave trade, use of the word "lively" meant the merchandise was attractive. So is the man described in this notice, from December 16, 1848:

RUNAWAY NEGRO. Ran away from William J. Johnson, living in Perry County, Alabama, on the 26th of April last, a negro man named TOM, of dark brown complexion, and long bushy hair and a heavy beard—low set, 30 or 35 years of age, weight 135 or 140 pounds; his two front teeth are large and twisted inwards. He wore off a Panama hat, brown coat with brass buttons, and striped pant.

He was owned by Mr. Baily of Cleveland County, N.C. and taken to Alabama by Andrew Hoyle of Hoylesville. As he had a wife at Squire Roberts', near Mr. Baily's in Cleveland County, he is, in all probability, making his way back to Cleveland County. He has been accustomed to work at gold mines and iron works. A reward of $100 has been offered for recovery of the negro.

In the spring of 1860, the *Yorkville* (SC) *Enquirer* announced the sale of 22 "lively Negroes" belonging to the estate of D. Birchett, who had lived in Cleveland County, North Carolina.

Bidding would take place on the square in Shelby. The lineup included: four men and seven boys—five women and six girls. Only one man was over 35 years of age, and only one woman over 28 years old. Of the boys and girls, nine were ages five to 13 years. Sold on a credit of six months.

The segregated "colored cemetery," where enslaved people and others were buried, on the west end of Sunset Cemetery. No markers yet remain in this large "empty" field although a WPA worker in 1939 estimated that the area holds around 300 graves.

A Cleveland County court matter-of-factly approved a list of deeded property businessman A.R. Homesley was to receive: a horse, bridle, saddle, three beds, a walnut sideboard and three Negroes—Jacob, Linna along with her child. Fendal Whitworth got a sorrel mare, road wagon, 30 head of hogs, 18 of sheep, and 14 of cattle, along with assorted household furniture and tools. And "ten Negroes." They were listed, and all their ages were approximate: Tobb, 36, Adam, 19, Esther, 17, Jacob, 13, Ben, 11, Titus 9, Vicy Ann, 2, Ann, 32, Milly Ann, 8 and Standford, 3.

Buying and selling enslaved persons: business as usual in the ante-bellum South. So were the county-appointed patrols. Like jury duty, every citizen had to serve from time to time. The patrols were organized because whites feared revolts and uprisings among enslaved persons. As patrols rode horseback around Cleveland County, they checked the passes of black people roaming the countryside. Some produced passes written by their masters and were told to be on their way. Free black people also had to show their papers. Black people who couldn't produce a pass faced severe punishment. The patrols also broke up large gatherings of black people and from time to time searched slaves' quarters. And they stood ready to chase runaways when called upon.

A Cleveland County court in 1845 made appointments to Capt. A.J. Jones' patrol. Serving were T.F. Elliott, A.M. Cabaniss, Albert Wilson, and Elsey Elliott. Patrol duty lasted 12 months, during which time the members were exempt from paying toll taxes. As to what they encountered during those 12 months, saddle sore from riding miserable backroads and combing every inch of this new county, no one will ever know. And most likely, no one will ever uncover all the names of the enslaved people buried in Sunset Cemetery. Some long-time Shelby residents don't even know there is a slave burial site. A historic marker would help everybody know more.

Wind doesn't summon the distant voices of Tobb, Vicy Ann, Jacob, and Linna here in the barren ground. Only silence. Meanwhile, on a cool autumn morning, with sun poking through a darkish cloud-cluster, a lone hawk sweeps across the sky, soaring over Sunset's graves, marked and unmarked, the black and the white citizenry. Encompassing all the cemetery, the hawk's movements may symbolize unity. The garden of the enslaved is no longer separate; it's part of the whole.

Damnatio Memoriae

June: In 1939, a Works Projects Administration worker named A[nson] G. Melton was one of two men taxed with recording the graves in Sunset Cemetery. He was part of Franklin D. Roosevelt's New Deal, a massive federal program that included ways to put people back to work after the Great Depression. The Works Projects Administration created the job of recording cemeteries, both by making lists of the names and dates of those buried in them, and by photographing tombstones and cemeteries. In Mississippi, a young Eudora Welty, the beloved American author, was hired to make a photographic record of graveyards in her state. Years later, her pictures would be compiled into a wonderful book, *Country Churchyards*.

The pictures in Welty's collection show mostly nineteenth-century gravestones. She photographed marble statues of lambs, angels, sleeping babies, women dropping flowers on graves, even a man in business attire. Each stone includes the names and dates of the deceased and sometimes an epitaph as well. Visitors in these cemeteries can find the graves of loved ones. Genealogists can trace family history. Cemetery buffs can enjoy the way the memorials invoke community values, admire the art work, speculate about the lives of those gone before.

Visitors can do all of these things today while strolling through Sunset Cemetery. That is until they come to the 1½–2 acre field at the west end. An 1886 map of Sunset Cemetery created by Paul B. Kyzer shows it divided into two sections. Approximately 2/3 of the area is a box labeled "Cemetery." A rectangular area west of this "Cemetery" is labeled "Colored Cemetery." Just to the west of that is another small area labeled "Col[ored] Baptist Church." The newer part of Sunset as it looks today is still a dairy farm in this map. The "Colored Cemetery" today looks like an empty field. It is mowed but full of depressions and small holes, which make it an unpleasant place for a stroll. It was even worse in 1939 when A.G. Melton saw it. On a page in his notebook, recently discovered among archival material from the old Cleveland County Historical Museum, he recorded his impressions: "Perhaps an acre and a half of colored graves are located here, all of which are grown up in weeds and small bushes, and now abandoned and entirely neglected. There are some three (300) hundred of these colored graves."

Melton's supervisor added a note at the bottom of the page: "The above was written by worker A.G. Melton on conclusion of listing of the colored graves ... and

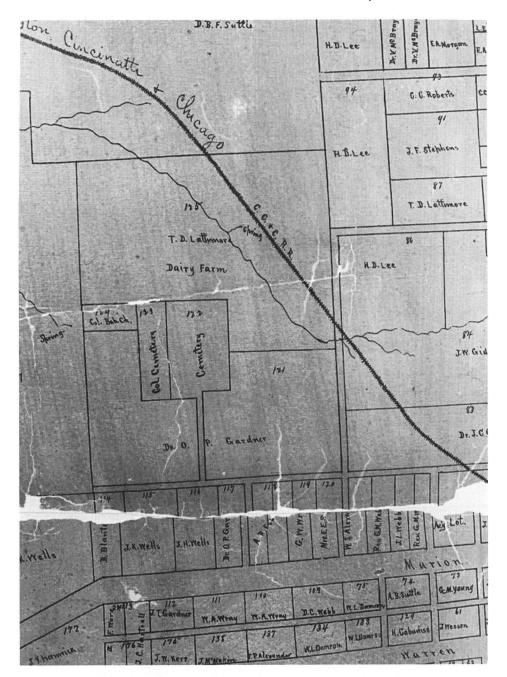

Detail of *Kyzer's Complete Map of Shelby*, NC, dated 1886 (courtesy Cleveland County Historical Collection located in Shelby, NC, photograph by Zachary Dressel).

seeing the negligent and abandoned condition of this colored section of Sunset Cemetery in Shelby, NC." Melton was so moved by what he saw that he felt inspired to compose a bit of verse and record it in his notebook. His compassion for those buried in unmarked graves is a poignant reminder that leaving no permanent record of one's life is a sort of second death, as if one had never lived:

It is enough to die
But oh, to be forgotten!
No deeds to raise a dust
When this frail flesh is rotten!
Oh! My God, let us die,
But never be forgotten.
　　This July 7, 1939
　　A.G. Melton, worker

Because of Melton's work, however, we can identify four people buried in the "colored" section of Sunset. Perhaps we will never know if these graves were marked at that time with, say, handmade wooden markers that have since deteriorated, if the markers have been moved, or if they are now hidden from view in the overgrown trees and brush at the edge of the graveyard. All four people died during Reconstruction or in the Jim Crow era. At least one was born during the time slavery was legal. Melton named two men and two women in his list:

Rankins, Leila, b. July 9, 1874, d. July 25, 1905
McCombs, Matilda d. January 5, 1889
Wills, Michael d. December 16, 1874 aged 64 yrs.
Thomas, William d. June 3, 1898, aged 20 years-old

A row of gravestones for unknown Confederate and Union soldiers in Sunset Cemetery. The stones for Confederate soldiers have pointed tops, and the stones for Union soldiers have rounded tops. O. Max Gardner III speculates that the Union soldiers died at the large residence that became Webbley, his family home, which was commandeered as a hospital by the occupation forces after the war. People leave pennies and pebbles for remembrance on these Union and Confederate gravestones in the old section of Sunset.

The segregated "colored" graveyard is mere yards from the graves of Confederate soldiers who died in the conflict or later. Even unknown soldiers are accorded respect in death if they are white. Their graves are well marked, and the burials of identified soldiers, we may assume, were attended by grieving family and friends who were able to buy appropriate tombstones for their loved ones. For example, Capt. Cicero A. Durham, who died a week shy of his twentieth birthday, is commemorated on four sides of an impressive marble obelisk. Durham, known as "The Fighting Quartermaster" of the 19th North Carolina T. Matt Ransom Brigade, lives on in memory as his best self. His stone records his last words: "I am dying. I do not fear death. I die for my country that holds my Mother's remains." Underneath is this tribute: "None more brave, gallant or beloved belonged to the Confederate army." In contrast, we know almost nothing of those buried in the field at the west end of Sunset. Though some of them were technically "free" at the time of their deaths, the "colored cemetery" is also the final resting place for people enslaved culturally by prejudice that deemed their lives unworthy of public remembrance.

What about their own memorial practices? What we know about burials during the time of slavery is mostly handed down orally. Lacking the resources and permission to enact burial customs that would be familiar to the white community or to erect professionally made monuments, Black communities in the South still found ways to honor their dead. In 2002, the revered civil rights hero W.W. Law, who died a few weeks later, described some of these to members of the Association

Detail from the gravestone for Capt. Cicero Durham of the Cleveland Guards. Known as "The Fighting Quartermaster" of the 19th North Carolina T. Matt Ransom Brigade, he left the D.H. Hill Military School in Charlotte to fight for the Confederacy and died at nineteen years old.

for Gravestone Studies as he led a tour in Laurel Grove Cemetery in Savannah, Georgia.

Rites for the honoring the dead vary from place to place, but Dr. Law, who has been described as a "griot" or one who maintains oral traditions for his community, explained what often happened at a burial for an enslaved person. First, burials probably took place at night illuminated by torches. Night burials meant that the community could gather without intrusion or punishment for shirking their work.

And then graves were marked with hand-crafted markers, including wooden figures shaped roughly like human beings with round heads at the top of elongated torsos. Sometimes wooden markers were simple boards. In her 1861 memoir, *Incidents in the Life of a Slave Girl*, Harriet Ann Jacobs of Edenton, North Carolina, described the grave of her father in "the burying-ground of the slaves" as "marked by a small wooden board, bearing his name, the letters of which were nearly obliterated." Such markers decompose within a few years.

Human nature being what it is, perhaps there was music. *Lay Down Body*, a history of African American burial grounds and customs, describes the antebellum Circle Dance brought from West and Central Africa and often practiced at burials of enslaved people. These are sometimes called "ring shouts" or "plantation walk-arounds" and involved singing and dancing in a counter-clockwise movement. We do not know these rituals ever took place in the west end of Sunset Cemetery, but we can imagine them.

Even today, Black Americans add distinctive cultural touches to burial grounds.

A gravestone in Eutaw, Alabama, that illustrates the African American custom of using the words "sunrise" for birth and "sunset" for death on tombstones. Photo by June Hadden Hobbs.

In African American cemeteries throughout the South and Southeast, visitors commonly find shells and broken dishes on graves as well as language that binds the community such as "sunrise" instead of "born" and "sunset" instead of "died" before the dates of the deceased. Although no markers remain in the garden of the enslaved, handmade or ephemeral grave goods may simply have not survived the years.

In ancient Rome, a ruler or government officials could punish wrongdoers or rivals by subjecting them to the process of *damnatio memoriae*, literally, condemnation of memory. Their names were wiped out of the record books, their pictures defaced, their statues removed. It was as if they had never lived. Something similar has happened to our neighbors in the west end of Sunset Cemetery.

Thomas Lynch, the poet undertaker of Milford, Michigan, describes the social contract of a cemetery near the end of his poem "At the Opening of Oak Grove Cemetery Bridge":

> A graveyard is an old agreement made
> between the living and the living who have died
> that says we keep their names and dates alive.

It is time for us to keep our end of the bargain by learning as many names and dates as possible and erecting a monument to these members of the community.

Bibliography

Books and Articles

Adams, Rebekah E. *Called to China: Attie Bostick's Life and Missionary Letters from China 1900–1943*. Huntsville, AL: Halldale Publishing Co., 2006.

Allen, Catherine. *A Century to Celebrate: A History of Woman's Missionary Union*. Birmingham, AL: Woman's Missionary Union, 1987.

Ariès, Philippe. *Western Attitudes Toward Death from the Middle Ages to the Present*. Translated by Patricia M. Ranum. Baltimore: The Johns Hopkins University Press, 1974.

Augé, Marc. *Non-places*. London: Verson, 1995.

Bachelard, Gaston. *The Poetics of Space: The Classic Look at How We Experience Intimate Places*. Translated by Maria Jolas. Boston: Beacon Press, 1994.

Bailey, Joe R. "'Tell Me About My Boy': World War II Graves Registration in Europe and the Repatriation of PFC Allison R. Jackson." *Markers: Journal of the Association for Gravestone Studies* XXIX (2014): 108–23.

Basbanes, Nicholas. *Cross of Snow: A Life of Henry Wadsworth Longfellow*. New York: Alfred A. Knopf, 2020.

Bishir, Catherine W. "'A Strong Force of Ladies'": Women, Politics, and Confederate Memorial Associations in Nineteenth-Century Raleigh." In *Monuments to the Lost Cause: Women, Art, and the Landscapes of Southern Memory*, edited by Cynthia Mills and Pamela H. Simpson, 3–26. Knoxville: University of Tennessee Press, 2003.

Blake, the Rev. M. "The Service of Babes in Heaven." *The Home Monthly*, July 1863–January 1864, 97–99.

Blumhofer, Edith L. *Her Heart Can See: The Life and Hymns of Fanny J. Crosby*. Library of Religious Biography. Grand Rapids, MI: William B. Eerdmans Publishing Company, 2005.

Braude, Ann. *Radical Spirits: Spiritualism and Women's Rights in Nineteenth-Century America*. 2nd ed. Bloomington: Indiana University Press, 2001.

Brentano, Florence. "Our Dead." *The Home Monthly*, January 1863–July 1863, 236.

Brundage, W. Fitzhugh. "'Woman's Hand and Heart and Deathless Love': White Women and the Commemorative Impulse in the New South." In *Monuments to the Lost Cause: Women, Art, and the Landscapes of Southern Memory*, edited by Cynthia Mills and Pamela H. Simpson, 64–82. Knoxville: University of Tennessee Press, 2003.

Campbell, Billy. "Saving One Million Acres for Two Thousand Years." Filmed May 1, 2013 in Greenville, SC. TEDx video. 13:45. https://www.youtube.com/watch?reload=9&v=OyA0VLzOPPA.

Carr, Nicholas. *The Shallows: What the Internet Is Doing to Our Brains*. New York: W.W. Norton & Co.: 2011.

Cash, W.J. *The Mind of the South*. New York: Vintage Books-Random House, 1941.

Child, Lydia Maria. *The Mother's Book*. Boston: Carter and Hendee, 1831.

Clark, Edward W. "The Bigham Carvers of the Carolina Piedmont: Stone Images of an Emerging Sense of American Identity." In *Cemeteries and Gravemarkers: Voices of American Culture*, edited by Richard E. Meyer, 31–59. Logan: Utah State University Press, 1992.

Clayton, Bruce. *W.J. Cash: A Life*. Baton Rouge: Louisiana State University Press, 1991.

Dean, M.A. "To That Mourning Mother." *The Home Monthly*, January 1863–July 1863, 157.

Deetz, James, and Edwin S. Dethlefsen. "Death's Head, Cherub, Urn and Willow." *Natural History* 76, no. 3 (1967): 29–37.

DePriest, Joe. *Voices in Time: Stories of the Banker's House*. The Banker's House Foundation, 2018.

Dixon, Thomas. *Southern Horizon: The Autobiography of Thomas Dixon*. Alexandria, VA: IWV Publishing, 1956.

Farrell, James J. *Inventing the American Way of Death, 1830–1920*. Philadelphia: Temple University Press, 1980.

Faust, Drew Gilpin. *This Republic of Suffering:*

Death and the American Civil War. New York: Vintage Books, 2008.

Fisher, Marc. "Why Those Confederate Soldier Statues Look a Lot Like Their Union Counterparts." *The Washington Post*, August 18, 2017, www.washingtonpost.com.

Gabel, Laurel K. "Ritual, Regalia and Remembrance: Fraternal Symbolism on Gravestones." *Markers: Journal of the Association for Gravestone Studies* XI (1994): vi–27.

Gardner, Fay Webb. Diary, 1929–1932. Fay Webb Gardner Collection, Gardner-Webb University Archives, John R. Dover Memorial Library, Boiling Springs, NC.

Gavin, James. *On to Berlin: Battles of an Airborne Commander, 1843–1946*. New York: Viking Press, 1978.

Hamrick, Mrs. C. Rush [Grace], and R. Hubbard Hamrick. *A History of the First Baptist Church, Shelby*. Shelby, NC, 1969.

Hamscher, Albert N. "Pictorial Headstones: Business, Culture, and the Expression of Individuality in the Contemporary Cemetery." *Markers: Journal of the Association for Gravestone Studies* XXIII (2006): 6–35.

Harris, Mark. *Grave Matters: A Journey Through the Modern Funeral Industry to a Natural Way of Burial*. New York: Scribner's, 2007.

Hawn, C. Michael. "History of Hymns: 'Precious Lord, Take my Hand.'" *Discipleship Ministries of The United Methodist Church*, July 31, 2014, https://www.umcdiscipleship.org/resources/history-of-hymns-precious-lord-take-my-hand.

Hobbs, June Hadden. *"I Sing for I Cannot Be Silent": The Feminization of American Hymnody*. Pittsburgh Series in Composition, Literacy, and Culture. Pittsburgh: The University of Pittsburgh Press, 1997.

_____. "Say It with Flowers in the Victorian Cemetery." *Markers: Journal of the Association for Gravestone Studies* XIX (2002): 240–71

_____. "Who Are We Baptist Women?" *Royal Service*, April 1985: 4–7.

Hobsbawm, Eric. "Introduction: Inventing Traditions." In *The Invention of Tradition*, edited by Eric Hobsbawm and Terence Ranger, 1–14. Cambridge: Cambridge University Press, 1983.

Jacobs, Harriet Ann. *Incidents in the Life of a Slave Girl*. 1861. Edited by Nellie Y. McKay and Frances Smith Foster. New York: W.W. Norton, 2001.

Jones, Jonathan. "Shelby's Monument to White Supremecy," *Medium*, June 26, 2020. Accessed June 28, 2020. https://medium.com/@jonathanjones9/shelbymonument-b4e9dac6e477.

Jones, S.C. *The Hamrick Generations: Being a Genealogy of the Hamrick Family*. Raleigh: Edwards and Broughton Printing Co., 1920.

Keister, Douglas. *Stories in Stone: A Field Guide to Cemetery Symbolism and Iconography*. Salt Lake City: Gibbs Smith, 2004.

Kelly, Suzanne. *Greening Death: Reclaiming Burial Practices and Restoring Our Tie to the Earth*. Lanham, MD: Rowman and Littlefield, 2017.

Lackey, Jack. *Ruth: Murder, Injustice and Life in the Rural South*. CreateSpace Independent Publishing Platform, 2016.

Lahr, Effie H. "Symbolism" [Address by Effie H. Lahr, Past Worthy Grand Matron, before the Fortieth Annual Session of the Grand Chapter Order of the Eastern Star of North Dakota]. https://www.ndeasternstar.org/wp-content/uploads/2015/10/F50–014.pdf/.

Linden, Blanche M.G. *Silent City on a Hill: Picturesque Landscapes of Memory and Boston's Mount Auburn Cemetery*. Amherst: University of Massachusetts Press, 2007.

Linden-Ward, Blanche [Blanche MG Linden]. "'The Fencing Mania': The Rise and Fall of Nineteenth-Century Funerary Enclosures." *Markers: Journal of the Association for Gravestone Studies* VII (1990): 34–58.

_____. "Strange but Genteel Pleasure Grounds: Tourist and Leisure Uses of Nineteenth-Century Rural Cemeteries." In *Cemeteries and Gravemarkers: Voices of American Culture*, edited by Richard E. Meyer, 293–328. Logan: Utah State University Press, 1992.

Little, M. Ruth. *Sticks & Stones: Three Centuries of North Carolina Gravemarkers*. The Richard Hampton Jenrette Series in Architecture and the Decorative Arts. Chapel Hill: University of North Carolina Press, 1998.

Long, Thomas G., and Thomas Lynch. *The Good Funeral: Death, Grief, and the Community of Care*. Louisville: Westminster John Knox Press.

Ludwig, Allan I. *Graven Images: New England Stonecarving and Its Symbols, 1650–1815*. 3rd ed. Hanover, NH: Wesleyan University Press, 1999.

Lynch, Thomas. *The Undertaking: Life Studies from the Dismal Trade*. New York: Penguin Books, 1997.

Mabelle. "To My Baby in Heaven." *The Home Monthly*, July 1863–January 1864, 289–91.

Morals and Dogma of the Ancient and Accepted Scottish Rite of Freemasonry. Charleston, SC: Supreme Council of the Thirty-Third Degree for the Southern Jurisdiction of the United States, 1871.

Morrison, Joseph L. *O. Max Gardner: A Power in N.C. and New Deal Washington*. Chapel Hill: University of North Carolina Press, 1971.

Norkunas, Martha. *Monuments and Memory: History and Representation in Lowell, Massachusetts*. Washington, D.C.: Smithsonian Institution Press, 2002.

Ochs, Carol. *Women and Spirituality*. New Feminist Perspectives Series. Totowa, NJ: Rowman and Allanheld, 1983.

Our Heritage: A History of Cleveland County. Shelby, NC: *Shelby Daily Star*, 1976.

Patterson, Daniel W. *The True Image: Gravestone Art and the Culture of Scotch Irish Settlers in the Pennsylvania and Carolina Backcountry*. The Richard Hampton Jenrette Series in Architecture and the Decorative Arts. Chapel Hill: The University of North Carolina Press, 2012.

Phelps, Elizabeth Stuart [Mary Grey Phelps Ward]. *Beyond the Gates*. Boston, 1883.

_____. *The Gates Ajar*. Boston, 1868.

_____. *A Singular Life*. Boston: Houghton Mifflin, 1894.

Reynolds, William J. *Companion to the Baptist Hymnal*. Nashville: Broadman Press, 1976.

Ridlen, Susanne. "Tree-Stump Tombstones: Traditional Cultural Values and Rustic Funerary Art." *Markers: Journal of the Association for Gravestone Studies* XIII (1996): 44–73.

Seemiller, Corey, and Meghan Grace. *Generation Z Goes to College*. San Francisco: Jossey-Bass, 2016.

Sloane, David Charles. *The Last Great Necessity: Cemeteries in American History*. Baltimore: The Johns Hopkins University Press, 1991.

Smith, Helen Sootin. Introduction to *The Gates Ajar*, by Elizabeth Stuart Phelps, v–xxxiii. Edited by Helen Sootin Smith. Cambridge: Belknap-Harvard University Press, 1964.

Stott, Annette. "The Woodmen of the World Monument Program." *Markers: Journal of the Association for Gravestone Studies* XX (2003): vi–29.

Stroebe, M., Gergen, M. M., Gergen, K. J., and Stroebe, W. "Broken Hearts or Broken Bonds: Love and Death in Historical Perspective. *American Psychologist*, 47.10 (1992): 1205–1212.

Taylor, Mark C., and Dietrich Christian Lammerts. *Grave Matters*. London: Reaktion Books, 2002.

Trevor-Roper, Hugh. "The Invention of Tradition: The Highland Tradition of Scotland." In *The Invention of Tradition*, edited by Eric Hobsbawm and Terence Ranger, 15–42. Cambridge: Cambridge University Press, 1983.

Vernon, Susie. "The Angel's Visits." *The Home Monthly*, January 1863–July 1863, 216.

Weathers, Lee B. *The Living Past of Cleveland County*. Shelby, NC: Star Publishing Company, 1956.

Welter, Barbara. "The Cult of True Womanhood: 1820–1860." *American Quarterly* 18 (1966): 151–74.

Welty, Eudora. *Country Churchyards*. Jackson: University Press of Mississippi, 2000.

Williamson, Joel. *The Crucible of Race: Black-White Relationships in the American South since Reconstruction*. New York: Oxford University Press, 1964.

Wright, Roberta Hughes, and Wilbur B. Hughes III. *Lay Down Body: Living History in African American Cemeteries*. Edited by Gina Renée Misiroglu. Detroit: Visible Ink Press, 1996.

Zipf, Catherine. "Marking Union Victory in the South: The Construction of the National Cemetery System." In *Monuments to the Lost Cause: Women, Art, and the Landscapes of Southern Memory*, edited by Cynthia Mills and Pamela H. Simpson, 27–45. Knoxville: University of Tennessee Press, 2003.

Newspapers

Anderson (SC) *Intelligencer*
Asheville Citizen
The Associated Press
Atlanta Constitution
Charlotte Evening Chronicle
Charlotte News
Charlotte Observer
Cleveland Star
Concord Daily Tribune
Lincoln Courier
Los Angeles Times
Morganton Herald
New Era
New York Times
Poughkeepsie Journal
Raleigh Christian Advocate
Raleigh News & Observer
Richmond Enquirer
Shelby Aurora
Southern Home (Raleigh NC)
Yorkville (SC) *Enquirer*

Index